# The Courage I Learned

# The Courage
# I Learned

Susan Hathaway – Saurman

Editor: Stephanie Viola
Cover Design: Erik Hornung

# Author's Note

When I decided to put my life's events down on paper, I wanted to bring awareness to breaking patterns of child abuse and domestic violence. The tragedies I describe in my memoir occurred more than forty years ago. Back then, law enforcement was not as successful as they are today in deterring domestic disturbance. Incidents of abuse were handled as "family matters" and led to warnings more often than arrests. Victims did not have as many resources as they do today. Laws, police response, and even the community's response to domestic abuse have changed drastically over the years. Now there are many services available to help. I encourage my readers to recognize the danger signs. Know that if you need help, you can change your life. You can make a new life and heal. Your future can be bright, even if your past wasn't. Please be a survivor.

# My Connection to Laurel House

Laurel House is dedicated to the vision of ending domestic violence in each life, home, and community. They were established in May of 1980, the same year my family was going through enormous trauma. We did not know about Laurel House in 1980. However, I was emotionally moved when I learned as an adult that they were working so hard to be a place of refuge for individuals and families at the same time our lives were in turmoil. I continue to be inspired by all they do to help our community. Their organization is remarkable.

## From laurel-house.org:

Domestic violence is a pattern of abusive and coercive behavior used by one person to gain power and control over another in an intimate relationship.

Although most closely associated with physical abuse, domestic violence can take many other forms such as psychological, emotional, verbal, financial abuse, sexual violence, and isolation. Laurel House staff members and volunteers are trained to help victims of all types of domestic violence, and to support their loved ones.

*If you or someone you know needs help, please reach out anonymously to:*

**Laurel House 24-Hour Confidential Hotline: 1-800-642-3150**
**National Domestic Violence Hotline: 1-800-799-SAFE (7233)**

*Skilled counselors are available to speak to you.*

# Table of Contents

# Introduction

*Every test in our life makes us bitter or better,*
*every problem comes to break us or make us.*
*The choice is ours whether we become victim or victor.*
Anonymous

Before my loving mother, Bunnie, was murdered by my father in 1981, she was a daughter, a sister, and an accomplished performer and singer. She was also a victim of domestic violence. She suffered greatly and, like most victims, she hid her fear well. Everyone who knew my mom, whether on or off the stage, saw her as a talented and beautiful woman who lit up every room and the hearts of everyone she encountered. When she died, the light dimmed for those who knew her. It dimmed for me too. But her absence in my life also inspired me to never give up, and ultimately, I was able to go on to live a happy life.

Many years after her murder, I received a few boxes of household mementos that a family member had held onto. In addition to a few knickknacks, the boxes included pictures of my mother and family. One of the pictures of my mom was a black-and-white photo of her looking right at the camera. I felt as if she was looking right at me through the photograph with her beautiful eyes and smile, and I was mesmerized. Receiving this and other priceless photos of my mother was an awakening for me and motivated me to search for more. Anything I could find to bring me closer to my mom was a gift. My hunt went on for decades as I periodically tried to connect with people my mother once knew through the theater or singing groups she had been a part of. Early on I was met with disappointment. Then, advancements in technology and the rise of social media gave me another opportunity. Miraculously, I was able to find a few individuals who had pictures and videos of her performing. In 2017, after two years of perseverance, I was flooded with responses. Numerous individuals who remembered my mother or had performed with her began to e-mail me. The empathy these individuals lovingly gave was inspiring. Former colleagues and archivists with these companies bent over backward to help me. I began to receive pictures I had never seen before, e-mails, and phone calls from individuals who loved and

1

admired my mother. I was overwhelmed with so many emotions at that time. Watching a precious video of her performing, I immediately felt elation hearing her beautiful voice once again after all these years. Then just as quickly came the overwhelming feeling of loss. Viewing these pictures, watching the video, and reading the messages of love for my mother filled me with sadness for her death all over again. Though mostly I was filled with pride, grief tugged at my insides for several days.

Remembering how much her absence always inspired me to never give up, I realized that what I had acquired was priceless, and these memories of her should be shared with everyone—not just my siblings, family, and friends. I continued to reflect on how memories of my mother were not only motivating to me throughout my life, but impacted others too. I wanted to do more. I wanted others to know how brave, warm, and amazing my mother was. I wanted the world to see how her memory and strength continued to influence me every day, kept me strong when life got tough, and helped me to always choose to be kind. Her life meant more than her death; her memories and legacy shine brighter than the tragedy that took her. Her struggle with domestic abuse, and the strength and courage she showed in leaving her abuser, were inspiring to me. I wanted to honor her by telling her story, as well as my own.

Deciding to write my memoir, I realized I would need to share my abusive upbringing. It would be necessary to provide background on my youth and to describe my father's violence. Peeling open old wounds and the deep pain of my past would not be easy emotionally. The prospect of looking back on my painful childhood memories and reliving my mother's murder frightened me. But I knew that in order for the reader to understand my family dynamic, I would have to dredge up the pain that I tried for years to leave buried.

Immersing myself back into the most painful moments of my childhood was awful. It was frightening how fast all the emotions came flooding in as I unraveled them onto paper. Recalling the last year of my mother's life, the separation from my siblings, and the murder trial awakened emotions I had suppressed, and my nightmares returned. There were times I wanted to give up the whole endeavor. I felt lost and stepped away from it several times. However, each time I quit, I kept thinking about my mom and all the strength she had possessed. She wasn't a quitter, and so, I wasn't going to be one either. I had to stay focused. I took several deep breaths and told myself, *you can do this.* I didn't stop writing until my journey was through.

Throughout the writing process, I used several resources to guide me: my memories, personal mementos, news articles, and court transcripts. The legal documentation helped me pace the memories I had of the trial and other documented events. These links to my past helped me fill in any gaps where my memory had faded over the years.

Descriptions of my father's violent actions and the pain he caused were a necessary evil. I needed to describe what he did to me, my mother, my siblings, and others to express this tragedy accurately and how we ultimately rose above it. But to be clear, any descriptions of my father in this book are not intended to idolize him. In fact, I would not publish my book while my father was alive because I refused to provide him with anything to feed his ego further. His opinions to me were moot. While his role may appear to be dramatic at times, my mother and family will always be more important.

I wouldn't have been able to complete this journey if it wasn't for my mother's memory and the influence of my grandparents who raised me after her death. My memoir is in gratitude to them. Without their love and support, I would not have become the mom, sister, wife, GG, and friend I am today. My hope is that after reading my story, others will be inspired to never give up.

**I am a survivor.** My personal journey has been just that, a journey through some of life's toughest challenges. The courage I've learned comes from all my life experiences, good and bad. It's also a product of how I embraced the inspirations in my life to guide me to never give up. My mother, grandparents, children, family, and friends are all stepping-stones of strength. I decided a long time ago to pick myself back up and take control of my life. I've held tight to *my philosophy* of not letting the anger, hatred, and sadness suck the life out of me. My father didn't deserve my anger or sadness. I wouldn't let him see my grief. My pain was not his to have. I felt if he saw my anguish, he would think he beat me. He didn't deserve to make me weak. I will not be weak. I am proud to be nothing like my father. I am better than him, and despite the atrocities my father inflicted, I survived. As the years go by, I continue to embrace all the lessons life has to offer. I realize as long as I am living there will be more to come.

# With Love

To my mom, Bunnie—Your love, courage, and everlasting light is always with me. Because of that, I never gave up. Your essence lives on. You are loved and missed so much.

To my grandparents, Ted and Kay—Thank you for being there for me. You gave me the strength to look beyond the next day.

# In Remembrance

Jim, you were a ray of sunshine in a time of true darkness. Thank you for making us smile and laugh when you were in our lives. And Teddy, I miss you, my friend. You left too soon.

# Prologue

My mom was like a warm hug. Gentle and caring. She had an inviting smile and sweetness that presented itself right away. Her face had a sincere glow, and if you knew her, you were blessed. She would brighten up any room with her beautiful smile. It lit up her whole face and was absolutely captivating. She was radiant. Her smile in pictures is a testament to my description. As a child, it was easy for me to idolize her. Sometimes when I saw her in her costumes and makeup for a show, I would think she looked like a princess from a fairytale. I still have these visions of her in my memory and I feel a warm, comforting feeling whenever I revisit them. She was my own personal Disney Princess.

As far back as I can remember, I loved to hear my mom sing. Her voice could take your breath away. Mom was often the female lead in shows, and she had to practice regularly. While sitting in our living room, I would listen to her practice. Her beautiful voice filled our home with song, echoing through the halls. On summer days when the windows were open to the world, the neighbors could hear her too. Everyone loved her beautiful songs. Mom's robust voice came in handy for other things as well. I remember fondly how she would holler out the front door for us to come in for dinner or lunch. Her voice was so intense, we could hear it loud and clear even if we were inside a friend's house. No phone necessary! My mom could out-yell anyone on the block. Years later, on the night she was all but silenced after a particularly brutal attack from my father, I would need to channel that powerful voice to stand up to him, to protect my family.

It started around 10:30 p.m. on October 11, 1980. I was in my room watching TV and I heard our parents leave their bedroom, sort of whispering as they walked down the second-floor hallway and descended the stairs. They both went into the kitchen and right away I could hear glasses clinking and other things rustling around. I figured they were making a snack. I heard someone twisting the toaster oven knob, setting the timer. (It always made this loud *buzz–click* noise when you turned the temperature knob.) I thought to myself, *I'm hungry too.* I decided to slip right into the pantry at the bottom of the back staircase and grab something to eat.

As I quietly went down the stairs, I began to hear arguing. Not yelling, more like muffled quarreling. I assumed they didn't want to wake up my brother and sister. I reached the second stair landing right before the back stairway to the kitchen, and I heard my father call my mom a whore. Mom said something back and the name-calling began. I stayed at the top of the stairwell and quietly waited there. I figured my father would just storm off in a huff to his music studio, his usual spot for solitary brooding. I stood there waiting and staring at the pantry door impatiently, completely irritated at this point. It felt like forever as seconds went by.

I was just about to give up and go back to my room when I realized how quiet it had gotten. The arguing had abruptly stopped, words shut off mid-speech. Then I could hear a banging noise and a strange shuffle, like the sound slippers make when they slide on the floor. *Bing!* The toaster oven timer went off, startling me. After that came a loud thud. I wondered what it was. Feeling uncomfortable and nervous, I silently began to ease my way back up to the second-floor hallway. The butterflies in my belly were churning as I thought with a sudden urgency, *I need to get back to my room.* I reached the second-floor landing and repositioned myself right by the third-floor stairs. At this point I heard gasping sounds. Then choking . . . lots of choking. Something was very wrong.

Full panic took over and I raced up the stairs as quietly as I could, trying to reach the third floor and my bedroom undetected. I stood in the doorway of my room. My thoughts were confused. *What's going on?* Seconds had elapsed and then I heard her. It was my mom. An awful screeching sound was coming from her mouth, her voice unrecognizable. I knew it was her, but the sound she was making was weird, unearthly. It sounded hoarse. Or maybe she was crying, it was difficult to tell. I was scared and began to feel the hairs rise on my arms and the back of my neck. Mom cried out again, straining to be heard. I can't even explain what was going on in my head. All I know is that I was frightened. When Mom tried to speak again in that strange, choked voice, it sounded like, *Stay away from me.*

Then, I heard my father. He sounded like he was crying, but also begging her, pleading with her, saying, "Oh please, please stop it, stop it." Over and over, he repeated, "Bunnie, stop it, you're overreacting!"

Mom's odd voice was downstairs, but in another area of the house now. *Maybe she's in the dining room? Or maybe the foyer?* Then I saw my sister standing in her bedroom doorway. She too had a terrified look on

8

her face. Our brief recognition of one another was interrupted by Mom's cries as she came up the stairs from the foyer. As I peered over the banister and down the staircase, I could see glimpses of her as she fled up the stairs. Her strange screeching, scratchy voice strained to shout, "Get away! Get away! Stay away from me!" My father was behind her, walking slower up the stairs, begging and pleading with her. When Mom reached the second-floor hallway, he was not far behind her.

I turned and headed for my bed. I jumped in it and a moment later, Mom ran into my room. She was standing near my dresser on the far wall of my bedroom, trying to speak to me, but her voice was hoarse. She said, in a high-pitched squeak, "He strangled me! He strangled me! He is trying to kill me!" At this point I understood what had happened, and I was even more terrified. I could hear my father coming. He seemed to be moving slowly. No sound of the keys he usually kept on his belt. It was his voice I heard coming up the stairs, still pleading with Mom to let him talk to her. It was only seconds before he walked into my room. He moved toward Mom and she put her hands out, motioning for him to stay back. Mom was terrified. He kept moving toward her. I was in the center of it all, sitting on my bed facing them, seeing Mom in this terrified state. Hearing her strained voice. Knowing now what he had just done to her. My brain was on overload with adrenalin, confusion, and worry. Then Mom looked at me, and in her hoarse voice she said, "Call the police. He tried to kill me!" My father kept begging her to stop saying that. She looked at me again, her eyes wide and fearful. The moments were sheer madness. *This can't be real.*

When my father tried to touch her, she recoiled up against my dresser in fear. He kept apologizing but was not leaving her alone. I couldn't stay quiet. Not this time. Suddenly, a courage I hadn't felt before welled up from deep inside. A primal anger, a rage that comes from being pushed past the threshold of fear. I stood up on my bed and screamed out loud at the top of my lungs. "GET OUT OF MY ROOM! GET OUT! GET OUT! GET OUT! GET OUT NOW! JUST GET OUT! LEAVE US ALONE!" There was sudden silence. My father stopped talking. His hands fell to his sides and his head slumped down. He turned and looked at me for a moment, then looked at Mom, and then turned away and slowly walked out of the room as if obeying my command robotically. It was the strangest thing to see. After he left, my sister ran up to Mom and threw her arms around her. They were both crying. I got off my bed and joined them. I could see a deep redness and fingerprint marks on Mom's neck. Every time she tried to talk, her voice sounded damaged and weak from his assault.

This incident would be the crucial change in all of our lives going forward – the last night we would live in that house. My mother's voice would recover, but I will never forget the look on her face that night. I will never be able to unsee that pain in her eyes. But I think about how I found the courage to speak up, for myself and for my family. This would not be the last time.

# CHAPTER 1

# Me as a Child

From the age of two until I was fourteen, I lived with my family in Lower Merion, Pennsylvania. It was a quiet, friendly neighborhood. Each home on our block had its own Main Line charm. My house was a six-bedroom, three-story colonial with a long walkway leading up to a gabled front porch. The walkway was lined on either side by a decorative white fence covered in ivy. Two huge trees towered above, and next to them were massive azalea bushes. There was an enclosed porch on either side of the house. On the left was my mom's porch, with lots of large windows that let in the sunshine. Alongside her porch ran the driveway, which led to a single-car garage. On the opposite side of the house was my father's porch—larger than Mom's, with blinds covering all the windows. We had a nice-sized yard that wrapped around from the right side of the house to the back. In the backyard was a swing set that was visible from the street.

*My house in 1980*

Before my brother was born, my bedroom was located at the landing of the second-floor stairs. The walls were light blue, and from the window I had a partial view of the house across the street where my best friend, Teddy, lived. Teddy was five months older than me and we had been friends since we were two years old. The old house he lived in was a mansion built in 1850, and it was huge! In its prime the house must have been stunning. Eight bedrooms, a fireplace in each of them. It took up a sizable portion of the neighborhood corner. From the street, you could see the large porch gable. The rest of the house was blocked off by the enormous trees that accompanied the property. It had a haunted-house appearance and to me, that was cool. I hung out at Teddy's house most of the time growing up.

Thinking back to my childhood, I can remember simple, normal times, playing with friends in the neighborhood. Kat was another childhood friend. She too came from a large family and we often played at her house. My time with Kat and Teddy filled up most of my out-of-the-house time. However, when I was about eleven, Kat and her family moved away. I was extremely sad when this happened. As time went on, Teddy became my closest neighborhood friend. There were good times at Teddy's house. He had a fort in his yard, lots of big trees to climb, and several places where we could access the roof and hang out. We even built a large rabbit run together, raised several rabbits, and shared in the responsibilities for them. I enjoyed being at his house; it was a nice escape.

From the outside looking in, my family life appeared to be privileged and relatively mainstream. At times, it would even seem glamorous. Both of my parents were known theatrical performers who acted in musicals and opera locally and abroad. They were involved with various performing companies—the Savoy Company, the Ardensingers, Rose Valley Chorus, Three Little Bakers Dinner Theatre, and Players Club of Swarthmore. My father did well in the printing business, and also had side work creating and selling reel-to-reel recordings of the many shows they participated in or attended. This provided a lucrative additional income, which contributed to our upper-class surroundings. I remember him telling me at some point that he had moved sixteen times in his life, and now he wanted all the things he never had. This included a nice big house and never needing to move again. My mom, Bunnie, was a stay-at-home mom, and my father's flexible hours allowed my parents to perform often and travel for shows abroad at least once a year. Over the years, they visited Spain, London, Rome, and other faraway places to perform. Even if you are not a fan of the genre, you would recognize the musicals or operas they had performed in: *The Pirates of Penzance, Ruddigore, The Mikado, The Sound of Music, A Funny Thing Happened on the Way to the Forum, H. M. S. Pinafore,* and the list goes on. Their passion for theater was a staple in our house. I recall my parents practicing at home prior to their shows, and other performers visiting our house to rehearse with them. The musical atmosphere my siblings and I grew up in was robust. It was difficult for me sometimes, having no musical or performance talent myself.

My mother tried. She enrolled me in ballet at age eight. As a child, I was very athletic and leaned toward boyish activities, and I think she wanted me to feel more in touch with my girly side. I tried to enjoy it and participated for about a year. Dancing with toe shoes and tutus, and all the rehearsals and the shows . . . I hated it. Whenever we had a recital, Mom would have to put makeup on me and do my hair. I would agree to pigtails, but sometimes I had to have a bun. Performing in recitals was a horrifying endeavor. I was petrified to be in front of all those people. My parents may have been talented performers, but I was not comfortable and did not enjoy it. After I complained for a solid year, Mom finally allowed me to quit.

*Me trying to like ballet*

Instead, she became very supportive of my athletic activities and was proud of my accomplishments, especially during my all-time favorite: Field Day. I excelled in sports, so it was something that didn't make me miserable. Broad jump, high jump, and relay racing were the events of the day. I was good at all of them and would always win several ribbons. Winning at something didn't happen for me often. So this was a big deal for me. When I came home with ribbons Mom was always so proud. She would stop what she was doing, and attentively listen to my excitement as I described each event. Then she would congratulate me, give me a big hug, and we would look at my ribbons together. This was the one time in my childhood life when I really felt proud of myself, and seeing my mom so excited for me was everything.

My second favorite hobby was art. I may not have had a stitch of talent in drawing or painting, but I loved to do it anyway. Mom loved all my projects. To her, they were all works of art. When I was in first grade I did a finger painting. She loved it so much that she had it framed and hung it up in the dining room of our house. It was a painting of our house, blue and orange with my thumbprints all around. Occasionally someone would ask about it and my mom would say with pride, "Suzie did that artwork."

I still have that painting. It now hangs in my office at home. When I look at it, I think of my mom and how caring she was.

One of my earliest memories of my mother involves a tooth I lost. I sat in the seat of a shopping cart as Mom wheeled me around the grocery store. I had a loose tooth that was ready to fall out any second. Occasionally I would wiggle it with my tongue, but I was too squeamish to yank it out myself. As we strolled around the store, Mom let me have a lollipop to keep me occupied. Shortly after I began sucking on the lollipop, I noticed a hole in my gum where my tooth used to be. I panicked right away. *Oh no! Where is my tooth?* I started to look around. When Mom noticed my odd behavior, she asked me what was wrong. I looked at her wide-eyed and flustered. "My tooth! I can't find my tooth! It fell out!"

Mom smiled and said, "OK, let's look on the floor." She bent down and looked all around the cart. After a few seconds of looking, she knelt down on the dirty grocery store floor and looked even harder to find my tooth. With no success, she stood up and replied, "Suzie, do you think that maybe you swallowed your tooth while eating your lollipop?"

I thought about that for a few seconds and was further panicked at the idea. I nodded my head yes and became even more upset. I burst out in tears, blurting out to her, "If I swallowed my tooth, the tooth fairy won't come. I have no tooth to put under my pillow for the tooth fairy!"

Mom was startled at my sudden sadness and said, "Suzie, don't worry, the tooth fairy will still come even though you swallowed your tooth. We will leave a note to explain." I immediately felt much better. Mom solved the worry. She knew exactly what to say and do to make me feel better.

Later when we got home, she helped me write a nice explanation letter to the tooth fairy, and before I went to bed, we placed the letter under my pillow. The next morning, I was so happy to find a bright, shiny quarter where the letter used to be.

That's who my mom was: my very own fairy princess. Thoughtful, warm, and loving.

# CHAPTER 2

# **Marylyn, Trey, and Me**

Though my mother was loving, the atmosphere of my home life didn't provide me with many positive feelings about who I was and what I looked like. I honestly never had any self-confidence growing up. I was very critical about my appearance and anything I did. I hated my red hair, all my freckles, my crooked teeth. And, to top it all off, I was academically challenged. This shortcoming would be my nemesis for years to come. Compared to my siblings, I just didn't measure up. I looked nothing like them. I felt I was the unusual child, socially awkward and shy. I was bullied often by other kids at school and had a hard time making friends. To make things worse, when I was six years old Kat's brother cut off one of my ponytails while we were all playing one day. It wasn't malicious on his part. We were just kids doing childish things. Nevertheless, the loss of my pigtail left my mom with one option: all my hair had to be cut off into a pixie hairdo. It was an atrocious look for me and added to my discomfort. Ladies at the grocery store mistook me for a boy. They would ask me if I wanted to take their shopping cart to their car. At school kids were mean and would bully me constantly about my new look. Not very pretty, and not very smart. It was a dreadful combination.

My sister, Marylyn, on the other hand inherited our mother's beauty with her big, brown eyes and lots of dark-brown hair. She picked up the outgoing, theatrical side from our mother as well. It was common for her to be flitting around the house singing, playing dress-up, and acting out pretend scenarios that I thought were hysterical. Sometimes she would act like she had a broken appendage, wrapping toilet paper around her arm or leg, and I would crack up laughing. She had a very bubbly personality, was very smart academically, and loved to be creative in everything she did.

*Marylyn and me*

Though I was four years her elder, she was the brave one. She enjoyed being around people, which wasn't me at all. When we had company, she loved to be in the middle of the celebration, talking to guests, sitting on their laps, and singing for them. I, on the other hand, would go up to my room, sit in my favorite chair, and hang out alone. Rocking in my chair and singing in private, I could stay up there for hours entertaining myself. Listening to the radio or watching TV—those things were more my comfort zone.

*Me, Mom, and Marylyn*

My earliest memories of my sister stand out in my mind and make me smile. Being the oldest of my siblings did afford me some opportunities to shine, such as when Mom asked me to hold Marylyn's hand while we walked around in a store. Marylyn held onto my hand and stayed with me the whole time. I enjoyed the feeling of pride that came with being her big sister. I can recall the two of us feeding ducks at a pond. We shared the bag of bread, and together we threw chunks of bread scraps to the ducks, giggling as they gobbled them up. There are many warm memories in my mind, but those two are delightfully happy.

*Trey*

When my brother, Trey, was born—a cute baby with platinum-blond hair, blue eyes, fair skin, and all smiles—I was practically an adult to him at age eleven. He did the cutest things, like sucking on two fingers on one hand while tugging on his ear and hair with the other. He'd scrunch up his face when he smiled, making a funny two-teeth *foo foo* face. When Trey began to speak, he had an adorable lisp. He called me Thusie.

When Trey was born, I was given lots more responsibilities with two younger siblings in the house and spent a lot of time taking care of my baby brother. I took him for walks in his stroller when he was an infant. Sometimes I helped feed him and gave him baths. As a baby, he simply hated the water and would scream the entire time as I bathed him. I also helped change his diapers. The new disposable ones were so expensive, and the tape they used would tear the diaper if you checked to see if it needed changing. Most of the time we used cloth diapers that had to be washed out in the toilet and then laundered. (I think I should have been given a medal for my valor.) But I enjoyed the challenge of being a big helper and wanted to show my mom I was good at something. When Mom praised me for my efforts, it made me feel proud.

*Two-fingers ear tug, and foo foo face*

Often, I had the opportunity to get him ready for bed, practicing the same routine Mom had: each night was a bath, and then she would sing him a few favorite songs in the rocking chair in his room. Mom sang those same songs to Marylyn and me when we were little. There were three I remember very well. The first was, "The Family Song," which repeated the same tune over and over as we named all the family, friends, and pets. It went something like,

*Mommy, mommy, mommy,*
*Daddy, daddy, daddy,*
*Sister, sister, sister . . .* and so on.

The second song was, "Climb, Climb Up Sunshine Mountain," and the third was, "I Can Sing a Rainbow." He loved these songs and would sing along when he was a toddler. When he would fall asleep in the rocking chair with me, it was gratifying. Despite my lack of musical talent, my singing was good enough for this tiny audience.

Chores and babysitting were a big part of my life. I did both after school and even on the weekends. It wasn't unusual for a kid my age to be watching her siblings, at least not at my house. I did a lot of it since my parents were often at rehearsals, parties, and social events. Two younger siblings could be very challenging at my age, but I knew how important my responsibilities were. In my home, following the rules was crucial. If I didn't do as I was instructed, the consequences would be dreadful.

It wasn't all bad. Looking back there are times I can remember just being a kid. The freedom of exploring the huge seminary up the street from my house. I could spend the whole day there. It was a huge property with lots of things to see. I always felt like I was on an adventure each time I hung out there. I also loved to run and often would test myself. I would run long distances, pushing myself to see how far I could go before I was exhausted. I occasionally ran all the way to Narberth, which was quite a few miles away from my home. There was a malt-and-burger shop across the street from the Narberth movie theater, a fun treat for me when I had money. The more I attempted this challenge, the better I got at running. On a few occasions it came in handy when I missed the bus going home after school. When that happened, I was never worried. I would take back roads and cut through some pretty interesting properties. Back then, walking home from school or walking home from anyplace, and being gone for hours at a time, was typical. We didn't have cell phones to check in every few minutes like today. I could be gone for hours and most of the time, that was not an issue. Most weekends or on summer days, I would leave the house around nine or ten o'clock in the morning. Then, maybe be back for lunch. After lunch I would be gone again until I heard my mom hollering out my name to come home for dinner. In the summer I would run right back out again after eating dinner and doing my chores, and would stay out until the streetlights came on. Those were the days . . . living the life of a child. It doesn't sound so bad when you reflect on the generic and simple things that went on in our everyday lives. Yet, what churned in the background behind the front door of our house was a much darker reality, and the truth was, I would rather be anywhere than at home.

# CHAPTER 3

# The Boogeyman in My House

When I was little, I suffered terribly from ear infections. I remember being miserable, and that Mom would put drops in my ears. She told me the reason I had a TV in my room at such a young age was because it was easier to put the drops in my ears when I was distracted by the TV. When I got a little older, Mom would hang out with me in my room and we'd watch shows together: *The Brady Bunch, Bewitched,* and of course, the Saturday morning *Looney Tunes.* Having the luxury of my own TV sometimes got me into trouble. I would sneak and watch horror movies against my parents' wishes. Only a couple gave me nightmares. One called *The Crawling Hand* made me scared to look under my bed for months. *Tarantula* and *The Spider* also stuck with me—to this day, I absolutely hate spiders. Mom would scold me and say, "Suzie, those are not movies for a little girl to be watching! See, you gave yourself nightmares. I warned you." She was right, but I couldn't help myself. For the most part, the monsters in these films never bothered me. I loved horror movies as a kid, and still do. I would watch them any chance I got, especially the classics. *Dracula* and *The Wolf Man* were my favorites. To me, they weren't anything to be frightened of. They embodied mystery, fantasy, and escape. Also, *power.* For a small child who so often felt powerless, I idolized these dark on-screen creatures.

Anyway, they were nothing compared to the monster that lived with us.

It was hard for me as a kid to recognize my father as a person. Most of the time, he was just the personification of my own fear, and being around him sucked the life out of me. I find it hard to recall more than a handful of times he was in a pleasant mood. All I can remember is the pain in my stomach each time I had to face him. As a child, I had no choice but to interact with him, to ask him for permission to go somewhere or to do things. It was a frightening experience both physically and mentally. At times it was so bad, I felt like my body was burning from the inside out. Something simple like asking him for help with homework would result in ridicule, verbal assault, physical assault, or all three. Out of all the nicknames bestowed on me by my father—*moron,* and *stupid,* to name a few—*pea brain* stands out the most in my memory. This title branded me for years and years, and would make me feel so useless. Academic struggles plagued me, and seemed to make me a target for his disdain. I had numerous learning challenges that made school difficult for me. Always in special education classes, I had to attend evaluation testing often. I struggled with reading and math. Because I wasn't learning at my age level, I felt awkward around kids my age. Although school was tough for me, it did have its advantages. It kept me away from my house for most of the week.

The mental and physical abuse I can recall began when I was around age six. There were normal everyday things that could set my father off. Normal kid things, like if I needed help with reading something, or I didn't clean up a mess. If I asked for permission to go somewhere or if I forgot to do a chore. Gosh forbid I wanted to attend a birthday party or a sleepover. Depending on his mood, they would result in one of two scenarios. If it was a good day, he would become aggravated and say, "Go ask your mother," or, "If your mother said yes, then fine," before promptly dismissing me. If it was a bad day, I would receive much worse.

Most days were bad days.

On one particularly bad day, I wanted to go outside and play. Mom said to me, "Suzie, you need to remember you have to ask your father for permission sometimes. He is your father." I always thought she was being mean to me when she insisted that I ask him for permission. (Little did I know then that as a victim of abuse, she was just trying to keep the peace and not stir the waters of violence of which my father was capable.) There must have been something so fun to do outside that I was desperate enough to risk it. I dragged myself over to the studio doors, took a deep breath, and knocked.

My father's studio was a scary place in my eyes. Located right off the living room, this room was a working man cave for him, full of all kinds of tape-recording gear, stereo equipment, a TV, and lots of records and tapes. Windows of the French doors that opened into the living room were covered on the outside with white curtains held tight with rods on the top and bottom. Whenever I had to approach these doors, the fear welled up in me.

He yelled, "Come in," and I entered the space like a spooked animal, hesitant, not wanting to anger the beast inside.

I gulped and said, "Excuse me . . . Mom said . . . to ask you . . . if I can go outside to play?" There was a long pause of dead silence. In my head I could hear crickets chirping.

"I don't know, *can* you go outside?" This was one of his frequent taunts, answering my question with a question. "You need to ask the right way." On this occasion, he continued to explain how I should have said, *May* I go outside. Then, "Since you can't remember to ask the right way, I wonder if you remembered to do your chores. Is your room in order?" As he was asking this question, I realized that I had better work some magic. I quickly asked if I may be excused to go take a second look to be sure everything was up to code. He rarely looked at me when we spoke. Most of the time, his back was toward me, his attention on his forty reel-to-reel tape recorders and stereo equipment piled as high as the ceiling in there. Most days he couldn't be bothered with me or anything that interrupted his agenda. So on this day, I had a chance to redeem myself and take a second look at my room. I slipped back out of the entryway of his studio, closed the door, and dashed upstairs. Hoping it was in proper order, I panned the room with my eyes. Suddenly I heard the sound his keys made on his retractable key ring that was clipped to his pants pocket. *Cling, cling, cling,* as the keys swayed back and forth. I knew right then, my "second look" opportunity had failed miserably. I was headed for a beating. The reason, who knows? Maybe I annoyed him. Maybe I asked him the wrong way. Whatever the reason was, it was my mistake and now I was going to pay for it.

The sound of him coming up the stairs put me in a panic. I paced back and forth. I started to feel hot and began to sweat. I wanted to hide but there was nowhere to go. I frantically tried to pull myself together, knowing that hiding would make it worse. My split-second decision was to stand in the middle of my room and face him when he walked through the door. Like a stone statue, I stood there, wide-eyed, fear heating up my body. When he entered my room, he looked around and surveyed the area, ready to point out anything he felt was not up to his standards.

"Come here," he told me, and I very reluctantly walked over to him, keeping some distance between us when I got closer. He said again, but angrier, "I said over here!" as he pointed to the spot on the floor directly in front of him. I crept closer until within reach. Then faster than you can blink, he grabbed my hair and pointed my head down toward the dust on my bedside table. On that table was an enormous old-fashioned radio, a record player, and a bunch of other odds and ends. Clearly, I had not dusted this table in a while. I could feel the blood leaving my body as it reacted to this realized error. I was now in huge trouble. Before I could even dwell on it for long, he lifted my head by my hair and shouted into my face, "Get this cleaned up, now!" along with something about how he gives me nice things and I can't even keep them clean. Then, he pushed me away by my hair and I toppled backward. I had experienced similar roughness from him before, but on this particular encounter I lost my footing and fell just short of my bed, hitting my back on the edge of the bed frame. The pain was immediate. I had scraped my lower back badly, but I dared not make a sound or even acknowledge the pain I was in. The tears were welling up already and I fought them back. I sat there holding my breath, waiting for him to leave my room. As he walked out my door, down the stairs, and out of sight, I immediately gasped for air and could feel the scrape throbbing. I took another deep breath and I sucked it up, along with my tears. After a minute or two, I got up and started cleaning up my room. I didn't go outside that day.

My father often used my academic shortcomings against me. He would frequently get frustrated when I struggled with math or reading, especially since he was very proficient in these subjects. If I ran into a problem, and that happened a lot, I would have to go to his studio and ask him for help. My experience with my father's outbursts in that room would result in a painful outcome, either mentally or physically. I would try desperately to understand my homework and not have to ask him for help. No matter how hard I tried, or my mom tried, I still struggled and regretfully, I would have to go and get help. He would start off trying to explain the lesson. But as I struggled to understand it, he would start to get angry. He made me so nervous that I would freeze up. I was so afraid of him I typically couldn't remember anything I had learned. Struggling to give a correct answer would lead to him mocking me for my stupidity, yelling at me in frustration, and dismissing me from his studio. On a few occasions he would throw my scholastic book at me in disgust, tell me I was a "stupid pea brain" and to get out of his sight.

Days or weeks would go by after these encounters without a word. Then one night he would popquiz me at the dinner table on a prior homework assignment. This was the Recall Game. The lesson taught here was that if I couldn't learn things, I would be mocked for it. Most times after a bad homework scenario, I would go back to my mom and ask her to help me, telling her I wanted to do better but he always yelled at me. She would say, "I have to live with him too, you know." Being a child, I couldn't see things through her eyes, only mine. And for me, things were tough. Years later, looking back, I saw clearly how truly diabolical he was. How he used his intelligence, alcohol, and cruel traits to knowingly abuse his family. He was cold and calculating, the perfect villain—and he was a ticking time bomb. A few days without having any confrontations with my father would put me into a state of false comfort. No sooner did that feeling settle in that I would be summoned into his studio or drilled at the dinner table, always regarding a prior lesson or some useless information he wanted to put in my head. Whatever it was, it wasn't going to end well for me. Inevitably I would say the wrong answer and end up being ridiculed, or worse. I was too afraid to learn, too focused on when he was going to backhand me. Throw me out of his studio. Stab me with a fork in my hand at the kitchen table or knock me backward off my kitchen chair. With these preempted visions in my head, I couldn't focus on what he was telling me. I only knew I would fail, and the result of my failures would be a painful consequence. Nothing was ever finished with him. With my father, everything always had a catch. The only lessons I learned were how to be nervous and how to get ready to protect myself for what was coming next.

Every confrontation with my father was different. Sometimes he got in my face, yelling and threatening. Sometimes, I got a fat lip when he kicked me forward as I tried to escape from him up the stairs. On one occasion he hit me repeatedly with a shoe I had left out on my bedroom floor. It was like playing the lottery in my house. Living was a game of chance. If I had avoided my father that day, then I was the jackpot winner. But one false move, like leaving the kitchen trash bag in our laundry–mud room unattended, would result in dire consequences.

On this occasion, I left the trash sitting there and our dog got ahold of it. As my mom scolded me, I hadn't realized my father was standing in the kitchen doorway. Just as I was about to take the ripped bag outside, my father seemed to levitate off the floor and over to me. He grabbed me by my arm and flung me like a rag doll right through the mud room door. My body hit the storm door with a huge crash. As my butt broke the lower glass pane window, the door flung open and I fell down the four cement steps outside. He screamed down at me from the doorway, "Next time do as you're told!" I sat there stunned for a few more seconds. When I tried to get up, I began to assess my injuries: a cut on my right arm, scrapes on my arms and hands from the rough cement steps, and later some bruises on my butt and thighs. I have no idea how I escaped from busting my head open on the cement steps. Mom came out to help me up and get me back inside. She patched me up, and not much was said. After that incident, the door was replaced with plexiglass and this weird-looking metal grating. It looked ugly, prison-like—a lasting reminder of my mistake and what I had paid for it.

My father was like a tiger, impressive at a distance with his talent, confidence, business savvy, and how he provided for his family. But step into the cage and you risked your life. He would try to lure me in some days, though I always knew better than to let my guard down. Out of the blue he would come find me and say, "Let's walk up to the seminary and hit some balls around." Or he'd want to shoot hoops in our driveway. I could never figure out what his end game was. Hitting balls to my father or playing twenty-one, it didn't matter how innocent it sounded. I was a nervous wreck. To this day I recall these moments with pure perplexity. This man had absolutely no tolerance for me at all, and yet, he wanted to hit some balls or shoot hoops with me? Hoops were easier, but not by much. I was better at this game, and he didn't seem to ridicule me quite as often. There were rare occasions when we finished the game, he gave me the ball and said, "Good game," and then walked away. It would stupefy me. Hitting a ball to him was a different story. Things would go as things always did. He would start out calm and during my epic failures to hit the ball, he would begin to get angrier and angrier until he'd throw the ball at me.

"Come on, Suzie, *jeezus.* What the hell is the matter with you! I have shown you a million times how to do this. Why are you purposely mocking me?" *Yes, that is what I wanted. To make you angry with me. Because I enjoy being treated like a piece of crap every day of my life.*

Then he would storm off, leave me there standing in the field with the bat and ball. I would watch him walk across the field, muttering out loud about how stupid I was and how he can't do anything with me. The farther away he got, the better I would feel. I would see him hop over the small, four-foot green fence that bordered the seminary, cross Wynnewood Road, and disappear down our block. I would take my time going back home, like usual. Sometimes he further ridiculed me when I got home. Other times, he stayed in his studio and nothing more was said.

*My father, me, and Mom*

To be fair, some pictures from when I was little reveal that at some stages in my life, my father seemed to have cared for me. Pictures that show me as a baby and toddler. Pictures of me being held by a smiling father. If I strain hard enough, I can even remember a few times I felt comfortable going into my father's studio. Once a year around Easter time when we would watch *The Wizard of Oz* together as a family. Another time, he let me fetch my mom her favorite candy, Peanut Chews, from a cabinet near the backdoor entrance to his studio. Even then, I felt so nervous. I quickly went to the cabinet and upon opening this large drawer, my eyes gazed upon an entire drawer full of candy! It was a huge stash filled with each of their favorites: Necco Wafers, Lemonheads, Good & Plenty, Charms Sour Balls, and Peanut Chews for Mom. If I had been more daring, or less terrified of my father's wrath, I may have sneaked in and grabbed some now and then. But I never did.

Nothing under our roof was safe from my father. He didn't discriminate in his violence—human or animal, all were equal targets for his anger. When I was about seven years old, my parents brought home two puppies, one an Airedale and the other a skinny black dog. Mom had them in the kitchen for what seemed like forever, trying to housebreak them. One day they got ahold of some clothes that were on the dryer in the laundry room and tore them to bits. My father heard Mom scolding the puppies and freaked out. I could hear my mom yelling and crying for him to stop hitting the puppies as he screamed at her, "It's your fault for wanting these stupid animals!" I went outside to the front of our house and sat on the side of our yard near the huge azalea bush. Looking at it used to calm me. When I finally did go back into the house, I could smell this horrible stink. The dogs had peed and pooped themselves all over the kitchen after being beaten by my father. My mom was in the kitchen crying and trying to clean up the mess. I began handing her paper towels as we sobbed together. Then we tried to sit with the puppies for a while, to calm them and ourselves. The feeling of complete sorrow and helplessness was overwhelming. A few days later the dogs were gone. No one really talked about them much after that.

Although my sister was four years younger than me, she didn't go unscathed from my father's fury. I remember numerous times she had suffered through incidents that were violent and unwarranted. When she was seven, our bedrooms had moved to the third floor of our home in preparation for the arrival of our brother. Out of boredom I suppose, Marylyn began to scrape the paint off the wall near her bed with her fingernail. When my father saw this desecration of the wall, he flew into a rage. I heard her spanking, and the yelling and the hitting was painful to me. (Years later, I would see her get a far worse beating.) Then, there were the times he would insist we read out loud to him . . . while he was in the bath. Imagine how awkward and embarrassing a "lesson" for him to force us both to suffer through as children. I was not a good reader and winced inside when he called upon me to read to him. Even though my sister was a strong reader, she loathed these valueless lessons too. I recall other days when Marylyn and I would take cover while my father redecorated our house out of rage, drunkenness, or both. These destructive outbursts usually revolved around ridiculous things. One time, he broke almost everything on the first floor of the house because Mom got a better part in a show they were in. It looked like a tornado had come through. Mom's knickknacks, chairs, pictures, keepsakes, some furniture, destroyed. My terrified sister hid in a kitchen cabinet next to our dishwasher, while I ran upstairs and peered over the banister of the second-floor hallway staircase. I can't remember where my brother was or if he was born yet. But I do remember I could see the occasional item smash up against the radiator cover below. Mom would always try to salvage whatever didn't get completely destroyed in his tirade.

Looking back and remembering the years we "functioned" as a family, I often wonder why my father was always so angry. None of it made any sense to me then or now. The pain he inflicted were not lessons learned. They were violent assaults with no merit. And the truth of the matter is, though we suffered together, there were lots of things we didn't know about each other's individual torment. There are some events my sister and I both remember, but I know there were things that happened to Marylyn I did not witness. We each experienced trauma that the other did not see or hear. For years I didn't even realize my mother was terrified of my father. We were all afraid and just living in our own bubbles, trying to get by day to day. Especially in 1980. That year, my sister and I really understood what was going on in our house. That year, everyone knew things were bad.

# CHAPTER 4

# **Buried Things**

Teddy and his family knew for sure there were issues in my house. I believe some of the other neighbors did too. But back then, neighbors simply minded their own business. My father was smart to serve blows in places that couldn't be seen. No one ever asked, and then again, I never talked about it either. Cuts and bruises from being kicked, shoved, smacked, and pushed were far less painful to me than the emotional bruises anyway. I often wondered why my father hated me so much, why he terrorized my mother and siblings the way he did. Another mystery my father kept hidden. Even as he projected to the outside world the confidence, charm, and persuasive manner that my mother had fallen for when they met, his true darkness would peek through. It wouldn't take long for her to realize who he really was. Things buried eventually come to the surface.

*Mom in elementary school, and her senior year.*

My mother's name was Bernadette Marie, but everyone called her Bunnie. She was born in Philadelphia on November 28, 1945; a beautiful little baby with lots of dark hair and deep brown eyes. My Grandmom knew she was something special the moment she saw her. She gave my mother the nickname Bunnie because, "Bernadette was too big of a name for such a tiny baby." Mom's upbringing was stern but loving. Raised

Roman Catholic, Mom attended church weekly with her family at the Queen of Peace Church located around the corner from their home. Mom and my Uncle Mike also attended Catholic school growing up.

Grandmom was right. Mom was something special. Admired by her peers, she developed many deep-rooted friendships in and out of school. My grandparents often described Mom as having a contagious personality. She oozed a sweetness and silliness that was irresistible, and her beauty and humor only added to her popularity. My grandparents would often remark how enchanting she was inside and out. It must have been all these qualities that caught my father's eye in late May of 1965 when they met. They were performing in a show together, and my father had noticed her during rehearsals. After a week went by, he struck up a conversation with her. Immediately smitten with Mom, he asked her out to lunch. Mom described my father at that time as very charming, funny, intelligent, and quite the gentleman. She was so awestruck she forgot to ask his name during the date.

Byron Groo, Jr., nicknamed Bee Gee.

My father was born on July 31, 1931. According to him, he had a very difficult childhood growing up. His family moved sixteen times by the time he was fifteen and he felt this unsettled upbringing kept him from developing any long-term friendships. He was a child of divorce and expressed that both of his father figures were unpleasant individuals. He also had a very strained relationship with his mother. Upon release from his service in the army during the Korean War, he lived a bachelor life and purchased his first home on Rock Hill Road in Bala Cynwyd, Pennsylvania. Working in printing and recording, business-savvy and established, there was nothing not to like in my mother's teenage eyes. Mom was nineteen and my father was thirty-three at the time of their first date. She liked that he was older because he had freedoms she didn't, and he treated her really well. In her eyes, he must have seemed like a gallant knight coming to take her away from her strict household. Soon they began to date exclusively.

After a few secretive dates, Mom invited him over to her house to meet her parents. While she was excited to introduce him to my grandparents, they were not happy about the relationship at all. Besides the fourteen-year age difference, my grandparents described my father as arrogant, egotistical, and manipulative. They didn't like him from the moment they met him, and they were very worried about his influence on their daughter, seeing that she was easily persuaded by him. This disapproval immediately flung my parents' relationship into a forbidden zone, fueling the fire, making them both more resistant and rebellious. It was this restrictive interference from my grandparents that caused their fast engagement. My father's side of the story was that when he first met Mom's parents, he found them to be very stern and controlling. He got in my mother's ear and did his best to cause a rift, encouraging my mom to reject the strict rules put on her by her parents. Bee Gee always got his way.

On July 31, while celebrating my father's birthday, they drove to Maryland and obtained a marriage license. Upon returning to Pennsylvania, they went and chose an engagement ring. Mom selected a beautiful marquise diamond ring with a platinum setting. That night, they announced their engagement and Mom showed the ring to her parents. The excitement turned sour quickly. Mom's parents were immediately upset. They firmly disapproved of the engagement and forbade Mom to wear the ring. This rejection didn't go over well with either of my parents. They both adamantly refused to pretend they weren't engaged. After a heated argument in their living room, my father left and Mom was upset at her parents' disapproval. The next day, additional restrictions were put in place. My grandparents made it very difficult for Mom to see my father. It was obvious Mom's parents were worried about this relationship. Things had developed so quickly, and they could see how impressionable their daughter was. Head filled with my father's persuasions, believing she was being unfairly controlled and restricted from what she wanted, my mother took action.

On August 10, 1965, Mom gathered a few things, slipped out of the house, and met up with my father. They drove to Maryland with the marriage license and her engagement ring and eloped that day. They came home in the early evening and went directly over to my father's parents' house. They announced they were married and were going to leave in the morning for their honeymoon. Mom had not told her parents anything yet, for fear of what the reaction was going to be. My father's parents advised that she needed to call her parents and let them know they had eloped. It was a very difficult phone call. Mom's parents were furious at the news. The call escalated emotions and things were left unsettled. Despite my grandparents' objections, my parents left for

Canada on their honeymoon for a week. When they came home, Mom moved into my father's home in Bala Cynwyd.

*Mom holding me in my christening outfit*

Nine months later I was born, a honeymoon conception. My arrival did help soften the strained relationship slightly with Mom's parents, but not entirely. Two years after I was born, my parents bought our home in Lower Merion from the sale of the Bala Cynwyd house. Together they began to fix it up. Fresh paint, a few needed repairs, and they were ready to move in. This house would be our home for the next twelve years.

The tension stayed thick for years. My mother was liberated from a strict household by an older man who supported her independence from her parents. She didn't realize then the freedoms she was giving up in return.

Prior to meeting my mother, my father had been engaged once before. The relationship had ended badly, and from what I learned, the woman had been harassed, stalked, and attacked by my father during and after the relationship. That's the most my grandparents would say on the subject. Not knowing this history at the time, could anyone have predicted what my parents' relationship would become? There were signs. My grandparents saw them, but my mother in the beginning of their relationship was enamored. Even when my father's violent nature began to show its face, Mom buried it deep down, wanting desperately to show everyone she was happy and living a dream come true. Mostly, Mom never wanted to hear her parents say I told you so. This propelled her determination to prove to her parents she had made the right decision in marrying my father.

As the years went by the contentious relationship with Mom's parents continued. You could sense this thick tension between my father and grandparents anytime we all got together as a family. I remember when I was younger, Mom always seemed on edge before her folks would arrive. I just thought she was nervous about cooking dinner. When I was older, she explained the reason. She was stressed, anticipating the pressure of the family tension. I knew most of what she said made sense. But I also knew there were lots of other things causing strain during their visits. Whenever her parents or brother Mike visited, she would try to prove how well she was doing by pointing out how she lived in a very nice home, was able to continue her theatrical interests, and was a full-time, stay-at-home mom. She needed them to see what her husband provided for her and the kids: her beautiful home, furnishings, clothes, trips, and so on. At the same time, she needed to feel confident about her choices, convincing herself that getting out from under her parents' thumb and into an independent adult life was a good decision. Well, that is what she was trying desperately to display. However, over time she recognized her husband's Jekyll-and-Hyde hostility. She saw his rage toward his family, pets, and others. She became increasingly frightened of him and desperate to try and hold things together. It was a slippery slope, and if you live with an abusive person long enough you become a victim too.

# CHAPTER 5

# **My Mother's Fear**

"Why do you always pick his side?"

As I began to clean up the mess in the center of my room that my father had left after one of his tirades, my mom came up to see what all the yelling had been about. She began to address the situation. I guess she had to put in her two cents and began nagging me about all the stuff I had in my room.

"Suzie, you have too much clutter! It looks like a pack rat lives here. You must get this room straightened up, right away!" None of what she was saying was helping me feel better at that moment. A little while earlier, my father had come up to the third floor and noticed one of my posters was coming off the wall. I had some very cool posters back then: Star Wars, Superman, Wonder Woman, the Hulk, and one very special Horror Classics poster with the Wolfman, Dracula, Frankenstein's monster, and others. I also had music posters with my favorite bands of that era ripped from *Creem* magazines. Since my ceiling was slanted, occasionally the tape came away from the wall and the posters would start to bow in the middle. I didn't know that this revealed where the tape had damaged the paint and old wallpaper underneath, a mistake I thought I had cleverly covered up. I began to panic as my father looked closer at my classic monster poster. He slowly turned and looked at me. I saw his face begin to change and I immediately became afraid. He looked back at the poster and in a flash, ripped it off the wall. Then he proceeded to grab another and another. He destroyed most of the posters I had hanging on the slanted ceiling. Then he stooped down to pick up a few that were stuck together on the floor, smashing them into a ball and throwing it at me. He walked over to me and I flinched, raising my arms to protect myself, thinking he was going to slap me.

Instead, he grabbed me by my hair, walked me over to the area in question, and said, "You see this! You will fix this mess immediately! You will scrape off these walls and repaint this room! Do you understand me!" I shook my head yes to acknowledge his question. He let go of my hair and said, "If you ever destroy this house like this again, you will sleep in the basement!" I again agreed, and he left my room.

So by the time my mother came in and began her nagging about my "clutter," I was so mad and frustrated that without thinking, I picked up a balled-up sock and threw it at her. The sock hit her in the arm and there was a split second of shock as we both looked at one another. She was stunned to say the least. It was obvious she couldn't believe I had actually thrown the sock at her. Frankly, neither could I. Then in a moment of realization, she fired back. With one fell swoop of her arm, she knocked all the things off my high dresser near my bedroom door. As everything came crashing down to the floor, I could hear all my possessions breaking. Included in this mass destruction was a beautiful white ceramic Clydesdale horse that I treasured. I was immediately devastated. In an instant, she had added more damage to the things in my sanctuary.

I lost every battle. There was no use even trying. With nothing to lose, I fired back by talking under my breath. In a low, angry whisper I said, "I hate you!"

"What did you just say?" she shot back.

"Nothing," I replied, and turned around to start picking up my broken possessions. Subconsciously I knew I could talk back to my mom. She was the more lenient parent. I knew she was not going to hurl me into a wall like my father would. I didn't hate my mom. I only said that out of anger. On the contrary, I desperately wanted her to see my side, protect me, and be my savior. The person I loathed was my father. He was nothing but fear, agony, and social withdrawal for me. I wanted my mom to be my fairy princess again, the one who would comfort me, praise me, and make me feel safe, like when I was younger. But now that I had entered my teen years, I began to feel anger toward her for allowing our abuse to continue. I often sensed somehow that she knew she had to find a way to alter things before permanent damage was inflicted on us. Unfortunately, her own fears, struggles, and position in our home overwhelmed her.

A few days went by and I began to fix the wall. To my surprise, Mom came to my rescue and helped me with the repairs. She also apologized to me for getting angry and breaking my things. She wanted to know if my horse could be fixed. I told her no, it wasn't fixable. I shrugged my shoulders in defeat like I always did. This was my life, the ups and downs of eerie calm and violent outbursts could and would take place throughout my childhood. I learned not to get too attached to things.

Being a child, I couldn't understand why my mom didn't protect me when I needed her most. However, as an adult, I learned to understand the reasons why she was not able to be more shielding toward her children. It wasn't because she didn't care. It was because she was living in fear too. A real day-to-day fear of her own that she kept hidden from us. I may have been too young at times to recognize the abuse she went through. My mom was a loving mother and a good person, but she was living in a world of *parental denial,* unable to acknowledge the truth. She was dependent on her husband and a victim of abuse herself. Victims make excuses at times, not seeing or hearing the abuse that is evident in order to cope in their own home. Her denial through the years is the only way she knew how to react to certain situations. She remained silent often for her own protection and due to her own misery. I found out when I was older how Mom never wanted her parents, family, or friends to know how unhappy she was, or how my father humiliated her and made her feel trapped. After my father was violent, he would plead with her and she would accept his apology as most victims do. She would think, *this time it will be different.*

My father was truly horrible. Yet, at the same time he could be so charismatic in his stage performances and encounters with colleagues. People who knew him would see two sides. He was either charming and funny or dark and sinister. Former colleagues even spoke of his arrogance and bullying. There were a number of people who were afraid of him and only tolerated him because they loved and admired Bunnie so very much. But he also had a persuasive way about him, which he often used to charm others into helping him get what he wanted.

With my mother, my father would profess his undying love to her and shower her with lavish gifts. These grand romantic gestures seemed so selfless; you would almost think he was a loving husband.

November 28, 1975 was Mom's thirtieth birthday. Mom was not in a very good mood. It was a milestone birthday, and she didn't like getting older. That morning, my sister and I went to present her with our cards and gifts, and found her sulking in her sun porch. When I asked her what was wrong, she explained, she thought maybe someone would have given her a surprise party or celebration. She was referring to our father, and was upset that he had not acknowledged such a big birthday for her. What she didn't know was, we had been told a few days before not to ruin the surprise he had arranged. The plan was to take her out to dinner with their good friend Bismark for a fun celebration. He told us he was going to purposely ignore that it was an important birthday in order to fool her. When Bismark showed up, she was so surprised to see him. He presented Mom with a huge box and told her it was for her birthday. Like a child, she quickly opened the gift. Inside the box was an authentic white feather boa. She wrapped it around her neck, looked at him with fluttering eyes, and squealed in delight. Moments later my father presented her with his gift, a stunning piece of jewelry, and announced that they were going out on the town to celebrate.

At Christmas, he would attach pantyhose to her stocking over the fireplace and fill them with an impressive array of individually wrapped gifts. The weight of the gifts made them fall to the floor and they continued across the carpet and stretched out into the room. When we gathered around to watch Mom open them up, my father was almost childlike with excitement. I couldn't help but think how clever it was of him to do this. I often wondered how he could be so crafty and yet so horrible at the same time. As usual, the truth always exposed his intentions. Power, control, and manipulation were always his motive. We found out later through court documents from the custody battle that he had a shoplifting habit, and some of her gifts were a result of that.

The older I got, the more I realized my parents' relationship was not normal. This revelation was additionally disturbing: since everything she did was always restricted or under his authority, she would do small things to rebel against his rules, like a kid would. I remember one argument when my father found out my mother was smoking. He told her if he caught her smoking again, he would take the car away from her. He was talking to her as if she were a child, always extremely controlling. Occasionally if we were in the car with my mom, she would have a cigarette and then tell me to throw them away before we got home, despite his threats. At the time I thought it was funny, in a way. I didn't realize the impact of my father's restrictions on my mother until I was older. She was kept from doing anything she wanted to do. Even going out with friends or participating in a bowling league caused fights. If she was late coming home or spent too much time at the neighbor's house, a huge argument would break out. Later I learned from many of her friends and colleagues that Bunnie was so sweet, but they could tell she was under his control. If she tried to be too independent, he shut her down.

This is textbook behavior for an abusive partner, I learned later. Domestic abusers are jealous, manipulative, and need to be in control. Because of their insecurity, they often want to encapsulate their partner in their life and in their home. Abusers are afraid on some level that their partner is better than them, or that they might leave them, so they use scare tactics to place a hold on their partner. My father did this often. Vulnerable and isolated, victims become entrenched in these tactics and feel it is unsafe to leave or confide in other people. They are too embarrassed to complain or seek help and feel somehow they deserve what is happening to them. Self-blame is common. So is feeling weak, helpless, and not having the strength to leave their abuser. Often, victims convince themselves that if they press charges on their partner and they are arrested, they will lose their access to finances, their home, and even their children. Instead, victims try to move past the event because they are too afraid of failure. They hope things will change, telling themselves it will get better, or tomorrow is a new day. If my mother accepted my father's abusive behavior and violent personality, it was because he made her feel she had no other choice.

Still, I can remember a few times my mother was not so complacent about my father's rage. Once in a while, he would act so horribly she would speak up. "Bee Gee, your anger is going to get you in serious trouble," she said to him after he intentionally rammed his car into another car over a parking spot. Then there was the incident when he hit a kid on a bike driving home one day. He blamed the kid and was more upset at the possible lawsuit or medical bills he might have to pay. My mother was appalled. "Bee Gee, could you be any more heartless!"

Alcohol would only amplify my father's violent reactions. Let me be clear—he was not an alcoholic. There was never any medical or psychological information that confirmed he had a drinking problem. He was a social drinker and an emotional drinker. He would pick and choose when he drank, just like he would pick and choose his assaults on his family. When he did drink it triggered all kinds of emotions. If he drank at parties for fun and was in a good mood, he might be arrogant or silly. However, sometimes provoked or not, his behavior would become combative and aggressive. He would lash out and be verbally abusive to others. At times his drinking would be triggered by disappointments, frustrations, and conflicts with my mom. When my parents' marriage took a disturbing turn in the summer of 1980, alcohol played a part on several occasions. Drinking was an excuse. It was the fuel he added to the fire burning in him already. It gave him the courage to initiate a stronger rage. My father was already aggressive. He already had no regard for anyone else's welfare. Adding alcohol made him rage on steroids. His fury and aggressive personality ultimately led to devastating events that destroyed lives that fateful year.

The older I became the more I thought about my father's actions. I realized there is a fine line between thinking about doing things and acting them out for real. Angry as he was much of the time, my father had a choice. You can choose how you are going to act. He chose wrong time and time again. Why? Because he wanted what he wanted. He used manipulation and various tactics to control what he felt belonged to him. This behavior paved the path for what came later.

# CHAPTER 6

# **Indiscretions**

I turned fourteen in late May of 1980, and I couldn't put my finger on it, but there were some strange things going on when June arrived. My parents were not themselves. It was very noticeable that my parents were not paying attention to routine things. Each of them was oddly distracted. For example, I had arrived home late from being out one night and no one freaked out on me. Then another time, I was on the phone for about an hour with my boyfriend and I didn't get grounded. It might sound odd that a teenager would not be thrilled about freedom from being reprimanded and punished, but I found it rather unsettling. Strange things were also happening with our house phone. For a few weeks we had been getting a lot of hang-up calls. I shrugged it off at first, but then after a few weeks, it seemed we had a serious prank caller on our hands.

While the weirdness nagged at the back of my mind, I was able to distract myself, spending lots of time with my new boyfriend, Patrick. What I didn't know was that my parents had decided to spy on me. My mother suspected I was being promiscuous and was concerned. Determined to get to the bottom of it, she asked my father if there was a way to tape-record Patrick and me talking on the phone. While this may sound like an extreme request, I believe my mother was worried about me moving forward too fast too quickly with Patrick, like she had with my father. She wanted to protect me.

A few days later, my father fulfilled my mother's request and hooked up a recording device to the phone. For the first trial run, he had it record all calls in our house for the day while he went to work. When he returned, he listened to a call that had been recorded. The voices speaking on the recording were not Patrick and me. They were my mom and another man. My mother evidently wasn't aware that my father had figured out how to get the recording device to work, and spoke intimately to the man, making it clear what was going on. Through this unfortunate turn of events, my father discovered my mother was having an affair. Days later, I found out those hang-up calls were from this man. He would call for my mom, then hang up if she didn't answer the phone. It was their secret code.

The entire situation to me was like an episode of *The Twilight Zone*. My parents tried to catch me saying something that would incriminate me. Instead, it backfired in the worst way possible. The days ahead in our house would get much, much, darker. My siblings and I continued to hear the fights between my parents and could feel the tension all the time. Now that the affair had been realized, we were getting pulled into the screaming matches. During one particular fight, my father revealed to me, deliberately, that my mom was the one who requested that the phone calls be recorded. He blurted out, "Your mother wanted to catch you and Patrick talking about what you were doing. Instead, she got caught being a whore." My father was enraged, cruel, and vile in his description of the events. Aside from being uncomfortable at how my father spewed out his anger, the news of my mom wanting to tape-record my conversations was a total surprise. He wanted me to know what a horrible person Mom was in his eyes, and how she got herself caught by being suspicious of me. I was stunned and embarrassed. I didn't know how to deal with this revelation. He continued to lash out, making it clear how Mom had been lying and sneaking around behind his back. The details of this affair were becoming very real, and everyone in our family was affected by it. The teenager in me was super peeved and bitter that my mom was trying to spy on me like that. *I can't trust either of my parents!*

However, the daughter in me was confused and sad.

*What's going to happen now? Are they going to get a divorce?* I felt like I had more doubts than ever before, thinking all kinds of things. The story was out of the bag.

Trying not to be pulled into the daily drama between my parents was difficult. One day we spent the day with Gram, my father's mother. This was a welcome time away from the constant tension in the house. I learned later that while we were gone, my father had held a shotgun pointed at Mom for several hours in their bedroom. He terrorized her and drilled her, demanding to know the name of the man she was having the affair with, only letting her go after he felt she had divulged all the information. Things that occurred in our house were often violent and weird, but this particular event was a different kind of scary. *Jeezus, when did he acquire a shotgun?* I thought. *Now we have guns in our house, guns my father has used to threaten Mom.* It was amazing that the police weren't at our house every week after that day. But Mom didn't call the police. Instead, my father belittled her into a corner every day for her betrayal. After the affair had been revealed, she hid on her porch most days. I saw that she was trying desperately to shield us from some of the marital issues. My father, on the other hand, didn't care to keep any of the details from his children.

Now that my father knew who the man was, he was not sitting quietly about it. She was having an affair with the church choir director. I vaguely remember him, an older man in his sixties, slender and bald. He directed the choir practice at the church and at my school. We had been attending mass at this church over the summer off and on. Mom enjoyed singing all the time and was asked to be the lead soloist there. She was very excited about the offer, and she thought it would be fun for us girls to get out of the house and join the choir there. The out-of-the-house part was awesome. However, for the most part growing up we were not church folks. I could count on my one hand how many times we had gone to church with our parents before then—once in a while for Christmas, or maybe Easter, when I was very young. Now, the reason was clear. What I didn't hear from my father directly, I overheard during his unfiltered fights with Mom. One detail my father repeated often was how old the man was, and how he could have been my mom's father. (I found that ironic, especially since my father was fourteen years older than Mom to begin with.) Days after my mother revealed the man's identity, my father confronted him in a parking lot somewhere and beat him up pretty good. The police came, but the man he beat up didn't press charges. *Later on, I learned from custody court transcripts that the man was also married.*

Events at home had flipped upside down with the recent happenings. I went from abused daughter, terrified of my father, to the daughter he would spill his guts to. He would corner me in different areas of the house and fill me in on details regarding their latest marital issues. I learned more about everything that was going on in our home than I ever wanted to know, and I couldn't escape him or the chaos, no matter what I did. I did try to push back on a few occasions during his exhausting rants. I took a stand and was bold enough to tell him that he needed to stop telling me all this stuff. He would look at me, with a brief epiphany in his face. I assume he realized he had said way too much to me. Yet, a few days later he would be right back at it again, coming up to my room unannounced. I would hear his keys as he came up the stairs and begin to panic, trying desperately to think of what I could have done for him to come up to confront me. But instead of screaming at me, he would come in all gloomy and tell me he needed to talk to me about things. Then, he would sit on my bed and begin speaking in a whimpering, apologetic tone of voice, blubbering about how much Mom meant to him, how our home and his family were his world. His worthless excuses were the same ones he would always give me after I received a severe beating or when he abused mom verbally or physically. I would say very little in response. Other times, the conversations were extremely uncomfortable because of the topic. He would disclose intimate details about their sex life, and he went into detail about the affair she had. Times they met up behind his back. The fight he had with this guy. All of it was more than any kid should know about such adult topics. To top it off, he would actually compare his relationship with Mom to my relationship with Patrick. "How would you feel if this happened to you?" he would say. I never knew how to respond. He even made me read a letter Mom wrote to him apologizing for what she did. Her words were so sad. She blamed herself for all of it. After I read the letter, my father leapt at the opportunity to express how he was trying to forgive her after all she had done. I just sat there.

A few times, he even took me out on car rides for private talks. He would go over all the same intimate details again and again, remarking how he couldn't even think about the church where she met this man or drive by that location without feeling sick to his stomach. He claimed that place would haunt him for the rest of his life. No sooner did he finish whimpering about the church, he would take a left turn emotionally and begin to probe me for information, asking me questions to see if I might have learned more from my mom. I would shake my head and reply, "No, I had no idea what was going on." That much was true.

By the start of June, I still hadn't brought up the topic to my mom. Things were tense and weird already, and I was too embarrassed. I just wanted to ignore it really. One evening, I went to say good-night to Mom, as I usually do. While bending down to give her a kiss and hug, she reached out and embraced me, and didn't let go. For a few seconds, it was that kind of awkward hug in which you're uncertain if you should stay hugging or separate. It caught me off guard. I tried to relax my body to be more accepting of her affection. As she began to let go, she placed her hands on my arms and looked me in the eyes. She had been crying. Her face was blotchy, and she had that nasal sound in her voice. She softly said she was sorry for hurting her family and my feelings. She knew that I was upset and hurt. She expressed she was worried for me and wasn't trying to intentionally hurt me. She explained her actions had been wrong and had nothing to do with me. This ordeal was her own mess and she wanted me to know that it was not my fault.

"I made a mistake, Suzie, and I'm trying to find the right way to fix things."

I didn't say anything while she was speaking. What could I say? My mom had an affair, and during her own indiscretions, she got caught by trying to spy on me and Patrick. How much weirder could it get? Then she continued to explain to me that she made a mistake and wanted the best for us kids. She said she was working through things with our father. She explained she wrote him a letter to apologize and in time she hoped things would get better. My mind wandered off.

*She's trying to work on things . . . Why? Nothing was ever good to begin with.* My mind then moved on to the unnerving recent developments, knowing my father had a rifle in the house and used it to threaten my mom. He was a scary man all on his own, and now he had a weapon. *Why would she want to work things out?* Mom must have been so miserable to have an affair with this much older man, yet now she's trying to mend her marriage. Having read the apology letter she wrote to my father, knowing she blamed herself and had asked him for forgiveness, I could only guess that she felt too humiliated and beat down to stand up for herself. As I drifted back into the conversation, she said she loved me, gave me another hug, and we both said good-night. I felt a little better that she had apologized to me. I loved my mom and disliked the estranged relationship we had. Most teenagers have difficulty talking to their parents. And in my house in particular, talking never made anything better. My emotions were so overwhelmed with everything I was personally dealing with that I couldn't relate to my mom. It felt like we lived in two different worlds under the same roof. Looking back now, I can recognize how alone my mom was. Alone and married to the monster who lived in our house. I truly didn't see what went on behind closed doors. It must have been incredibly scary for her to be in that physical and mental place. Feeling scared and backed up against a wall. As the months unfolded, I saw with my own eyes why she behaved the way she did. She was a victim just like me. Imprisoned, fearful, and helpless.

# CHAPTER 7

# **Distractions**

My mother, siblings, and I came home from grocery shopping one day. As we headed into the kitchen, I smelled alcohol. I saw a huge bottle of liquor in the sink, a broken flowerpot with dirt all over the place, and broken dishes. It looked like my father had thrown the bottle into the sink and knocked everything off the windowsill leaving a huge mess of broken glass and dirt. It stunk of alcohol. We began to put the groceries away. As we emptied the bags, we could hear him yelling from his studio, inaudible things. He was clearly angry. He stayed in his studio until later that night when we were sitting at the table having a snack. Mom had come downstairs after taking a shower and had a towel draped around her neck. My father came into the kitchen, opened the fridge, got out a soda, and poured some of it into a glass. He walked over to our mom, stood next to her, called her an *f-ing whore,* and poured the remaining soda over her head. Then he calmly walked out of the kitchen and back into his studio. We all sat there stunned for a few uncomfortable seconds, staring at Mom, who clearly was shocked. She started to cry. We quickly got up and gave her hugs. There was nothing else we could do. It was the way things went in our house. We brushed it off and kept going.

After my father found out about my mother's affair, there was a new outburst each week that I would see or hear. Emotions were fluctuating daily. As usual, being outside the house offered welcome distractions. This particular summer provided me with a huge one: dating Patrick.

My first introduction to Patrick was at Teddy's house that summer. Teddy had met Patrick at the alternative school they both attended. Patrick was two years older than both of us at age sixteen. Unimpressed with Teddy's new friend, I barely acknowledged him the first time we met. I was known to be shy and antisocial, so most of the time, I was oblivious to what other people were doing and preferred to be alone.

The next day I stopped over to see Teddy, and Patrick was there again. Teddy started to poke fun at me, like usual, saying stupid crap about my clothes or my hair—typical annoying boy-teasing stuff. I would always fire back and tell him to shut up. It was our normal. We would joke with each other all the time. However, lately when he was hanging out with his new friend, he became extra annoying. I could tell he was showing off because he was really being an ass. Patrick didn't seem impressed with Teddy and his continual wisecracks at me. On a few occasions, he even told Teddy to knock it off. This didn't go unnoticed by me or Teddy. I thought it was rather interesting that Patrick would come to my rescue. Teddy would get irritated by it.

Despite the occasional squabble, I began having fun hanging with them. Patrick had a comedic sense of humor and could do that funny eyebrow raise that John Belushi used to do. Once or twice he did this for a visual effect when joking around with us. He had a quick wit but also a mysterious aura about him. I liked how he could make me laugh, something I didn't do often. It was then that I noticed his facial characteristics kind of reminded me of Robin Williams from *Mork and Mindy*. The more I got to know him, I learned he lived in the same township as us and also struggled with school. In the beginning, we all got along really well, hanging out, teasing each other. Then one day, a few weeks after we met, Patrick threw a wrench into things. Out of the blue, he asked me out on a date. I was completely caught off guard and didn't know what to say. At first, I thought it was a mean joke and became annoyed. I responded back in a smartass way saying, "You're such an asshole."

He looked at me rather surprised and said, "Hey, I'm not joking." Again, he repeated his question, but this time he was more serious. I stood there for what seemed like an eternity, trying to wrap my head around the request.

I finally responded with, "Maybe, I'll tell you my answer tomorrow." Then I ran off home, leaving him standing there. I can only imagine what he must have thought, but at that moment it was the only way I could think of to escape from the intensity of it all. Honestly, I was really confused. Why did this kid want to go out with me? I wasn't a good-looking girl. I never wore makeup and wasn't ladylike by any means. My ugly red hair cut into a Dorothy Hamill style, crooked teeth, and let's not forget those plentiful freckles everywhere. As a teenager, I still had that ugly duckling syndrome, so being asked out by Patrick was unfamiliar territory for me. I was suspicious and yet also feeling a strange electricity. The emotions spinning around in my head were overwhelming. I had a hard time sleeping that night, thinking about his question.

The next day my parents went out early for some dinner rehearsal thing. Teddy and Patrick came over to my house while I was babysitting my brother and sister. They arrived at the back door. Teddy knew to go to the back door when my parents weren't home, to have better cover. Teddy also knew they had to be very careful doing this. Teddy tried to fill Patrick in briefly about my father, telling him that my father was a psycho. I'm sure at the time, Patrick must have thought Teddy meant my father was protective. Later on, he would learn that was not exactly what Teddy meant, but at the time Patrick was clueless.

After they came in, we all hung out in the mud-laundry room. (This way they could leave fast if necessary.) When they arrived, I was folding laundry. We all talked while I folded, and listened to music on the portable radio we had in the room. My sister and brother were watching a TV show in my mom's sun porch. Neither of them had heard us chatting. Otherwise, they would have been in there too, thwarting Patrick's intentions. Shortly after arriving, Teddy said he had to leave, but Patrick stayed for a little while longer. Not much time passed before he repeated his question from the day before. While I had thought about it the night before and all day long, I wasn't sure how to respond. I was afraid and inexperienced, knowing nothing about boys and dating. Then, a song that I really liked came on the radio: "Let's Go" by The Cars. I began to sing along, swaying back and forth while still folding laundry. Suddenly, before I had a chance to react, Patrick lurched forward and kissed me! I was backed up against our washer and lost my footing. I could feel his body weight on me and smelled his cologne. I remember the rush of adrenaline through my body as the song seemed to get suddenly much louder. The kiss only lasted a few seconds. Then he backed away slightly and was inches from my face. I probably looked like a total spaz and felt like a space cadet. But he smiled and said, "So, will you go out with me?" I felt so flushed. I bet I was beet red! The entire situation was awkward and weird for me.

I tried to collect myself and, stuttering, I responded with, "Um . . . yes, OK, yes . . . I will." With my emotions all out of whack, I suddenly felt super anxious and paranoid. I promptly told him he had to leave. I walked to the kitchen phone, grabbed a piece of paper, wrote down my phone number, and told him to call me when he got home. I stammered trying to explain that I would get in huge trouble if my parents found out he had been there. He seemed a little confused but politely agreed. "I will call you later," he said, and left out the back door.

My father and Patrick's mother thought the whole idea of us dating so young was ridiculous, and there was some concern about Patrick being two years my senior. I almost laughed when my father played the "concerned father" act. But, after some discussion and setting of ground rules, both our parents agreed to us dating.

Patrick filled my days with something to look forward to. We talked a lot on the phone at night, hung out during the day at each other's houses. Sometimes we went down to Merion Station Pizza. A few times we even went with his parents to huge outlet stores or museums, which was interesting and fun for me since I had never been to any of them before. Occasionally if I was hanging out with Patrick at his house, his parents would drag us to the grocery store. You would think a trip to the food store with Patrick's parents would be boring. Nope! He would do all kinds of goofy, crazy antics, like yelling out in the aisles some outlandish remark that would make people turn around and stare. I spent half my time with him blushing from laughter. Sometimes, we would just hang out and listen to music. One night while I was babysitting, Patrick showed up at my house with his friend Chris, and something under his arm wrapped in tinfoil. I had met Chris once before at a wrestling match earlier in the summer. He had weak legs from a childhood illness as an infant, but he was always super positive, which I admired. Patrick handed me a vinyl record covered with foil. It was not just any album. It was Pink Floyd's *The Dark Side of The Moon*. We were all huge fans of their music. Sitting around listening to Pink Floyd with Chris, Patrick, and my siblings is one of those rare happy memories from that time of my life.

Then there were the times we were typical sneaky teenagers. We would plot secret meetings when Patrick's parents were away on a business trip or at work. Those were the days we had alone time. I had already seen his room a few times before when his family was home— door open, of course. His room was on the third floor of his three-story colonial home on the same side as my room was in my house. It felt oddly familiar every time I visited. He had a queen-size bed, bare wood floors, and a black-and-white picture of the band The Doors hanging above his headboard. On one side of the room was a record player, with several vinyl records on a stand next to it. On either side of the room were large speakers spaced apart for proper sound exposure. On the walls he had hung some interesting artwork. A few vintage stained-glass windows leaned up against the wall and antique novelties sat on his shelves. I thought all of his stuff was super cool. He had a very eclectic style. I noticed that his family had a flair for antiques and historical décor as well. We both had parents who enjoyed classical music and were well-educated. It was interesting that both of us had similar parental issues too. His difficulties were with his mom and mine with my father. Ironically, despite our highly intelligent parents, we had similar learning problems and had both spent years in special classes. Neither of us was fond of school, but we liked a lot of the same things: listening to music, solitude, art, cooking, and travel. These similarities helped our relationship blossom. About a month into our relationship, during one of these unsupervised hangouts, I lost my virginity.

My memory of this pivotal moment in my life is a combination of excitement at first, and embarrassment during. I was super nervous and at the same time felt a little uncertain. I do remember tenderness, and that is the most important thing of all. That was not something I had often experienced in my life. Oddly enough, I remember the music he had on. It was the Genesis album *And Then There Were Three,* and one of the songs that came on as we peacefully hung out in his bed was "Follow You Follow Me." From that day on, it was our song.

These new emotions whirling around in my head regarding Patrick were perfectly normal teen feelings. However, for me having a boyfriend was still very unfamiliar territory. I still couldn't wrap my head around the fact that a boy liked me. Even after a few months, I was still feeling awkward and insecure. My thoughts would turn to all the new experiences we had had together, and I would get a rush of happiness. It was nice to feel cared about. He really did make me feel special, buying me gifts and taking me to interesting new places. It was puppy love for sure, and it was slowly boosting my confidence. That was something I truly needed. As days ticked by, I started to feel that maybe, I was not that ugly duckling after all. I was happy and that was a nice feeling for a change. I honestly had something nice to distract me from my usual misery at home.

As usual, good things for me didn't last long. The happiness of my first boyfriend was short-lived, our closeness eventually leading to my mother's suspicion and my father's dark discovery. My only escape was when I didn't have to deal with what was going on with them. Luckily, they were so preoccupied with their own marital problems, I was able to have a few moments during that month when I could enjoy my own life. One such day was when Patrick and his parents invited me to go on a day trip with them to the Reading Outlets. It was nice getting away from the house and having a fun day. When I got home, I was excited and couldn't wait to tell Mom about the day's events. Walking into the foyer, I put my things down and called out for my mom. She responded, her voice coming from my father's studio. I immediately thought that was weird. She was hardly ever in there. Then I saw that the studio door was open. Double weird. I could hear music playing, but I was so lost in my own thoughts, I didn't stop to think before I walked to the studio door entryway and peered around the corner. I could see her sitting on the couch along the left-hand wall of his studio, my father standing in front of her. Raising my voice above the loud music, I said, "I'm home! Wow, what a day I had! It was so cool. We went to–"

Before I got another word out, my father shouted out, "ARE YOU DEAF! Can't you hear that I'm listening to music with your mother?" Before I could even react, he took a few steps toward me, grabbed my arm and, practically picking me up off my feet, threw me through the entryway of his studio. I fell right on my butt and bit my tongue hard.

As I scrambled to get my bearings, I began to crawl crab-like to get away. I could hear my mother screaming at him, "Bee Gee, stop it! She was just trying to tell us about her day." My father stood there glaring at me.

I pushed myself back up onto my feet and tasted the blood in my mouth. I was so thrown off by this hostile encounter. Things had been good between my father and me for weeks. Before I even realized it, anger boiled up inside me and I shouted out, "You wonder why I hate you! I hate living here. I hate the way you treat me. I can't be happy about anything!" There were a few seconds of eye contact, and then I turned around and stormed off toward the kitchen. I didn't have time to process what had just happened. All I could think about was the disgusting taste of blood in my mouth. It overwhelmed my senses and made me feel ill. I needed to rinse my mouth with water.

As I walked away, I heard my father say, "I don't give one iota how angry you are." I suddenly realized at that moment I had lost my temper and talked back to my father! The feeling of immediate terror and the pain from my tongue had me dazed. *Shit, I'm going to get it now. He's going to come into this kitchen and beat me to death!* My thoughts were interrupted as I heard my mom saying something to my father. I don't know what it was. I just kept walking to get to the kitchen. Their talking sounded more like arguing now, ending in a loud exchange of words that I could not make out. I reached the kitchen and stood at the sink, using water to wash away the blood in my mouth. The sting of pain coming from my tongue was terrible. As I bent over to let the water run over my tongue, I thought to myself, *Do I need stitches?* I turned off the water, grabbed a paper towel and moistened it. Then, I opened up the freezer, grabbed a cube of ice and wrapped it in the wet paper towel to soothe my injury. I thought about my stuff in the foyer, wondering if I should dare go get it. I was unsure where my father was, but I was so discouraged about everything at that moment that I decided, what did I have to lose?

Walking out of the kitchen into the dining room, I practically ran right into my mom. We startled each other, then I stared at her with a disapproving look while holding the wrapped ice on my tongue. I removed the cold compress to say, "I still have my stuff in the hallway, and then I'm going to my room."

"Suzie, you must understand that when you interrupt your father and rush into his studio like that, it makes him angry." I looked at her with a glaring smirk. I was feeling two things at that moment, pain and immense anger.

My response to her was pure frustration and irritation. "Mom, I was just trying to tell you about my day. Why do you defend him all the time? Why? This is not my fault! He treats me like shit all the time—"

She immediately interrupted me, telling me not to curse and to keep my voice down. I was so mad at her. I was mad at everything and she knew it. Again, she said to me, "Suzie, you need to think before you do things, and I will talk to your father."

"Nothing is going to change. I can't wait to get out of this house!" She again raised her hands to her lips, signaling to keep my voice down. She looked at me, paused for a long moment before she spoke again. "Let me see your tongue." I stuck it out for her to see, feeling silly as she looked at it. She let out a sigh and said, "I hope the bleeding will stop soon. Go up to your room and I'll be up in a little bit. You can tell me about your day. I'm sorry this happened." She gave me a hug and said she loved me. I immediately felt calmer but at the same time unsettled. My feelings often felt confused after the attacks from my father when my mom tried to calm things.

I softly responded, "I love you too, Mom." We parted ways and I went to my room. I put away the things I had purchased that day, tried to soothe my wound with ice and water, and watched some TV. Mom did come up to my room to hear about my day. I showed her what I bought, and she was happy I had a good time. I had calmed down and my tongue felt a little better. Later that night, I lay in bed and tried to focus on having fun with Patrick and chatting with Mom, falling asleep to good thoughts.

As I think back to these times, I wish I had embraced those moments more with my mom, having a hug from her or sitting and just talking to her. I would give anything to have them back.

At the start of July, my parents seemed a little calmer as they left for England to perform. They planned to extend their stay for a vacation as well. Marylyn, Trey, and I left to stay with our grandparents as we did each year. Time spent at my grandparents' house was usually really boring. There was nothing for us to do there and the neighborhood had no children our age. So we looked forward to the portion of our visit when we would head down to the New Jersey shore. Depending on the year, we would either stay in Margate at my grandparents' shore home, or sometimes we went and stayed at my Grandpop's brother's shore home in Cape May. Both places were really nice and provided us with fun beach distractions. If we were at the Margate house, we would have beach days, catch frogs at night, and go to the boardwalk in Ocean City. If we were at the Cape May house, it was the beach, the boardwalk, and an awesome bay area where I used to find all kinds of really cool seashells. Sometimes, lots of horseshoe crabs would wash up on the beach, covering the sand. We would strategically walk around looking at them. It was a strange sight but fascinating at the same time. At night we would visit Wildwood boardwalk and enjoy the rides.

While our parents were away, Mom sent us a postcard as she always did when they traveled. This year, she sent one of a beautiful cathedral she had visited called Hereford Cathedral. It looked quite impressive from the picture. Having this postcard arrive was a nice reminder that soon Mom would be home, and we would be heading back to our house to continue our summer with our friends in the neighborhood. During our visit that summer, I was allowed to talk to Patrick a few times on the phone. Good thing, because I really missed him. I even wrote a few letters to him while we were apart. This year we went to the shore on the second half of the visit. I remember when Mom got back from her trip, she came down to the shore to visit with us. We all went to the boardwalk together. Mom stayed for a few days with us, and our father came down for a day and then left.

When I got back from vacation, Patrick and I spoke on the phone and couldn't wait to meet up. We got permission to see each other later that day. When he came over, he surprised me with a gift. I opened the box to find a really pretty necklace. He told me how much he missed me while I was away. I have to admit, he made me feel very special. Later that night, my parents gave each of us little gifts from their trip. There were moments like that, when I felt maybe my life was getting better.

how I felt. I didn't know how. I also never told her she was right about me and Patrick sleeping together, mainly because that would be a huge issue. She had a right to be worried. However, I was a teenager and it was tough to see beyond my own needs and feelings. Looking back, each of us were going through difficult times. For me, teen angst and growing rebelliousness. For Mom, a midlife disaster and reckoning over the choices she had made.

After hearing about all the recent scary outbursts, my grandparents started calling more often than usual. Mom spoke more to her parents in the coming weeks and months than I had ever been used to. She had a tough relationship with Grandmom for a number of reasons. One was being criticized if she wasn't attending church each week, and the other was my father. My grandparents never liked him and always let her know it. Now, she had to disclose so many family secrets she had kept hidden from them for years. She was frightened and needed their counsel, so skeletons that were unknown to our grandparents had to be released from the closet. Lots of secrets spilled out, and I'm sure it was not easy for her. How does anyone begin to explain what went on in our home? The abuse, the lies, all the things Mom kept hidden from her parents for years and years? I am sure telling them about the affair alone must have been incredibly difficult. Everything was coming out and none of it was pretty.

By September, all the grandparents were coming over more often. Gram, my father's mother, visited us even more frequently than my mom's parents—about twice a week. Gram used to have a nice relationship with my mom. I say *used to* because when Gram found out about the affair, her attitude toward Mom changed quite a bit. Gram was furious learning she had been asked to watch my brother a time or two while unknown to her, Mom had met up with the choir director. When Gram found this out, she defended her son and remained on his side. This brought more tension to our household, and my siblings and I were stuck in the middle as usual. I remember tiptoeing around the house for new reasons, trying to do my normal day-to-day living.

After the summer break ended, I was back at school, drenched in stress both in school and at home. It was overwhelming. The only people I could really talk to about anything were Patrick and Teddy, but they didn't go to my school. Jodie and Rick were friends of mine since our elementary school days. My girlfriend Jodie was always nice to me and we hung out often at her house. She lived with her mom and brother, and her mom was kind. Jodie was a year older than me, had pretty Italian features, and was very outgoing. I didn't reveal to her the struggles I had at home, although I sensed she knew things were strange, especially since I rarely asked her to come to my house. I didn't have friends over very often. When Jodie and I hung out, it was at her house most of the time. I remember we always had fun and sometimes we hung out with Rick too. However, with the recent stresses at home, I was feeling more alone than usual. School was a diversion, but the days still moved along like molasses. I was so beat down with all that was going on with my family, I simply arrived at school in the morning, went to class, and then left. One day I remember in late September, the news broke that John Bonham from Led Zeppelin had died. This news totally sucked. I was pretty sure they were supposed to come to the US on tour later in the year, and I had hoped to see them with Patrick and Teddy. I assumed the band would break up after this disastrous loss. What more could go wrong that year! At least this distraction changed the subject for a moment and took my mind off homelife issues. And that was a good thing.

# CHAPTER 9

# Same Crap, Different Day

"Stop! Stop! Bee Gee stop! Don't hit her anymore, you have to stop!" My father was already at the second hallway landing, and I could hear him coming up the third-floor stairs. I took a huge, deep breath. Then I could see him. He reached the third-floor landing and then he started down the hall. He had something in his hand. What was it? What did he have in his hand? He reached my doorway and the light illuminated what it was.

*Where did he get a hockey stick?*

Then, like a flash of lighting, he was in my room raising that hockey stick up in the air. I saw it come down. The sound echoed through my chest as the stick cracked across my legs. He raised that hockey stick again and hit me over and over and over on my legs, back, and arms. He hit me anyplace I moved to protect myself. I remember him saying over and over, screaming at me, "I will make sure you never walk again!" He repeated that several times. I felt as if I wasn't attached to my body anymore. I knew this was happening to me, but at the same time, I could feel myself drifting away, hiding inside my mind someplace as I had done during other attacks. I don't know how long it went on. It felt like time had stopped while this moment played out.

I could still hear things, like my mom in the background yelling over and over to my father, "Bee Gee, stop, stop, stop!" Suddenly, I realized he had stopped. Then, he abruptly left my room. I don't know how long it was before I regained my composure. I do recall sitting there thinking to myself, *Even if I had told the truth and said that yes, Teddy and Patrick stopped by and hung out for a while, it wouldn't have made any difference. No or yes, I still would have suffered the same fate that night.* It never mattered if I was honest or not. With him, the outcome was always the same in the end: pain and humiliation.

Earlier that night, I had to babysit while my parents went to a rehearsal. We all knew no one was allowed in the house, but of course, we ignored the rules. When Patrick and Teddy stopped by, we all hung out anyway. Not long after they arrived, we saw the lights of a car pull into our driveway. My parents were home way earlier than expected!

Teddy and Patrick bolted out the back door. My brother was still up so I knew it was very early for them to have returned home. They came in through the front door and my father saw me first. For some odd reason he immediately asked me point-blank, "Was anyone in the house tonight?"

Of course, I lied right through my teeth and promptly said, "Nope! No one was here." Then I quickly tried to change the subject by letting him know I had vacuumed downstairs while they were gone. In my mind, I thought I sounded pretty convincing. But he was not convinced and glared at me in disapproval. I began to slowly inch myself away from him, thinking that despite his look and the feeling in my gut, maybe I had satisfied his suspicions. I turned around and made my way across the threshold of the kitchen door, intending to get myself a snack and then go watch TV in my room. However, he followed me into the kitchen and this time in a much deeper and authoritative tone he said,

"Was anyone in this house? And you better tell me the truth."

I lied for a second time, but this time I was less convincing. In a flash, the entire universe began to spin in slow motion for me. Time stopped for a few seconds while my face slid off its skull. I knew immediately what was coming. Seconds elapsed and he was upon me. I felt his rage explode on me as he screamed, "You're a goddamn liar!"

He slapped me hard across my face and head, knocking me off balance. I moved back, raising my arms up to protect myself the best I could. He came at me again. This time he hit my chest with both of his hands full force. I fell backward onto our double-oven cabinet. The force from hitting the bars so violently was incredibly painful, but I quickly forgot about it as he jumped into action again. Without hesitation, I fell to the floor trying to avoid getting hit again, then scooted sideways to get away from him. Trying to avoid another blow, I wound up cornering myself up against the bottom kitchen cabinets. Trapped in a corner. This time his attack changed to kicking me. I curled up into a ball and tried to cover my head and face with my arms. He kicked me so many times I lost count. With each kick, I would try to protect myself, occasionally attempting an escape between blows. He continued to kick me and I could still hear him yelling, "You damn liar! You're a damn liar!" and my family in the background screaming too.

Mom was yelling, "Bee Gee, stop it, stop it!" My sister and brother were crying and huddled with Mom by the kitchen table. In between blows, I could hear their crying swirling all around me as I desperately tried to look for a way out. My mind was telling me I had to get away from him. I had to escape.

Then, there was a brief moment when he was interrupted by my mom trying to grab him while pleading with him to stop hurting me. It gave me the opportunity to scoot over toward the kitchen steps. At that split second, I leapt up and headed for the two stairs at the back entrance of the kitchen. I could see our walk-in pantry door there on the landing. I was free to scramble up the back stairs to the second-floor landing. From there I had nineteen more stairs to go before I reached my third-floor bedroom. I raced down the small hallway into my bedroom and I paced back and forth. I finally sat on my bed, trying to catch my breath. I didn't feel any pain really. Not yet anyway. I felt sweaty and my heart was pounding along with my head.

At some point Marylyn had made her way up to her room. I am not sure if she did this before or after I got upstairs. She came in my room, asking me if I was OK. I know she was trying to help. I could tell she was scared and upset, but I didn't want to talk to anyone. I just wanted to be left alone. Finally, I caught my breath and all kinds of thoughts raced through my head. Only a few minutes had passed before I heard that dreaded sound . . . *cling, cling, cling.* It was coming from the stairs. I could also hear my mom yelling,

"Stop! Stop! Bee Gee, stop! Don't hit her anymore, you have to stop!"

After the beating with the hockey stick, I sat there alone, wondering where my mom was. Maybe she was comforting my brother? Marylyn again came in to try and check on me. I was overwhelmed with emotions. I couldn't think clearly and I asked her to leave me alone. I slowly tried to get up. My legs were weak and my whole body felt oddly shaky. Yet, at the same time I was full of energy, like I had chugged down a two-liter bottle of soda. I steadied myself, walked over and closed my door a little. After pacing around my room, I finally decided that I was not staying in that house another second. I began putting a few more layers of clothes on, preparing myself for an exit out of that house. I had to be smart about it. Taking what I could to keep warm, I grabbed some cash I had saved and stuffed it into my pockets. I put on a few shirts, doubled up on socks, and shoved a few things into a big purse that I had. Then I stood up on the second twin bed in my room, which was under a small window. I opened the window and looked out, studying it for a minute to assess if I could climb out. It was a small casement attic window that opened out with a swing-hinge sash, directly over my father's studio. I didn't dwell on things. I just followed through. I was able to maneuver my way out of the small window but had to hold on with all the strength I had left.

I knew I had to manage this escape with total precision, especially with his studio being below. My adrenalin was pumping madly as I wiggled out the window. I put one leg through while holding onto the window frame. Then, I maneuvered my other leg through. Using the frame as support, I was able to grab onto a thick black wire that ran down the side of the chimney. Gripping onto the wires for dear life, I shimmied my way down onto the roof below, being extra careful to land really quietly, ninja-like. Next, I walked gingerly to the edge of the roof. I knew at that point, jumping off the studio porch roof would be fine. I would land in the grass and then run. The leap off the roof was a good eight- or nine-foot jump, and I landed hard. Success! I was so relieved. I stood up, took a deep breath, and got myself ready to run. After taking a few steps toward the yard, moving in the direction of the sidewalk, Teddy and Patrick appeared out from the bushes, scaring the crap out of me! Both of them whispered back and forth, firing off questions.

"What happened?"

"Are you OK?"

"What did he *do* to you?"

They looked at me wide-eyed like they had seen a ghost, each saying they heard me, my father, and my mom screaming. I felt like I was being interviewed by two news reporters. But I didn't have time to chat with them. "We need to leave, *right now!* I don't want to talk about it here. Let's go!" We all ran up the street into the darkness.

We ran for a long time, trying to figure out a good place to go and hide as we ran. Teddy made the first suggestion. He explained he would tell everyone I hitched a ride down to Wildwood, New Jersey, to throw them off the trail. Patrick offered, "Let's go to Ardmore. I have a friend who has an apartment there. I can ask him if he can help us out. Maybe we can stay there and hide out for a few days." We continued on, staying clear of the main roads as much as possible in case my parents realized I was gone and called the police. The roughly three miles took longer with all our detours, but it was worth it to keep out of sight. This place Patrick suggested was near the Burger King in Ardmore. When we got to the apartment, the guy wasn't home. We hung out in the hallway of the apartment complex, not knowing what else to do. Patrick was confident this guy would be home soon or at least show up at some point. No such luck. For several hours, we all talked and plotted what we could do while sitting at this guy's door in the hallway. After a while, Teddy decided he better go home so his parents didn't wonder where he was. It was about ten o'clock by then.

Before he left, he said again, "If anyone asks where you are, I will tell them you hitched it to Wildwood."

Patrick and I stayed in that hallway until morning. It was a long, cold, and uncomfortable night. I must have dozed off at some point from pure exhaustion. I woke up to the daylight peeking through the window. We decided to leave the duplex and go get something to eat, both miserable from lack of sleep. I tried to stand up, but my body hurt so bad. It took all of my willpower and Patrick's assistance to get my muscles to work. I thought, maybe some food and hot coffee would help. We left the apartment building and headed toward Burger King. It was a nice day out. As we exited the building and walked down the street, I began to think, *What am I going to do now?* Just then, we saw a cop car go right past us. *Shit!* We looked at each other in panic. If he turns around, the jig is up. Sure enough, that is exactly what happened. We kept walking, picking up the pace. Then I told Patrick to take off before the police car got back around to us. He looked at me and asked why. I told him there was no reason for him to get in any trouble. So he popped into a parking lot and took off. Seconds later, the cop pulled up slowly, sounding his siren one time. I stopped and stood on the sidewalk. He got out of the car, walked around to the sidewalk, and asked for my name. My heart was pumping furiously. I told him.

"Do you know how worried your parents are about you?" I looked right at him and laughed obnoxiously.

"My parents don't give a shit about me! That's why I'm out here. My father beat me up with a hockey stick last night. I am not going back!" The officer looked right at me, totally ignoring what I had said. He told me to get into the vehicle, and that he was taking me to the police station where I could wait for my parents to come get me. I was confused and peeved at the same time. Did he not hear me? I again explained what had happened to me the night before. I even tried to show him my injuries. My arms and my face. I said he should see my legs. I again went through details of what my father did the night before during the whole five-minute ride to the station. All my ranting fell on deaf ears. He wouldn't listen to me.

I assumed my parents must have told the cops some wild, crazy story about me being a typical troublemaker teen, because he looked at me and said, "How can you say things like that about your folks? You teenagers give your parents such a hard time, you're lucky they don't throw you in juvenile hall."

I sat there stunned. What was wrong with this guy? *Are you kidding me!* I was so annoyed. I couldn't believe I was telling the police that I was beaten up by my father. I have all these bruises. I have *proof!* But he is making me feel like I'm the criminal because I ran away.

When we got to the station, he allowed me to walk in on my own and told me to sit in this room in a chair near the front counter. I kept blurting out what happened and why I ran away.

"You are sending me home to a crazy man! What do I need to do to prove to you that I live in a horror house! I'm going to be killed if I go home!" The desk clerk and another officer stared at me momentarily, and then went back to whatever they were doing. I gave up, it was useless to continue.

A few more minutes went by and my mom arrived to pick me up. She walked in and I could see the annoyed look on her face. She spoke to the officer and had to sign some paper. I stood there glaring at her. Again, I said loudly, "You know what's going to happen when I get home. He's going to beat me to death." I looked at my mom and said, "Why are you even here?" She told me to not say another word. I rolled my eyes. I was so mad, I had nothing to lose. I said whatever came to mind. It didn't matter now. I knew then that my life was meaningless. I wasn't going to even try anymore. Right or wrong, for me, I was always on the losing end of the stick. This time, a hockey stick.

During the car ride, the discussion took on a whole new vibe. Mom began to apologize for me getting hurt. "Your father was wrong, he went too far! You shouldn't have suffered such a beating."

I glared at her, and in my teenage rage, I told her off. "You don't even protect me! Why didn't you tell the police what he did to me? Why!" She responded back, insisting that if I had told the truth none of it would have happened, trying to communicate with me but blame me in the same breath. Again, I lashed out, "Speaking of lies, *that* is a lie. All you do is defend him. No matter what I said he still would have kicked my ass. Either way, Mom, either way! Look what he has done to *you,* Mom!"

I know she understood what I meant. He was a monster; not even she could deny that. Before we got home, she started to offer me some advice. "When you get home and you see your father, apologize. Just apologize for lying and try to look remorseful." I looked at her like she had ten heads.

"Mom, he hurts me! You saw it, you were there. He hurts you too. We need to get away from him. Why do you stay with him? *Why?*" Suddenly, she pulled the car over. I panicked, thinking she was going to smack me. She was quiet, the tension was horrible. Then she looked at me. Her face changed, and I could hear the strain in her voice.

All of a sudden, she interrupted me and blurted out something I will never forget. With extreme distress in her voice she said, "Suzie, *we have no place to go!* I don't know what to do. I tried! I tried! I can't get away from him. He will never let me go! You just don't understand. *He will never let me go!*" After she spoke, she turned her head and stared out the front window. The silence was deafening. I sat there. I heard every word she had said. I really heard her. It was a haunting moment. I remember how urgent she sounded. She looked like a scared little girl. She looked like me. Her admission caught me off guard. For a moment I felt sorry for her. However, at the same time I was so angry that I had nobody to protect me. Before I could think of anything else to say, she put the car in gear, and we drove home.

When we arrived at the house the exhaustion began to overwhelm me. I knew I was going to face my father, but at this point I really didn't care. I didn't have the energy to exert any emotion. I walked through the front door and into the foyer, put my stuff down, and then walked into the kitchen with Mom. My father was descending the back steps into the kitchen. He approached me, looking at me with that familiar irritated look on his face. He said, "You are such a disappointment." There was a brief pause, and then he went on, "You will go to school today. Your mom will drive you, since we can't trust you. Then, she will tell the principal you are not to leave the school." He paused again, looked at me and said, "Do you understand me?" I nodded my head in response. He turned and walked out of the kitchen. Mom told me to go change and meet her at the front door. I sluggishly walked out of the kitchen and back into the foyer to get my things. Then I started up the stairs to my room. Each step I took made my legs feel like I was carrying a thousand pounds. I finally reached my room and began to tenderly take off my clothes. Every inch of me hurt, and I had more bruising than the night before. I looked like I had been hit by a car, and felt like it too. I put on some clean clothes and went back down the stairs. My legs were on fire.

The drive to school was quiet. I think I might have dozed off. We pulled into the school parking lot, walked in through the lobby, and went into the office. As we sat in the waiting area, Mom gave me her explanation of what she felt was the right thing to tell the principal. She said she would tell him I ran away and was behaving in a typical rebellious teenage manner. I didn't respond. I was exhausted and had given up trying to fight the losing battle that was my life. None of it mattered anymore. After she spoke to them, she came over to me and said, "Suzie, do not leave this school, please. Do you understand me? Let's try to move past all of this, OK?" I shrugged and nodded my head. The secretary gave me my hall pass and I went to my first class—English with Mrs. Nelson, thank goodness.

Mrs. Nelson was a teacher who cared about her students, and I never forgot her passion for helping us learn. She had a strong presence, but also a heart of gold. The moment I walked into the class, she looked at me with this odd stare. I gave her my hall slip and she told me to go sit at my desk. I sat down and listened to her give the class some instructions. A few minutes later, she came back over to me and asked me if I was OK. I said, "I'm fine," of course. What else was I supposed to say? *Hey, by the way, my father is a lunatic. He mentally and physically abuses me and treats me like a freak. Can you save me?* I couldn't tell her the truth. How does a kid like me tell anyone what is really going on at home? Sitting at my desk, the exhaustion was overtaking me. I put my face in my arms and fell asleep. Mrs. Nelson never said anything to me, and I didn't get detention for sleeping in her class that day.

I kept my jacket on the entire day at school. No one could see the bruises on my arms. I couldn't cover all my face bruises entirely with makeup, but if anyone were to ask, I would have simply said I had a run-in with a ball or some other stupid answer. I was a quiet kid and not popular, so I really never had to explain much of anything to anyone. Patrick and Teddy went to an alternative school, and I wondered how things had been for them since we parted ways. When I finally saw them after a few days confined to my house with no phone privileges, I filled them in on all the details and my parents' reactions. Neither of them was shocked.

*Same crap, different day.*

Later in life, I thought about what my mom said to me in the car that day. *"He will never let me go!"* Her words will always haunt me. They make much more sense now that I'm an adult. But back then, my pain and fears distracted me and overshadowed everything. I couldn't really let what she said fully sink in. At that moment in my life, I was so angry at her and everything else. I felt betrayed by her. Betrayed by both my parents, by life itself. I look back now, and I know she loved me. But she also had no idea how to handle all of this horror.

My personality morphed following the events of the previous few months. I wasn't sure what was going on entirely, but I had this *I don't care* attitude. Maybe it was typical teenage angst. Maybe I was just tired of being afraid. Or, maybe it was just a mental breakdown. I didn't know exactly. Whatever it was, it was a huge change in the way I handled future confrontations with my father.

A few weeks after the hockey stick incident, there was another showdown between my parents. This one had a strong effect on me. I was in the kitchen preparing a bagel and watching TV, and my brother was upstairs with Mom. I thought my sister was too, but apparently that was not the case. Earlier, Marylyn had witnessed my father go into my mom's music bag, pull out some sheet music, and tear it up. Then he put all the pieces back into her bag, went back into his studio, and slammed the door. Marylyn promptly ran to tell Mom about what he had done. Minutes later, I could hear them all come down the stairs. Mom began to yell out loud enough for my father to hear, "Oh, how childish. He's ripping up my things now." Well, this woke the sleeping lion who had been brooding in his studio. Seconds later, I could hear my father come out of his studio into the foyer. He began to roar obscenities at Mom. I recall, my brother was near the stairs, and my sister was closer to the credenza along the foyer wall. Mom screamed back at my father. The knife that I had been using to cut my bagel was still in my hand when I walked out of the kitchen to the entryway of the foyer. As I entered the scene, my father turned his rage to Marylyn, calling her a little bitch for tattling. Then he started screaming at Mom saying he didn't give a shit about her feelings or her ripped-up sheet music.

He continued to scream more obscenities and then unexpectedly kicked Mom's music bag, which had been on the floor leaning against an antique chair. The bag landed near Marylyn and without hesitation, she went to pick it up. Seeing this, my father, in one swoop of his hand, hit my little sister, knocking her to the ground. Then, he kicked her, causing her to retreat into a curled-up ball on the floor. The moment I saw him hit and kick my sister; the anger surged up in me. He had backed away a few inches by then and was standing in front of her. It was then I realized I still had the knife in my hand.

The whole situation played out in slow motion. I stepped forward, held the knife in front of me as if it were a sword, then yelled out, "Don't you touch her again! Get back! Get back! Leave us all alone!" It felt like forever as we all stood there motionless. Those brief seconds, everyone was stunned. Frozen like statues. Then, he took a step back, looking at me the whole time. It was terrifying. I have no idea what he was thinking or what was going to happen. Is he going to lunge at me? The suspense was distressing, but I held my ground. I never moved. He glanced around at us all for another second and took another step back. Then, he turned around and walked back to his studio, shutting the door slowly. Not slamming it like he usually did. All of us stood there frozen. My hand was shaking, still holding the knife. Marylyn was sobbing, and my brother cried along with her, holding onto Mom's leg. Mom jolted me back to reality when she spoke.

"Suzie, can you please go put the knife back in the kitchen?" I unfroze from my position and robotically obeyed her request. I walked back into the kitchen, placed the knife in the sink, and stood there staring out the kitchen window for a while, lost in my own thoughts. A little while later, we all gathered in Mom's porch and clung together for support. That night we kept the door closed, watching TV until it was time for bed.

When October came, the tension in the house had changed. The atmosphere had become eerily calm again. I noticed my parents were trying to communicate more. Instead of screaming, they were talking, and spending more time together too. My father was home a lot more often when I got home from school. That was odd. He started having dinner with us again during the week. I'm not sure if they were seeking counseling or what. I simply noticed they were back to being preoccupied with their own issues and not paying attention to my teenage life. It actually seemed as if they were trying to work things out. You would think that was a good thing, but it wasn't comforting to me at all. The weirdness detector in my body was going off all the time. Little did I know, the next time things would erupt would be the last time I would call that house home.

# CHAPTER 10

# Leaving

Thinking back to the night my father strangled my mom, the night I stood up to him, the night before we packed up and left that house for good, I remember Mom sitting on my bed showing Marylyn and me the marks on her neck. Through tears, she said, "Never forget this, he tried to kill me, he tried to kill me." We sobbed together, huddled on my bed. Suddenly, Mom seemed panicked again, saying she needed to call her parents. She guided my sister off to bed, and then, surprisingly, circled back into my room. She sat down next to me and I could feel her trembling. It was then I told her what I had heard in the stairwell. She looked at me with frightened eyes and I could tell she was still in a daze after my father's horrible attack. She repeated the same phrase over again, "He tried to kill me, he tried to kill me," while rubbing her hands back and forth over her neck. She was overthinking every action, wanting to leave my room but afraid to, terrified my father would come after her again. Moments went by and then she stood up, startling me with her sudden movement. She repeated, "I have to call my parents." She walked out of my room and I was left alone with my thoughts – all the weight of the world on my shoulders.

One . . . two . . . three . . .

I began counting objects, staring at different items in my room, counting things and trying to calm down. It was a weird thing for me to be doing at that moment. Randomly looking around my room, scanning it. Thinking about the disaster of a life I had.

About half an hour went by and Mom came back up to my bedroom. She was too afraid to fall asleep in her own room and remained on my other twin bed for a long time. I stayed up most of the night, on guard, waiting for something else to happen. I could hear her sniffling from time to time. I wanted to stay awake. I had to be ready, just in case. Suddenly I woke up and realized it was morning.

Mom was no longer on the bed across the room. I heard voices coming from downstairs. I jumped out of bed, threw on some pants, and quickly ran down the stairs toward the sound of my grandparents' voices. I was

75

relieved that they were already there. They had arrived much earlier and had already taken Mom to the hospital for evaluation. Mom's injury was very evident now. You could see the strangulation marks on her neck, clearly indicating what had occurred the night before. This visual was a harsh reminder of the frightening events of just hours earlier. Mom had filed a report of the attack, but once again, she had not pressed charges. My grandparents called the police anyway, wanting to have an officer at the house while we moved out to be sure there were no issues. When I came downstairs, the officer was parked out in front of our house, there to enforce the peace while we gathered up whatever possessions we could. My father was holed up in his studio. At some point through all the commotion, I began to understand that we were actually leaving our house. I stood there frozen, stunned that it had finally come down to this.

I was brought back to reality when my Grandpop came over to me and gently pulled me aside. He said to me, "The doctor said your Mom's vocal cords may have been damaged. She may never be able to sing properly again." He was all choked up as he spoke, and I struggled to process this news. I couldn't imagine life without my mom singing. That was what she loved to do. Had my father destroyed that too? Just as I began to dwell on this new horrible possibility, my Grandpop's voice became firm as he said, "That man tried to kill our daughter last night. I'd like to see him come out and try something when I'm here!" I had never seen my Grandpop that upset before. Then he turned his attention to me, saying more gently, "I'm proud of you, Suzie, protecting your mom and your sister. Good girl." I was caught off guard, needing a moment to understand what he was congratulating me for. Then it dawned on me that Mom must have filled him in on how I had stood up to my father last night, ordering him to leave my room after his attack on Mom. For a moment, I felt proud. But it was short-lived as I was shocked back to what was unfolding at the moment. My mom was gathering things from various rooms, and my Grandmom was too. Grandmom came over and asked us to continue packing up everything we could so we could get out of there as quickly as possible. We were moving out, and it was happening now.

The tension and the entire situation were uncomfortable. During the boxing and bagging up of household items, my grandparents would intermittently let out a rant, projecting loud enough so my father could hear them from his studio. Grandpop was yelling loud and clear how he felt about his daughter's attack. Who could blame him? He shouted, "He is a violent man. He tried to kill our daughter. He should be put in jail!"

Then my Grandmom would say, "He is evil. I knew it from the moment I met him!"

All of this was going on as my siblings and I were standing open-mouthed, trying to figure out what to do. I could tell my mom was frantic. She told me to focus on getting my things. It was weird to hear her speak. Her voice still sounded so hoarse. She reiterated that we only had room for the necessities. I stood there for a few more seconds, watching everyone carry things out of the house. I was pretty sure the neighborhood was in gossip mode by then, especially with a police car out front. I grabbed a few coats from our foyer closet to take out to the car when I saw Teddy standing across the street. I knew he was wondering what the heck was happening. I placed the coats in the car and walked over to talk with him. I quickly tried to fill him in, but my Grandpop called me back inside and instructed me again to get what I needed.

"Gather your things, we need to go!" he said.

I ran up to my room with two large green trash bags and a box. I put as many things into the two trash bags and one small box I had, realizing quickly I would have to leave a lot of my belongings behind. I grabbed clothes, toiletries, personal stuff, and whatever I could possibly take right then. As I was doing this, I suddenly felt panic. This was it. It finally was happening. We were leaving. The anxiety slipped into a kind of nausea. My friends, my school, my life, it's all here. Despite all the years I wished I could leave that house, now that it was happening, I was terrified. Even though I felt like I was sinking in quicksand, I didn't have time to dwell on my feelings.

My Grandpop snapped me out of my thoughts when he called out, "Hurry up, we need to leave!" I dragged my bags down the stairs and ran back up to get my box, feeling like I was outside my body. The chaos in our home was my normal. There were so many serious confrontations in the past. But lately, things had gotten worse and worse. Last night's incident was the icing on the cake. My father's actions the night before had resulted in a life-or-death situation. We had to get out of there. I loaded my stuff into Grandmom's car. Grandpop's van was already full. My mom's car had enough room for us in the back seat. It was time to leave. We were going to live with my grandparents where it was safer, forty-five minutes away in Ardsley. Moving there would get us far away from him.

There was no good-bye. It was a swift exit. I climbed into the car and gazed out the window, watching the house I grew up in disappear as we drove around the bend. When my house was no longer in sight, I felt a sudden rush of anxiety. What was going to happen now?

# CHAPTER 11

# New Surroundings and a New Predicament

My sister and I had spent a few summers with our grandparents while our parents did theatrical tours. Staying for a week or two was not unfamiliar. Moving in, however, felt very strange. The smells, the surroundings, even being in such close proximity as a family was awkward. We had full run of the upper portion of their house. There were two bedrooms and one bathroom. The larger room was given to Marylyn and me. We had never shared a room before. Being a teenager, adjusting to close quarters with a ten-year-old was difficult to say the least. My brother stayed with my mom in the smaller room. Mom had grown up in that house, and it must have been a weird experience for her to be back home living with her parents—especially since she left under strained circumstances so many years ago. Over the next couple of weeks, Grandpop and Mom went down to the house a few times to gather other items that we were not able to take with us during our hurried exit. Grandpop set up space in their basement for the extra stuff. There was furniture, boxes, a rack of my mom's clothes, and other odds and ends. Meanwhile, we settled in best we could under the circumstances. We got up very early five days a week to take the forty-five-minute drive to our schools. After school, we took the bus back to our old house in Merion and hung out at Teddy's house until our mom or grandparents came to get us. That was a plus. Each day we got to see our friends, and I got to see Patrick. Within a week or so, we had all gotten into a normal pattern.

While waiting at Teddy's after school, I often found it so odd that I couldn't go into my home. There it was: my house, right across the street, and I couldn't go in. Not that I missed it or anything. Except, I sort of did. I had horrible memories of that house for the most part, and yet, it was the home I grew up in. It was awkward now to be an outsider looking in. And nothing was ever going to be the same again. Mom had filed for divorce and custody. With financial help from my grandparents, she now had an attorney. Mom was looking for a job and trying to find a place for us to live. Soon I would be going to a new school. There was so much going on in such a short span of time. Everything was changing.

I felt sick to my stomach.

Leaving home and getting far away from my father, I thought I would feel less anxious but that was not happening. I felt horrible all the time. I began to wonder if I was coming down with something. *It's just nerves,* I would tell myself.

Then, near the end of October, it suddenly dawned on me that I hadn't gotten my period in September. I was very late, and now very worried. I thought maybe all the stress had something to do with it. So after school one day at Teddy's house I pulled Patrick aside when he arrived to see me and explained my concerns. He was immediately freaked out. He stepped back and blurted out, "It's not my problem, it's your problem." It was heart-wrenching to hear him say that to me. We argued back and forth, both of us scared and unsure of this new terrifying possibility. It was an ugly scene. Then, in the midst of our heated argument, he broke up with me on the spot, saying, "I don't want to have a steady girlfriend anymore." I was totally devastated, and at the same time, humiliated.

After he left, I stood on the sidewalk in front of Teddy's house feeling lost. I was scared and overwhelmed, with no one to talk to. Everything was happening all at once. I felt a wave of emotions come over me. As I sat down on the curb, I thought about how I had given him my trust. What an idiot I was. My father's nickname for me came into my thoughts. *Stupid pea brain.* My father was right. How could I ever have thought Patrick loved me? Or that I was worth anything? All the ugly things that my father had said to me for years came gushing into my head. As usual, I had to deal with this alone. My thoughts raged on.

*Fine. How much worse could things get! My life is complete shit anyway. I'm living a nightmare. My whole life is upside-down. My father's a psycho. My parents are getting a divorce. I'm living at my grandparents' house. My boyfriend doesn't care about me. Oh, and let's not leave out how dead I'm going to be when my parents find out I might be pregnant!*

Still sitting on the curb in thought, my grandpop arrived to pick us up. I had to pull myself together. It was a long drive back to my grandparents' house. During the ride I had a full plate. Alone in my pain and thoughts, I had to pretend nothing was wrong. I couldn't disclose how devastated I was in front of my sister, grandparents, or my mom. They would wonder what was going on. So I buried it and swallowed my pain. The fear of my predicament was enough to keep me quiet, and not knowing the answer for sure was a heavy burden all on its own.

Honestly, I was unsure how to approach this dilemma. So I asked a friend at school, ". . . hypothetically, for a friend." She suggested Planned Parenthood, explaining that anyone could go there, talk to someone in confidence, and get help. I looked up the information in the phone book and called from a pay phone at school. I was able to make an appointment pretty quickly. The day of my appointment, I cut school later in the morning, so I was already logged in for homeroom. Then I walked to the facility, which wasn't too far away.

When I got there, I answered a few questions and gave a urine sample. Then, I waited in the exam room for a long time. Finally, the nurse came back in and told me the result of the pregnancy test was positive and, "the doctor will be in shortly." Panic hit me like a brick to the head. *I am in so much trouble. What the heck am I going to do? I can't have a baby.* My thoughts were interrupted as the nurse and female doctor came in to do an exam. The situation was an unfamiliar and scary experience. It wasn't unusual for me to feel lonely and scared. Just this version was different. The exam was awkward, and my drifting thoughts were interrupted by questions from the doctor: Did I know the father? Was this a consensual conception? What was my plan? I told her I had a boyfriend, and yes, it was consensual. But I had no plan. I didn't know what I was going to do, how I was going to manage this huge new burden. While the doctor tended to my chart, I told the nurse I needed to think first, and maybe I could try to talk to my mom. The doctor made another appointment for me and left the room. I sat on the exam table, wearing a paper cloth, feeling numb. What was I going to do? My head was filled with more questions than answers. Like a zombie, I got dressed and left the office. On the long walk back to my neighborhood, I had lots to think about. When I arrived at Teddy's house, I acted like things were normal and waited quietly for my mom or grandpop to pick me up.

After a few days went by, the weirdest thing happened. My mom noticed that something was not right with me. She confronted me down in the basement while I was getting laundry. Even with all the stress she was going through, she didn't miss a beat! "Are you pregnant?" she flat-out asked me. I was stunned. My mom was so smart. I stood there frozen in place, my mind racing.

I thought to myself, *I know the facility wouldn't have told her. It's all confidential. This has to be Mom-intuition. I have no choice but to come clean.*

I'm sure my face said it all before I opened my mouth to confirm her suspicions. She was silent for a few awkward moments. Let's just say, she was not happy. We had a very tough, heated, whispered conversation in my grandparents' basement. She expressed how disappointed she was with me and a few other unpleasant things. But after her initial shock and hurt she went on to say we would need to go to the doctor. That's when I told her I had already gone to Planned Parenthood. Her mouth fell open for a few seconds in utter surprise. She was stunned hearing that I had taken it upon myself to handle this first step all on my own (and that I had broken some rules to do it). When the shock wore off, she asked me what they said. I told her the results were positive and I had another appointment set up. I think at that point she was so overwhelmed with so many thoughts that she didn't know what to say first. She stood there for what felt like a very long, silent moment. Her head was down. She was thinking or trying to take it all in, I guess? A few moments later she looked up at me.

"Do not tell anyone, not my parents or your father, no one!" Her worry over my secret getting out must have been spurred by thoughts of my Roman Catholic grandparents, not to mention my father who would surely try to use it against us. Then she paused and said, "Does Patrick know?"

"I tried to talk to him. He freaked out and broke up with me saying it was my problem and I had to deal with it."

"Let's leave it there then. Do not talk to him. Do not tell him anything. We need to deal with this together." She put her arms out. I was hesitant to move. Then she said, "Come here," and I walked into her arms, and she hugged me. I was so emotionally knotted up I couldn't cry.

"I'm sorry, Mom," was all I could say. I believe she knew I was sorry for being so stupid. Everyone in their lifetime has done something they regret. I could feel she understood.

"Suzie, remember, do not talk to anyone but me. I need to think this over and we will address this more later." I agreed and went back upstairs. I felt really horrible that my stupidity caused her even more stress. *Yay me.*

One day after school, Teddy asked me why Patrick wasn't around. I told him, "We broke up, and I am not his keeper. I really don't care, anyway."

Teddy being a wiseass said with a laugh, "Why did he break up with you? Did he find out you're pregnant or something?" I looked at him with eyes as big as saucers.

"What? How did you know!"

Teddy looked back at me with the same wide-eyed look, surprised by my reaction as well. "I didn't," he replied, "I was messing with you. Wow, holy shit, you're pregnant! Really? And he broke up with you? What a dick!" We stood there for a few seconds and then he said, "What are you going to do?"

I told him I had no idea. I filled him in on my mom's reaction and told him he couldn't tell anyone, especially Patrick. My mom would be so peeved if anyone found out, especially my father. Teddy agreed to keep the secret. He knew my father finding out could result in me and my mom getting hurt. We sat there for a while saying nothing. I think we both needed to think about things. Teddy at times could be a really good friend. He was someone I could trust, and at that moment in my life I really needed that.

I thought back to things Teddy knew about my life and felt grateful for his friendship. He always had my back and knew life was hard for me. He had also had his own struggles, and I guess because of that we shared a special bond. A few minutes later my moment of reflection was interrupted by my Grandpop arriving to pick up my siblings and me.

In the last week of October, Mom secured a job as a secretary at a home security company in Bryn Mawr. This was the change she had been hoping for. By the second week in November, it was time to move again, this time into our own place.

Mom found an apartment in Sussex Square Apartments in Plymouth Meeting. It was down the street from a big mall, and she was really excited about it. We were on the list for a three-bedroom that wouldn't be available for a few months. So we made the cozy two-bedroom apartment work for us. My grandparents helped a lot during this tough time. Aside from paying for Mom's attorney and being there to emotionally support my mom, they cosigned for the apartment, paid the security deposit, and covered the first month's rent. They also helped us move in. We were very thankful.

Our new place was nice, but small. Mom tried to make things as fair as she could, giving my sister and me the larger master bedroom and en suite bathroom. For Trey's room, she turned the very large walk-in closet across from her room into a mini toddler bedroom. It was a little unconventional, but it worked well for him. Mom took the door off its hinges and placed a cot for his bed. Then she added his toys, boy's decor, stuffed animals, and a small dresser. He was three years old and this little room fit him perfectly! The living room was a nice size and there was a small dining area off the kitchen. I remember the grounds were nice too, and there was a pool in the middle of the complex. Our future bus stop was at the entrance.

Mom was trying to get us registered in the new school district. However, it didn't happen overnight. So we still had to be driven down to our old schools and get picked up from Teddy's house. During this period of time, things had become even more complicated with Patrick. I felt like he simply showed up at Teddy's house on his way to Merion Station Pizza just to annoy me. One day he tried to apologize to me, and asked me what happened about my "situation." Keeping my promise to my mother, I told him there was no situation. It was a false alarm. I felt it was best to listen to Mom for once and I refused his apology. I was extremely upset about how he bailed on me when I needed him most. I was disgusted with him and myself. I think I even told him I hated him at some point. Maybe he was trying to make amends. Maybe he missed me? Whatever the reason, I didn't want to be hurt again. The pain from our breakup had reaffirmed to me what a loser I was, and I could no longer trust him. The pregnancy alone made it risky to be around him. There were days it was hard to stay sane with my emotions and hormones going crazy. I didn't want to give him any reason to think I was pregnant. So I had to focus on listening to my mom. I needed to stay away from Patrick, and he needed to stay away from me.

This was difficult, since he was always turning up.

While my parents were separated and since the attack, I had not seen my father or spoken to him. We didn't have any kind of set schedule to see him at that time. Visitation had not been settled yet, and Mom didn't want us around him alone for very long after his attack. However, we did talk to him on the phone occasionally after we moved into the apartment. Conversations were short. During one of the calls, I told my father Patrick and I were no longer dating. He asked why. At the time I said we got in a fight. I didn't elaborate much on anything with my father.

We ate dinner at his house one time before we started our new school. It was very weird being in the house after we had moved out. The appearance was altered from the move. Most of the furniture and all the pretty things Mom had contributed to were gone. It was a shell of a house now. All that was left was the hideous living room furniture they had purchased before my birthday—a dark-brown leather couch and loveseat with antique brass nailhead trim running up the sides of the arms. In the center of it all was a large, matching square ottoman. His opera pictures were still hanging, but the rest of the walls had noticeable fade marks from where pictures used to be. I observed boxes he had begun to pack in the corners of each room. The dining room was now so strange. Notably, none of Mom's knickknacks were in the display cabinets. Her sun porch, once homey with furnishings, hanging potted plants, a television, fully adorned shelves, and a huge gardenia bush—looked naked. Only the couch and chairs were there now. Our bedrooms, of course, were bare. One bed and one dresser remained in each of our rooms. The house echoed as we spoke from the lack of furniture. The empty house and having to see my father again added anxiety to my already overstressed state, not to mention the extreme nausea I felt most of the time.

During this dinner visit, there was a knock at the back door. Moments later, I saw Patrick walking into the kitchen with a pizza box. I couldn't believe my father had called the pizza place where he knew Patrick was working! My father was well aware we were not dating anymore, so I was immediately upset to see him in our house. I cursed out loud in front of my father and siblings. Then, they all witnessed a fight between Patrick and me, each of us spewing nasty comments at each other. The stunning aspect of this scenario is that my father didn't knock me into next week when it happened. He must have been trying to be on his best behavior because of the court stuff going on. Otherwise, I would have been severely reprimanded. After the fight, I walked out of the kitchen and went into Mom's porch. I could hear my father say something to Patrick as he walked him to the back door. After Patrick left, I had no choice but to eat the stupid pizza. I was starving.

Later my father asked me why we broke up. I fibbed, saying that Patrick thought I was too young, and I now lived too far away. I said he was a jerk. My father didn't question it. Instead, he took the opportunity to compare my experience to his own.

He said to me, "Oh, now you know how I feel, Suzie. How heartbroken and pulled to pieces I felt after your mom did that to me. You now understand how it feels to be hurt by the one you love." In my mind I thought, *Ummm, no . . . I don't. I was not married, and he had no idea what I was feeling. Gross, do not compare yourself to me.* Every time he would get emotional with me or start to cry about his situation with Mom, I wanted to vomit. I couldn't stand hearing about it or being in the middle of it. I had my own problems to worry about. Staying far away from Patrick was one of them, and my father was making that impossible. Despite my attempts, Patrick would show up in the neighborhood or at my father's. He also had this bizarre friendship with my father even after we broke up. I guess it was because of the work he had done around the house for my father while we were dating, like painting our shutters and other odd jobs. My father had him doing stuff for him still. I had no idea why.

The pregnancy was one of several things weighing on my mind. About a week before I started at Plymouth Meeting Junior High School, I was required to take evaluation testing because I had been in special education classes. The testing took place on a Monday, one week before my scheduled doctor appointment with my mom. I felt horrible that morning. I had the worst cramps and felt miserable. I tried my best to get dressed and function, not wanting to bring any attention to my discomfort. Mom dropped me off to take the placement testing not far from our apartment. I didn't tell Mom I was feeling miserable. She had enough going on. Before I got out of the car, Mom told me she would pick me up after she ran a few errands.

I walked to the office, and then I was escorted into the testing room. I sat at a table and tried to focus on completing the testing, but I was barely able to finish. I fought back the discomfort as best as I could, sweating and still really crampy. Once I finally finished all the questions, I asked to go to the bathroom. While walking to the bathroom, I began to feel even worse. It felt like I was having my period but the pain was awful! I was sure I was bleeding, and the cramps kept getting worse. With each step I took, I tried to catch my breath and broke out in a sweat. In the bathroom I discovered I was right. *Holy crap!* I was really bleeding badly. My underpants and pants were already soaked with blood. I tried not to panic as I wadded up a ton of toilet tissue to make a makeshift pad, hoping to keep from bleeding further through my pants. It was dumb luck that I had black pants on that day. The whole time I was thinking, *What does this mean? And why do I feel so scared?* I began to realize as the minutes passed that maybe I was having a miscarriage. I knew enough from health class and from what my mom had told me about her own miscarriages to assume that's what was happening. I tried to get my emotions together before leaving the bathroom.

I walked over to the office to await my mom's arrival, standing, so I didn't stain the chair. When she got there, I walked right up to her and whispered in her ear that I was bleeding. She looked at me, stunned, and said, "We have to go to the hospital."

On the ride over, Mom told me about a few of her miscarriages and how hard they were on her. She expressed her sorrow with me but at the same time she wanted me to know how serious the situation was.

"Don't rush to grow up, Suzie. Don't rush. Take my advice, slow down. There is plenty of time to have relationships and children. You want to find the right man. I am telling you, take your time. I made many mistakes and I do not want you to make them too."

We arrived at the Suburban General ER and I was evaluated. I had blood work done. They confirmed I had a miscarriage and would need to follow up with my doctor in a week. A million emotions swirled around my head. Feelings of sadness, stupidity, and relief. I was emotional for lots of reasons. I had caused additional stress and worry for my mom, especially at a time when she didn't need any more on her plate. I also felt very guilty about getting myself into this situation in the first place. I was young and in love with Patrick, my first boyfriend, the first person I thought really cared about me. Our love was real for me. But like everything else in my life, he let me down. It felt lonely, even with my mom sitting there next to me. Only fourteen, and I felt like I had lived a lifetime already. It was a huge wake-up call telling me I needed to slow down, take a few steps back, and not be in such a rush to become an adult.

When we got home, Mom had to call and explain everything to my father. It was necessary because of the hospital visit. He would have found out regardless. We were all still under his insurance. This situation caused more stress for Mom. Of course, he would try to place the blame on her.

The next day while I was recovering, my father came to the apartment to visit me. He wanted to take me out for lunch. I felt better physically so I was able to go. This was a horribly awkward visit. Part of the awkwardness was knowing he knew what I had been through, and the rest was driven by his strange behavior. I was used to him being either a violent monster or a blubbering, emotional mess. But in the car, he acted concerned, playing the loving parent act. I held back the vomit in my mouth.

*Spare me the concerned talk, I know you're faking.* Then he began to softly scold me for not telling him what was going on.

*Wow. Who is this guy? Am I still on Earth, because I am pretty sure this is not my father.* I must have had my Wheaties that day because I had the brawn to talk back to him. I was irritated and sharp with him, saying something like, "Oh, sure. After the great father–daughter relationship we have had all these years, you feel I should have told you about my problem? I didn't even tell Mom! She found out on her own."

He sat there motionless, staring at me, looking confused. Now he knew the truth. I confirmed that she too was clueless, until I told her. For a moment after lashing out at him, I wasn't so sure he wouldn't punch me in the face. I braced myself thinking he might. As we sat in the car, I awaited a possible hostile reaction. But to my surprise, he lowered his head for a moment, as if he was in thought. Then he looked up at me and began to talk, once again sounding sappy. "Suzie, I am not perfect, I can only ask you for your forgiveness."

Crickets chirped in my head as I sat there, mouth open. *What just happened? Is he asking me for forgiveness? Is he sorry? Is he crazy? What is going on?* I can only remember feeling confused and sick to my stomach at his strange, uncomfortable demeanor. His new way of dealing with me was awkward. He was like a stranger from the Body Snatchers movie. An alien pod came and took my father away, replacing him with this weird guy. I didn't trust him before or now, and I sure wasn't buying all his new mushy father crap. I knew he was up to something. Not to mention, I knew he harbored a horrible temper and soon it was going to show up again. All he needed were a few buttons pressed and he would soon blow.

# CHAPTER 12

# **Friends, Love, and Freedoms**

My first day at a new school and I didn't really give a crap. Mom met me in the kitchen and asked me if I was ready. I nodded yes. I hadn't done much to prepare. What was the point? I didn't know anyone. So I put on my typical jeans, T-shirt, and a pinch of makeup, and ran a comb through my hair. I had sort of a Joan Jet thing going on at the time. Lots of layers with long bangs. Nothing I did with my poker-straight hair ever made any difference anyway.

I thought about how I really never had any sense for fashion. If I see pictures of me as a kid, I cringe. The clothes and hairstyles Mom chose for me were, in my opinion, awful! I remember complaining most of the time when I was old enough. Buying clothes for me was always a challenge for her. I absolutely hated the stuff she would pick out for me: floral and fruit patterns, crazy shapes, and lots of color. *Good grief!* I didn't find the finer outfits or fashion statements exciting at all. Mom dressed me in all that goofy clothing and added pigtails. In my eyes, I looked like Pippi Longstocking tripping out, but I know her heart was in the right place. Even though I was not into the girly stuff, I still appreciated all she did for me. I never gained her fashion or beatification skills. Even now, I have no interest in fancy hairstyles, applying makeup properly, or getting my nails done. I always wanted simple things: jeans and a T-shirt, especially when I was little, before I had a choice. Thank goodness my sister came along to appease Mom's fashionable nature. Otherwise, I would have driven Mom crazy.

As I walked toward the door to leave, Mom said, "Have a great day, everything is going to be fine."

I responded back with an unconvincing and weak, "Thanks, Mom."

My stomach was in knots already as I walked to the bus stop near the entrance of the apartment complex. I kept telling myself, *just breathe.* I waited there with a few other kids. Finally, the bus arrived, and I got on. I gazed down the aisle, trying to walk and look at the same time. Maybe there would be a seat open near the middle or back of the bus. That was where I liked to sit.

I was about four rows from the back when I heard this girl say, "Hi, you're new. Here, you can sit with me." She had this huge smile and was so friendly and pleasant. I sat down and she told me her name was Katie. I felt oddly at peace sitting with her. Katie was very pretty, and outgoing. She was tall and slender, with blue eyes and light-blond hair that hovered above her shoulder in a wispy layer cut with a little bit of a soft curl. Katie was naturally attractive. I don't recall seeing her wearing a stitch of makeup. She was also very forward, asking me my name and lots of questions. Her genuinely nice personality made it easy for me to feel welcomed. We hit it off right away. If it had been up to me, I would have sat alone and walked around that day alone. But Katie had this sweet way of talking, you could tell she had a genuinely good heart. She glowed with that very normal-loving-family vibe, something that I was not familiar with. I learned she lived with her parents and sister right around the corner from the apartment in Plymouth Meeting, which was awesome.

During my interaction with Katie on the bus that day, there was another person who was inserting himself into our conversation. His name was Sam. Man, was he a character! One of the first things he said to me was, "Wow, you look like Pat Benatar," and he kept referring to me as *the Pat Benatar look-alike.* How he came up with the assessment that I resembled a popular, cool rock singer, I will never understand. But I wasn't complaining. Sam was also very outgoing and kind of pushy, but in a very nice, comical way. He had a round face, big green eyes, brown curly hair, and a thin frame. He was super animated, and when he spoke to me his green eyes sparkled. It was totally hypnotic and captured my attention. That day on the bus, he made it very clear he was interested in the "new girl."

When we arrived at the school, both Katie and Sam helped me get to where I had to go. I was happy to have their guidance. Sam was especially accommodating, escorting me to most of my classes whether they were near any of his class locations or not. As he walked me around the halls, I noticed he had cowboy boots on and walked with kind of a bowlegged swagger. Old cowboy movies flashed into my head, and not in a bad way. It actually made me smile. As we walked down the halls of my new school, I couldn't help but admire that Sam dressed nicely, sporting tight jeans and a button-down shirt. Despite my distraction with his attire and walk, his help to some of my classes made my first day a surprisingly smooth experience.

Both Sam and Katie showed such enthusiasm and were so nice helping me out, it was overwhelmingly cool. I kept thinking, *How can this actually be happening to me?* I was awestruck at how nice they were, and yet at the same time, leery. Was I on the TV show *Candid Camera*? Maybe I was in a movie like *The Stepford Wives,* but a high school version. It was a little unsettling; I didn't expect my first day to be like this. When Mom came home from work later on, I couldn't wait to tell her all about my two new friends. All through dinner, I rambled on about my radical first day at school. Mom was very happy to hear things had gone well. My sister had been in school a few days prior to me, and so far, she was doing well too. It felt like things were finally looking up for us. And there was more to come!

My second day on the bus, Sam seemed determined to impress me. He handed me a wrapped package. I was stunned, while Sam bubbled with joy.

"Open it, open it. It's for you." I looked at him and shrugged my shoulders.

"OK." I tore open the wrapping to uncover a black-and-white pastel painting of John Lennon. To put it mildly, I was shocked. *Wow!* He doesn't even know me, and he gives me this awesome gift. *I love John Lennon,* but then again, who doesn't love John Lennon? Sam revealed that he had actually made it for me. I was completely caught off guard. I quickly managed to say thank you several times, telling him his choice regarding John Lennon was brilliant. As I sat there admiring this work of art, Katie asked me to hand it to her so she could take a look.

Suddenly, Sam blurted out, "Let me take you out on a date." I was overwhelmed with all the excitement and unsure how to respond. His personality was very forward, and yet, I didn't feel threatened. I thought for a moment. *What should I do?* I wasn't sure if I wanted a relationship right then. I wasn't with Patrick anymore, but I was still conflicted about him and afraid to trust anyone after our falling out. I was still emotionally beat down from the miscarriage and depressed about how I hurt my mom. My family life was a disaster. Should I even consider a new boyfriend? My subconscious was in overdrive, trying to weigh things out: *Sam is really fun. He's interesting and seems so uncomplicated. He makes me feel special and overwhelms me with his humor and charm. I feel like my feet are being swept out from under me.*

If I recall, Katie told Sam to give me some space. "Good grief, Sam, she needs a minute." So after thinking it over briefly, feeling a little overcome, I told him maybe. I wanted him to meet my mom and family first. He was immediately pleased and agreed with no hesitation. That made me feel even better.

Sam and Katie came over the next day to meet my family. The introductions went seamlessly. Mom really liked them, and we all got along so well. This unusual happy vibe going on was unfamiliar to me. I felt like I was in a dream sequence on a TV show. Hanging out, laughing, and being normal. I was not used to feeling relaxed. Don't get me wrong, I liked the change. I wanted to let it sink in. What did I have to lose? Especially since up until that point things had been awful. I wanted to trust my new feelings, go out on a date with Sam, and embrace my new friendship with Katie. But the last few months had been a train wreck and I was still trying to ease into the new home, school, and changes to my family life. I needed this positivity. And with each day that went by, miraculously, things did improve for the better.

As the weeks passed, the dynamic of all our lives was improving immensely. My mom, my siblings, and I were so much happier than we had been before. Normal day-to-day things that used to be dreary were now new and fun. Each day I woke up happy and looked forward to the good stuff for once. School with my new friends was actually enjoyable. After school I would pick up my brother from the babysitter, go back to our apartment, and keep an eye on him. I did Mom's ironing while watching *General Hospital* (I loved Luke and Laura!). I made dinner, and sometimes if I had time, I would make a dessert, all before Mom got home from work. On one occasion I made an apple pie, and even made the crust myself from scratch. Another time, I made apple-and-raisin popovers. I remember those two desserts so clearly, because Mom was very impressed with me and made sure to let me know how much she loved them. My sister got home from school a little later than I did. She had a few chores to do, and when she was finished, she would run off to play with a few of the kids she had met around the apartment complex. Mom would get home from work around 5:30 p.m. We would eat dinner and catch up on what we did during the day. Sometimes Katie would come over and have dinner with us. Hanging out in the apartment with our new freedoms and friends was giving us all our strength back. It was a new beginning. A life like normal families had. As for me, I was feeling inspired.

I felt like a changed person, happier. Katie was a wonderful influence on me, always in a good mood. We were polar opposites on lots of things, but still became good friends. In and out of school, we were almost inseparable. She would come over to my apartment after school and sometimes stay for dinner. Katie often told me how she really loved my family. That was always nice to hear. Occasionally, I slept over her house. Sleepover nights were fun. I remember hanging out in her room or sitting in the kitchen talking to her mom. Katie had a close relationship with her parents. It was comforting to be around such a calm, normal family. Often we stayed up late watching TV or waiting for the HBO Saturday night movie special to come on. At that time, HBO only had one channel. The dramatic theme music signaled the new movie was starting, and we were excited to watch whatever it was. Hanging out with Katie was always cool. She was a happy, positive friend to me and my family in a moment in our lives when we truly needed it.

It didn't take long for my friendship with Sam to blossom into a steady relationship. Dating him was melting away all the pain of my prior experience. For the first time in a long time, I felt comfortable and calm. Sam was a wonderful morale booster, a friend and a boyfriend—caring, funny, and fun to be around. His family was very nice too. He had two older siblings and his parents were divorced. His mother was kind to me, and I always felt welcome at his house. Sometimes we all hung out together; Katie and her boyfriend would double-date with Sam and me. If it was just Sam and me, we loved to listen to music. We had different music tastes, but that made it interesting. He introduced me to Elvis Costello, Split Enz, REO Speedwagon, and Tom Petty, to name a few. Looking back, every time I hear songs from these bands now, I still think of him.

At that time in my life, with these new friendships, I was truly happy. I think back fondly to normal kid pastimes, like sitting at lunch with a bunch of Katie and Sam's friends, trying to avoid getting hit when a food fight would break out in the lunchroom. Or, roller-skating at a rink called Ridge Runner on Ridge Pike in Norristown. Roller-skating was a popular activity in 1980, and this place was frequently our weekend hangout. Even now, any time certain songs from that era come on the radio, I will immediately go right back to those memories of skating around the rink. Queen's

"Another One Bites the Dust," David Bowie's "Ashes to Ashes," "Kiss on My List" by Hall & Oates, and "Hit Me with Your Best Shot" by Pat Benatar fling me back in time. Walking around the mall was another favorite thing to do. Grabbing something to eat or playing at the huge arcade, popping quarters into *Pac-Man, Centipede, Defender,* and *Frogger.* I really loved the game *Galaxian* (later in 1981, my favorite was *Galaga*). That game was so radical, and I would play it for hours! My name was at the top of the high-score leaderboard several times. If I had the chance to whoop your ass at *Galaxian,* I would. Even Sam was impressed with my game skills. It didn't really matter what game we were playing. We always had fun.

Having Katie and Sam in my life helped distract me from thinking about my old neighborhood. Sometimes I couldn't believe I even missed my old home, especially since most of my memories from there were horrible. I think I just missed my old friends and the familiar setting, but I definitely didn't want to return to the pain and fear associated with that house. I wasn't afraid all the time like before. I had joy in my life. And I even liked going home now.

The change was noticeable in Mom too. Her new job at the alarm company was giving her new confidence. After being a stay-at-home mom for over fourteen years, she jumped right into her new breadwinner role. She was making a new life for herself and for her kids. Not long after she was hired, she met a very nice man named Jim. He was separated from his wife and in the process of divorce too. I often wondered if this was part of the reason they became friends, having similar circumstances and all. I remember Mom telling me that Jim had escorted her to her car a few times for safety reasons. My father, who had a history of violence, was caught on a number of occasions stalking her. There were quite a few times Mom would go out to lunch or leave work to find that her estranged husband was following her. He was always trying to confront her about something, sometimes showing up at her job or other places she went. So Jim would walk with her to her car or stay close by knowing that at any point her hostile husband could show up. I assume this act of chivalry is how their relationship began, along with other interests they shared. Mom was a very attractive lady and her sweet, friendly, outgoing personality must have also contributed to her catching Jim's eye.

When we finally got to meet Jim, I could clearly see why Mom liked this guy. He was a very attractive Italian man with handsome features to match: thick, dark hair, tan skin, brown eyes, a mustache, and a cleft chin. In addition to his physical attributes, he loved to sing. I knew Mom liked that. He was very charming right out of the gate, with an inviting and pleasant personality, warm and caring. It was easy to like him the moment we met him, and very quickly we learned that Jim was lots of fun to be around. He knew how to make us laugh, lightening the mood and brightening everyone's day with a goofy look or joke. Gosh knows, during this time in our lives, we all needed that. Jim was twelve years younger than Mom, born in March 1958. This fact would be brought up over and over by my father in the coming months. "This guy is almost your age, Suzie, and he's still married," he would tell me. But Jim seemed very adult to me. He had an old-fashioned way about him, an old-soul vibe in his personality. Loving and warm, Jim's demeanor was soothing. We all felt calm when he was around. It was also nice to see Mom happy. She really beamed whenever he was visiting, laughing all the time and truly radiant. This new freedom for her and for all of us was a breath of fresh air. We were all soaking in these new feelings, making new memories, bonding, enjoying a more relaxed environment at home. It was an incredibly nice change.

In addition to all this new happiness, things were changing between me and Mom. I was getting to know her in a new and wonderful way, watching her come into her own and be her own boss, free of her possessive husband. You could tell she was visibly more confident and motivated. She also began to show a fun side I had not seen before, lighthearted, laughing more often, funny, almost silly. Maybe I just noticed it more now that I was happier as well. Ever since we left the Merion house, Mom and I had begun to bond again, talk more, and share our thoughts. She took a genuine interest in what I was doing, and I felt closer to her, began to trust her. The sense of fear and uncertainty I used to have was slipping away.

This new life was surrounding us like a warm hug. We were functioning like a normal family, and the energy was amazing. Mom really liked her job, and her boyfriend was awesome. I had new friends and a great boyfriend too who got along with my family. I enjoyed seeing Marylyn giggle with laughter, my brother beaming with that funny *foo, foo* face he would make. My family was smiling and laughing more than I had ever seen before. The chemistry of each of us had changed, and it was a good change. The scary home life we lived in before was melting away from our daily existence, and I was seeing and feeling what it was like to be a normal kid—like a ray of sunshine after a long darkness. These pleasant distractions made it easy at times to forget about my father and the fear we once felt living with him. But it seemed that the more our confidence and happiness grew, the more unhinged my father became. He was furious about Jim, jealous and angry that Mom was living her own life. And in the coming weeks, he would go to great lengths to try and regain the upper hand.

Shortly after leaving my father, my mom had filed for divorce, which began a string of calls with lawyers, paperwork, and meetings about which my mom would only share limited details. On one occasion back before I started my new school, I had to attend a legal meeting with my mom, her attorney, and a psychologist. After my father's last violent act, Mom wanted to keep our visitation with him limited. I remember I had to answer a bunch of questions. They asked me to review with them in detail all the violence that took place in our house in the past, the events leading up to our moving out. I told them what I heard and saw the night my father strangled Mom. I told them how he physically hurt me all the time, including the hockey stick incident. I told them about the time he hurt my sister in the foyer. I told them about all those long, weird conversations he had with me after he learned about the affair, how he would either come to my room, corner me in the house, or take me on a drive in the car to vent his marital frustrations to his fourteen-year-old daughter. I told them everything I could possibly think of, including why I didn't want to live with my father. It's hard to imagine the custody battle being any battle at all, considering my father's actions. But through the legal back-and-forth, we had a few sporadic visitations.

He would come to pick us up at our apartment for a quick dinner on a school night, or take us out to lunch or dinner on a weekend. During two visits, he brought Patrick with him. My mom and I were stunned when he showed up with Patrick in the car. My father was well aware my relationship with Patrick had ended. He also knew I had suffered a miscarriage, which Patrick was not supposed to find out about. The whole thing made my mom and me uncomfortable, wondering, *Did Patrick know about the miscarriage? Had my father told him? Why was he along for the ride?* I also noticed that Patrick seemed different. I was not sure exactly what vibe I was feeling, but something was off. Maybe it was just me being on guard. I still didn't trust him and I was suspicious of his visits to my father's house. *Why is he here? Why is my father allowing us to still socialize?* I could not pretend; I had to ask Patrick what was going on.

Patrick was very forthcoming with information. He explained to me that my father wanted companionship on the drive to our apartment. He thought maybe if Patrick came along, things would be less stressful. I thought that was a lame reason, but OK. Shockingly, he told me my father had tried to kill himself a few weeks ago and felt better when he had people around. I was stunned to hear this and asked him what happened. Apparently, they found my father at a park lying on a bench a few weeks ago. He had called my mom after taking a bunch of pills, saying he wanted to die. My mom and Gram called the police and he was taken to the hospital. *Wow*, Patrick knew a lot about this! This was the first I was hearing this news. I assumed Mom didn't want to burden her children with what had happened. Suspecting Patrick may not know the entire story, I decided to question my mom later about it.

After my father and Patrick left, Mom and I talked in detail about the weird visits. We both knew something was going on. My father always had an angle, and the fact that he was allowing Patrick to come on the visits was very strange. Mom asked me lots of questions about what I thought might be going on, and I answered them all the best I could. I told her I thought Patrick was trying in his own way to stay in touch. Maybe he felt bad for dumping me. I was pretty sure he had no idea about the pregnancy because he never asked me about it, and he seemed curious about our new life at the apartment. I didn't tell him about Sam. Neither of us was sure what was going on exactly, but we were pretty positive my father was up to something. Then I asked her about what Patrick had told me. Had my father attempted suicide? Had he really tried to kill himself? She explained what she knew, verifying it was true. Our mom-and-daughter powwow ended with us having more questions than answers. Everything my father did had a catch to it, and we sensed that something was way off.

Things got even weirder when Mom started to notice how my father would bring up topics she had never discussed with him. When he picked us up for visitations or spoke to her on the phone, he would blurt out comments about Jim, her job, times Jim ate dinner at our house, and other information no one had shared with him. It was becoming clear he was listening to her phone calls or had somehow spied on her conversations.

Things were made clear soon enough. In December, my mom, grandparents, and I attended a court hearing. Since I was only a minor, I was only brought in at specific times when my testimony was needed, but I heard later the real reason why Patrick had been along for the ride so-to-speak during my father's visits. A sick plot twist that only my father could think up, he had manipulated Patrick into spying on us and performing other intrusive acts by convincing him we were in danger. Yes, my father had brainwashed my sixteen-year-old ex-boyfriend into believing that my mom's new boyfriend was a drug dealer, that we were all in danger, and that he needed Patrick's help to get the proof he needed to protect us. This was complete nonsense, of course, but Patrick didn't know Jim. My father told Patrick he needed him to listen closely when he was around our house, and ask questions to find out when Jim would be coming over. Then, on a few occasions, my father took Patrick with him to our apartment at night. My father, equipped with a tape recorder, brought Patrick down to the basement of the apartment and placed the tape recorder under a specific crawl space. Patrick did not realize that it was directly under my mom's bedroom. Later, they would go back again to pick up the recorder. Through acts of obvious invasion of privacy and stalking, my father was taping my mother's private conversations and manipulating a teenager to accompany him. We were outraged and alarmed at my father's devious and downright creepy actions. This shook my mother up even more. The things my father could convince people to do was astounding. Patrick was a kid, and he didn't know or realize that his actions were illegal. He was convinced that he was helping my father and doing a good thing to help the family. My father openly admitted he was doing this at the court hearing. He was so narcissistic, he always felt the things he did were justified and right. This, of course, did not sit well with the judge.

That wasn't the only secret revealed during that court hearing. The next subject up for discussion was me. My father's attorney brought up my pregnancy. His attorney tried to say my mom withheld information from him, and allowed me to see Patrick unsupervised. After a lengthy battle back and forth between attorneys, the judge determined the timeline of my pregnancy occurred back in September when we were living as a family in Merion. He said it was inadmissible. Good news for my mom, but humiliating for me. Now everyone in the room knew what a total loser I was, including my grandparents who were at the hearing.

Afterward, I stood in the hallway of the courthouse waiting for Mom. My Grandpop pulled me aside and told me he was very sad about the entire situation—and he was going to pray for me. I was so mortified. Another notch in my belt toward my forever-complicated, crappy life. I was so angry. Angry that my father used such devious tactics against me and my mom. Angry he used Patrick. I remembered how my father acted worried about me after my miscarriage. Not so much when he was in the courtroom. All his sappy father crap. Now I knew why he was so interested in being father of the year. He didn't care about me or Patrick. He simply wanted leverage. Why was I even surprised? I should have known he would use my predicament for his own gain. Thankfully, this time his scheming would be used against him in the custody battle, and only burned him in the end.

# CHAPTER 13

# Songs, Photographs, and Holidays

*Mike, Grandpop, Grandmom, and Mom*

My mother was always a wonderful singer. My Uncle Mike once told me his favorite memory of Mom was the time she participated in the Bishop McDevitt High School talent show. I can just picture her waiting backstage in her 1950s-style below-the-knee dress with her dark-brown hair styled in soft waves above her shoulders. As my uncle tells it, she took the stage and approached the microphone to begin her performance. High school sound systems being what they are, each attempt to sing into the microphone was answered with a horrible screech that reverberated throughout the auditorium. It took only two unsuccessful attempts before she took things into her own hands. With the calm and ease of a seasoned performer, my mother moved the microphone to the side of the stage, stepped up to face the audience, and belted out her song. She won the talent show that year.

*Mom on stage*

Years later, and throughout my childhood, I was lucky enough to attend many of her shows and loved to watch her perform. Mom was often the female lead in shows, so she had to practice regularly. Her voice filled our home with song on a regular basis. Notably in 1974, Mom was Maria in *The Sound of Music* and did a dozen or more performances. Practice makes perfect, so she sang constantly. My sister was only four at the time, but I remember when she was older and Mom would sing around the house, Marylyn would love the songs from that show. The song "My Favorite Things" is still one of her favorites.

*Pictures of Mom from show promos*

With the Players Club of Swarthmore, Mom played the beautiful Marietta in the show *Naughty Marietta*. Many of her fellow colleagues spoke so highly of her and often expressed how wonderful she was in her role. She did several performances with the Ardensingers and the Rose Valley Chorus in the seventies. In 1976, she sang in *Gondoliers*; in 1978, she played Phyllis in *Iolanthe*; in 1974, she played the part of Saphir in *Patience*. Then, in 1975 she did *The Pirates of Penzance*. She played the part of Mabel in this show, and really showed off her extraordinary vocals singing "Poor Wandering One." In the second act of this performance, Mom and Frank Reynolds, a tenor, perform a duet together. To this day, it is one of my all-time favorite pieces of music she has ever sung. "Stay, Frederic, Stay" was her half of a duet from the show, and she performed this song on a number of occasions. Growing up I became familiar with this song. It was so hypnotic and soothing. Like a lullaby sang by my mom.

*Frank Reynolds and Mom*

She performed often with Frank. They were good friends, and his tenor voice complemented Mom's soprano sparkle. They did many shows together through the years, most of them Gilbert and Sullivan productions. *The Zoo,* a farcical story, was another show they acted in together. Mom was Laetitia and Frank Reynolds was Carboy. Mom's last performance was a 1980 production of *Ruddigore.* It was her last show with the Ardensingers. I remember when I found the article written April 25 about her performance in this particular show, I was full of pride at all the beautiful things they said about my mother. "Bunnie Hathaway is the perfect embodiment of the lovely Rose, who lives by her book of etiquette. She is pretty to look at and delightful to listen to." Other reviews written were also very complimentary. Each review made me smile.

My mother's musical exploits made up a large portion of my fonder childhood memories. Once back in the seventies, Mom even had the opportunity to be on TV to promote an upcoming show. She sang on *Captain Noah and his Magical Ark,* a children's TV program. At the time it was a pretty cool thing to know my mom was going to be on television. Dressed in a costume from *The Pirates of Penzance,* she sang "Poor Wandering One." When the episode aired, we all watched it together on my mom's porch.

My parents were also good friends with several celebrities in the music and theater clique. In the early to mid-seventies my parents became friends with Deborah Cook, an operatic soprano. I remember Mrs. Cook when I was little. She was very nice to me whenever I saw her. I even have a few photos of her holding me as a child. She had beautiful, long, black hair and a very pretty smile. There were two other performers that I remember: Marylyn Mulvey and Victor Borge. Victor was a comedian and pianist. Marylyn was a first-place soprano winner of the Metropolitan Opera National Finals and accompanied Mr. Borge on stage. Together they had a very amusing stage performance. Victor would play the piano and Marylyn would try her best to sing while Victor interrupted with silly antics. He would fall off the piano bench in surprise when she hit a high note or made silly faces and so on. Their performance together was hilarious. Today you can watch it on YouTube. During those years, Marylyn would come to our house off and on to visit. She was tall and slender and quite beautiful, with blond hair, blue eyes, and always very nicely dressed. She and my parents became good friends. They even asked her to be my sister's godmother. (Hence, my sister's name.) As for Mr. Borge, I can't recall any specific memory. However, my mother told me that when I was four years old, Victor decided to bring me into the fun one night during a show. We had second-row seats, and he called out to my parents, who then brought me up on stage to sit with him at his piano. He carried on with the show for a little while as I sat there. Mom said it was quite adorable.

Aside from her show performances, Mom sang on other occasions too. Christmas songs were popular—I loved her version of "Silver Bells"—and she also did a few renditions of church hymns. She sang as a soloist for different types of celebratory events: weddings, church functions, and holiday parties. Through word of mouth, our family and friends would often want her to sing for them. Her precious gift of song was a true talent. She beamed with happiness when she sang. I believe it was her true calling.

## Winter 1980

Mom seemed to be a changed woman in this new peaceful life we had in the apartment. I took notice of her happiness whenever we spent time with Jim. He was a very positive person in her life. He made her happy and treated us lovingly. The negative things we endured in the past seemed less upsetting as each day went by. Our environment may have been suffocating in the past, but not anymore. That winter in the apartment, despite the custody battle and all the change we had undergone over the last few months, my family found music again.

When Jim came over, the fun would begin right away. We would listen to music, dance, and sing together. Jim would always belt out the Dean Martin songs he loved: "On an Evening in Roma" and "That's Amore." Today when I hear certain songs, my heart and mind go right back to these happy moments with Mom, Jim, and my siblings. Through sheer silliness, Jim was somehow able to get us all singing and dancing to those songs. It was hysterical to hear him and watch him be so goofy, making funny faces while he sang. He would sashay all around the apartment, pretending he was dancing with someone. Then he would grab one of us to dance with, singing out loud and proud. Another song I fondly remember was "Lady" by Kenny Rogers. Jim would sing to Mom, dedicating the song to her. Whenever we would go out for a drive in his Bronco truck, we would all chime in singing these songs and others. We had happy dinners together, funny food fights, and water fights. Being around Jim was invigorating for all of us. The singing we did together was bringing out Mom's natural passion. You could see the joy in her face as she sang along. When Jim was around, we could see mom enjoying herself again. They both oozed with happiness. She even began to sing songs that I never heard before. I began to realize she actually liked different types of music besides musicals or opera. I guess I never really paid attention until now. Mom was really opening up, or maybe I was. Regardless, it captured my attention that new songs were rubbing off on her. I was surprised when she told me she liked songs like Ronnie Milsap's "Smoky Mountain Rain" or Neil Diamond's "Hello Again." She was even interested in listening to my music. What a change that was! I was really into The Cure's album *Seventeen Seconds,* and played the song "The Forest" all the time. One night after school I played it for her, and she said she really liked it. That made me very happy, especially since I thought the music was amazing. She also liked when I played the new album from John Lennon, *Double Fantasy*. We would feel sad momentarily remembering his death from earlier in the month. She even tolerated my Pink Floyd, ACDC, and Ozzy obsessions. Idolizing my mother's musical talent from a young age, I really appreciated her open-mindedness and feedback. I had never shared my enjoyment for music with my parents before. My strained relationship with them had made it hard for me to open up to them about my passions. Now that we all felt safer, not scared and tiptoeing around like we had in our old home, I realized I had a common interest with her and that was important to me. I desperately wanted to feel close to my mom, and sharing my love for music with her was a perfect start.

One day after dinner, she told me she loved that I was so diverse in my musical interests. She said she thought that was wonderful, and her positive reinforcement made me feel amazing. When I had the time to listen to my music at the apartment, I would feel more inspired knowing she approved. As I lay on the floor between the two record player speakers, eyes closed, with a pillow propped up behind my head, I would escape to my music neverland. At the time, I didn't have any headphones. So this was my way of listening and feeling at one with my music. I would listen to an entire album, front and back. For me, it was like seeing a movie in my head. The story and songs whisked me away to another place. For an hour or so, I felt the melodies and rhythms flow through my blood. Mom was very tolerant, and she let me enjoy the escape.

Christmas that year was calm, and that was a noticeable change. Thankfully, there was no need to ask my father to participate in decorating or for help with the lights. (One year, he became so irritated he threw the tree into the foyer screaming, "I don't have time for this!" He bent the stand and stepped on the remaining lights he didn't realize were under his feet, breaking several of the bulbs before storming off to his studio.) In our new home, we had our tree, our ornaments, and together, we enjoyed decorating. No stress! I remember Mom took us to a new church for services on Christmas Eve that year. It was a Roman Catholic church called Epiphany of Our Lord, located about five minutes from our apartment. This church had really high ceilings and reminded me of the church my grandparents attended. The holiday service was long, and my brother fidgeted through most of it. He was a great distraction in boring moments. When I wasn't holding in my laughter at watching his antics, my mind wandered to memories of Christmas growing up. Believe it or not, Christmas in the old house did have some good times.

For instance, baking chocolate chip cookies with Mom was an event I would look forward to each year. She would let me work the mixer and spoon out the dough onto a cookie sheet. Sometimes we'd make sugar cookies, having fun with the cutouts and decorations. On a few occasions I came down with a stomach bug near the holidays and couldn't help with the cookies. To make myself feel better, I would lie down in Mom's sun porch, gazing at the lights blinking on and off. They hung from her windows and sparkled with all the glass around them. I also enjoyed watching a holiday show on TV while I lay there soothing my stomach. To perk up my spirits, Mom put two sandwich bags of cookies away for me. Days later when I felt better, I gobbled down all of them in one sitting only to get sick all over again from eating too many cookies. I didn't care. It was totally worth it!

Mom always tried to make the holidays special. Despite my father's distaste for festivities, she remained positive and happy on every holiday. Christmas day after presents and breakfast, we would drive all the way to my grandparents' house to eat. Entering their home, you could smell spice and clove. I would become bored while waiting to eat. There was nothing to do until then, and waiting for dinner seemed longer than it was. The TV was turned to either a sports event or a church choir singing. The appetizers were horrid: smelly anchovies, a few slivers of weird cheese, and a few crackers. This fare was not kid appealing. Grandpop's famous eggnog was fun to hear about, even though I was too young then to try this amazing concoction. He would say it was "powerful stuff" and would "put hair on your chest." (Years later when I was old enough to finally try it, I discovered he was not kidding about how strong it was.) Meanwhile, my Grandmom was busy in the kitchen, wielding her spoon, stirring gravy, and checking on the foods in the oven. Mom would go in and try to give her a hand. When everything was ready, we would all take down a dish of food and find our spot at the very long table set up in their finished basement. Each year, Grandmom would decorate the table with pretty holiday linens, decorative place settings, and ornaments she made herself for each of us. The food was placed all along the table and we would pass things around. Everything about dinner was spectacular and super yummy. I really looked forward to a few signature foods: the carrot salad, dry stuffing with Grandmom's famous gravy poured on top, and of course, the dessert handcrafted by my Grandpop: ice cream parfaits, which he would top with creme de menthe, whipped cream, and a cherry. I remember being wide-eyed in delight as I walked off with my dessert. Other desserts that hold rank in forever favorites are Grandmom's pound cake and her Scottish shortbread cookies. To this day, Christmas is not complete without the Scottish shortbread. Thankfully, my brother has the knack to make them exactly like Grandmom's.

After dinner and dessert, we were ready to open the presents! Crinkling paper wrapping flew everywhere as everyone simultaneously opened up a gift. It was exciting chaos watching and listening to all the *oohs* and *aahs*. Then, we received a calming serenade before the night was over. Mom and Grandmom would sit at the piano and sing Christmas carols. I loved to hear them sing, and I even enjoyed singing with them. They both had lovely voices. The night would end with peaceful versions of "Silver Bells" and "O Holy Night" sung in unison.

As my thoughts came back to the present and we filed out of the church, I couldn't help but feel a little nostalgic for the Christmas of my childhood.

*Trey and Marylyn Christmas 1980*

Everything about Christmas was different now, but I recall Christmas morning that year had two very nice memories. Jim arrived early that day and Mom and Jim presented Trey with a large gift. A huge fire truck! He totally loved fire trucks, and he danced around the room in excitement when he saw it. It was big enough for him to ride on, with a siren, blinking lights, and a large rescue ladder that extended up. My brother had a noticeable lisp when he was little. So when he said the word fire truck, it came out *fire fruck*. We would all giggle at him.

The second memory made Christmas that particular year extra special for me. I got a camera—my very own camera. It even had a built-in flash! I was super excited that I didn't have to use Mom's Polaroid anymore. I liked her camera; taking a picture and seeing it develop in a few minutes was neat. But now I had the freedom to take pictures without having to ask permission. This was the best gift I could have received. It molded my love for taking pictures, and to this day photography is a passion of mine. Not in the professional way, but more in a personal and memorializing way. I feel pictures are so important. They capture loved ones and life in a frame of perfect immortality. Without pictures, I would feel lost. This camera took some of the best pictures over the next few months. Some of them are the last pictures I have of my mom.

# CHAPTER 14

# **Kidnapper**

One day in January 1981, Mom took me and my siblings roller-skating. She even strapped on roller-skates and got out onto the rink with us. We had a blast. I have a picture of that day—a precious memory and photo to match. Mom was hysterical going around the rink. She kept looking as if she was going to fall, but she stayed pretty steady the whole time. This is how I remember my mom during that time in our lives: always teetering on the brink of a stumble, but remaining upright, on her feet. She was so strong.

*Roller-skating fun—Marylyn, Trey, and Mom*

At the same time, my father was digging his own hole, and I think Mom knew she would win custody. But there were some precautions that we had to keep in mind. Mom asked us to be careful how much we divulged to our father about Jim and our private life. She predicted he would push us for more information during visitations, and she explained it was none of his business. My sister and I did our best to keep things private. We were glad to comply. In our eyes, Mom had the right to be happy. She had the right to have friends and enjoy time with us, regardless of who was involved. However, that didn't stop my father from trying to use everything my mom did against her.

I would get so upset when my father's miserable outlook on everything would interfere with our happiness. I was in a good mood most days, except when we had visitation. Going to see my father was like an imposition on his time. He never asked how we were doing in our new schools or how we were feeling. All he did was drill us for information. Exactly as Mom suspected, he would ask us questions in a very sneaky way to try and get us to slip up. My siblings were his prime targets for information. They were younger, and both would slip sometimes and tell him things innocently. It was totally normal for them to be excited about what was going on in our lives. A few times they expressed how much fun an event was, or talked about someplace we went. My father would ask, "Oh, who did you go with?"

Usually, one of my siblings would say, "We went with Mom's friend Jim," and my father would be *very* interested in that information. Then, he would completely turn his focus to drilling them with questions.

That's when I would get furious with him, tell him to stop it, and remind him how old they were. I thought to myself, *What an awful person he is, trying to drag information out of my three-year-old brother.*

He would get frustrated with me and say nasty things about Jim like, "He is closer to your age, Suzie. Don't you see that!" When he said stuff like that, it upset me so badly.

I threw that brass attitude I had developed right back at him, saying, "Mom is allowed to have friends, and we don't ask you what you're doing!" He would then shut up about stuff for a few minutes. But it was never over. "Your mother is still married, and so is that guy. She is being a horrible example of a parent in front of my children." I looked at him with a stunned expression, but then almost laughed out loud.

How laughable coming from him. Was he mental? He was the tyrant, not Mom. He was the worst example of a parent ever in the history of parents and yet, he had the nerve to criticize other people. I really didn't see what the big deal was. My parents were separated. In fact, he had tried to kill her! Not to mention the abuse he had inflicted on all of us for years. It blew my mind how delusional he was. This was all his fault. Did he even stop to think about that? Nope, he never did. Mom was trying to live her life. She deserved to find happiness away from him. Nobody in their right mind would want the terrible life she had while living with him. The truth was, she was legally separated from him and had every right to meet people, make friends, and start a new life.

To add further insult to the situation, it was obvious that my father already had a lot of information about Jim, and he was just playing games with us. He would blurt out his knowledge of Jim. It was completely ridiculous. Putting us kids in the middle of this nasty custody and divorce battle was bad enough. Saying horrible things about Mom and Jim was completely inappropriate. He made the entire time with him miserable.

I would get so peeved. "Why are we even visiting with you? All you do is talk about Mom, Jim, and how terrible they are. You make us uncomfortable all the time. I hate these visits!" Then he would stop and apologize to us and try to carry on with the visit. But the damage was done. The tone was set, and no one wanted to be there. He just didn't care about us, plain and simple. He just wanted anything he could use against Mom so he could win.

On a few occasions he would end the visit really early. When we got home, I would fill Mom in about the visit. She would get very upset and call her lawyer, telling him what was going on during our visitation. I was always hopeful the lawyer would say we could end the visits, but no such luck. Maybe the judge would lessen our time with him, or maybe even say we didn't have to go. Unfortunately, we would have to play by the rules and wait for the final results of the custody hearings.

However, my father never played by the rules.

On February 5, Mom had let my father pick up Trey and take him for the day. He was to bring him back to her at her job. Panic sank in when he never showed up. She couldn't reach anyone at the house or get any answers out of Gram. She called the police and her parents. When I got home from school, I knew something was wrong right away. It was like walking into a scene out of a TV crime drama. Mom was home, and she was crying, shaking, pacing back and forth in the living room. My grandparents were trying to calm her down.

"What happened?" I asked.

Mom tried to fill us all in. It turned out she left work thinking my father might be waiting at the apartment or left Trey with the babysitter. But when she got home, no one was there. That's when my father called and told her he was on his way to Florida on the Auto Train. He explained he

was simply taking a trip with their son and there was no need to panic—
he had family there and Trey was safe. Regardless of what he said, Mom
had every right to be hysterical. My father had kidnapped Trey and was
taking him to Florida without her knowledge. What a total jerk he was for
doing this to her and us. Everyone was upset. I was so angry.

My mind drifted back to yesterday, watching my brother play with our
new puppy, a little husky we had gotten a week earlier. She was white
with blue eyes and black markings on her face and body. We named her
Monique, but called her Neeki for short. My brother wanted to pet her
and hold her, but as puppies do, she overpowered him and nibbled at his
fingers and face, or licked him into giggles. He laughed and clapped his
hands as I tried (against Mom and Jim's advice) to teach Neeki to howl.
Then, he would try to pick her up and carry her into his little bedroom to
keep her to himself. It was so adorable, and watching him brought me so
much joy. My father always found a way to ruin good things for us.

They were gone for fifteen agonizing days. My mom was distraught the
entire time. It was an incredibly heart-wrenching time for Mom, for all of
us. Knowing my baby brother was in my father's custody made me really
furious and very worried.

The thoughts that filled my head were overwhelming. Was he going to
return with my brother? Was he going to stay in Florida? It was obvious
he was being vindictive, and had planned all this behind my mom's back.
This was just another example of how unkind and manipulative he was. I
was scared and I didn't want to say anything that I was thinking. The last
thing I wanted was to further upset my mom. After things calmed down a
little, our grandparents went home. I called Sam and Katie to fill them in
and made a simple dinner for us. While I was on the phone, Jim arrived.
He tried to comfort all of us. I could see the stress on his face. That night
was the first time I had ever heard him get upset and actually swear. He
made a few references to what he thought of my father. We all were in
shock. What would happen now?

During the emotional couple of weeks while my brother was gone, we
had to continue functioning in our daily lives. Normal day-to-day routines
were tense in his absence. The sounds of his giggle and toddler silliness
were missing from our apartment. I kept momentarily forgetting he was
gone. Out of habit, I would stop by the babysitter to pick him up, or set a
place for him at the table and then realize he wasn't going to be there.
Seeing the empty place at the table would make me upset. I missed giving

him a bath and singing to him before bed. Seeing his little room dark and empty was heartbreaking. Each day I would do something out of instinct and feel hurt all over again, remembering he was in Florida. If I was experiencing all these emotions, I can only imagine what Mom was going through. I am sure it was far worse for her.

We tried to fill the void of his absence. It was hard to do. While my brother was gone, it seemed awkward to laugh or want to go out and do things. His absence weighed heavily on our hearts. Katie would come over to visit with us. Wanting to be supportive, she would offer kind words of encouragement. None of us felt much like having fun. So having her come over was a comforting distraction. That weekend we all hung out with Katie and Sam at the mall. We walked around and tried to do anything to keep our minds occupied. The days went by painfully slow.

Valentine's Day arrived with a somber tone. Despite the mood, Sam and Jim tried to make the day special. Since it was on a Saturday, Sam came over to our apartment. He greeted me with a card, flowers, and a huge box of chocolate. Jim arrived that afternoon with flowers for Mom. He even made sure us girls had flowers too. At dinner time, Mom continued her tradition of giving us cute little gifts. Her efforts to make every occasion special made me smile, and I thought about how she always did something sweet on even the minor holidays. Each Valentine's Day and St. Patrick's Day, Mom would have a few small gifts and candy for us at the dinner table. I still have one of her gifts in my memory box today: a white horse brooch pin. I loved horses as a young girl, so that pin was perfect. I cherish memories of her and the lovely things she did for us.

The day my father and brother were expected back, I wanted to stay home from school. I argued that it would be too hard to focus, waiting to get home to see my brother. Mom, on the other hand, wouldn't let me miss school. Meanwhile, she waited impatiently to hear when she could bring her son home. Around lunchtime she received the call from her attorney and the news was not what she had expected. He explained to her that her husband had no intentions of giving his son back. My father had consulted with his lawyer while he was away, expressing that he was going to keep him in his care until the next custody hearing. That was a dagger in my mom's heart! She was hysterical all over again. Her attorney took immediate action. He drew up a petition for contempt of court, requested full primary custody, and asked for an emergency hearing.

In the meantime, Mom begged to see her son. My father was not having it. It was difficult for me to understand how he was able to hold my brother hostage. Why was he allowed to keep him? I had a million questions spinning in my head when I heard about this, and I had a very hard time trying to understand the legal loops he was able to jump through. Mom had to explain to me that he was breaking the rules, but the judge had to review all the facts. Once that happened, custody could be finalized. All we could do was look forward to when the judge reviewed the case. Even though the situation was temporary, it was maddening nonetheless. Now the only time we could see my brother was during our visits with him. I wondered if that would even happen.

Each time I saw my father in the coming weeks, he had a smug attitude that was infuriating. He was so sure he would gain custody of his son in the end. (Believe me, we could only hope that would never happen.) I was right to doubt that my father would let us see my brother during visitation. During our drop-off or pickup, most of the time he would leave my brother with Gram, hiding him away as if Mom would run off with him. My blood would boil when he did that. He was so mean. So egotistical. He acted as if he was the only injured party in this mess. Everyone was wrong but him, and it was my mom's fault that all this was happening. Her fault for cheating, for leaving him, for meeting someone else. Did my father ever think that maybe Mom found happiness in others because he was such a horrible person? I wondered how he lived each day thinking he was so blameless and everyone else was wrong.

A few times during visitation, I had words with my father about what he did. He continued to bad-mouth Mom, saying things like, "I didn't want my son around Jim or any other loser your mother hangs out with." This was how the visits would go. Nothing but nasty comments and frustration. He had no regard for how his actions and his outbursts affected his children. Marylyn and I would get upset all the time. Thankfully, my brother was too young to understand how reprehensible his father was. He had witnessed terrible things, but he was too little to comprehend any of it.

During one visit with my father, I found out he had enrolled Trey into a day care center. The odd part was, it was located inside the same church where Mom met the man with whom she had the affair. This was extremely odd, notably because of the conversation he had with me during the summer. He had told me over and over again how sick to his stomach he would get even thinking about that church, how that place would "haunt him" for the rest of his life. In my mind, if that location was so traumatizing to him, why would he ever enroll his son there? Now he would have to drop off his son five days a week to the same location that allegedly brought him so much heartache. I couldn't shake how very, very, weird it all was. I was so puzzled by it that I asked Mom why he would do that. Her response was, "He is probably trying to rub it in my face." At the time, that actually made sense. But it still nagged at me.

My brother stayed with my father for the rest of February. We got to talk to him on the phone sometimes, and one time we saw him at the house in Merion during visitation. I couldn't wait until my father's spiteful actions bit him back, and I hung onto hope that the lawyers and courts could see loud and clear how nasty he was. The only good news we received was that the hearing was set for March 31. Even though it felt so far away, it gave us something to look forward to.

# CHAPTER 15

# February 18—The Next Attack

On February 18, another scary situation unfolded for Mom. My father attacked her again, this time outside, in the open. Mom arrived at a bank, and my father showed up. He must have been following her. He begged her to get back together, trying to bully her into submission like he always had in the past. During this encounter, he noticed she didn't have her wedding rings on. He freaked out, shoved her up against the building's exterior wall, and literally tried to force his wedding ring down her throat. Then, he punched her in the mouth. She screamed and screamed, and strangers driving by the bank as well as customers began to notice what was happening. Apparently, a man pulled over and got out of his car. He and others arrived on the scene. Someone called the police and my father left. Mom waited in the bank until the police arrived.

By the time I got home from school, my grandparents were already at the apartment. Everyone was very upset after hearing what had happened. Mom was on the phone with her attorney in the bedroom. After she got off the phone, she filled us in on what my father had done. While she was talking, I couldn't help but stare at the injury to her lip from the attack. My stomach was upset seeing her injury and I could clearly see that she was feeling afraid all over again. This attack flung her right back to the incident at the house, all the fear from when he had tried to strangle her now fresh again. It scared Mom enough to say those frightening words out loud again. She blurted it out, in front of us all: "He is going to kill me. It's just a matter of time. He is going to kill me."

My grandparents were very emotional knowing their daughter had been through another assault. I could see how hard it was on them. Grandpop was beside himself, saying things like, "Over my dead body will he hurt you again." After that incident, Grandpop carried a bat, golf club, or a large cane with him wherever he went. He had every right to be vigilant, fearing for his daughter's safety. She had been attacked several times. Someone had to protect her. But inside, we all felt powerless.

In my mind, I was screaming, *Why! Why is he getting away with all this? How much more can she take! Every time we find peace, he finds a way to take it away from us.*

That night Mom had an emotional meltdown, exhausted from all the attacks, missing her son, and the legal drama. She was at her wit's end and continued to say she was sure her husband was going to kill her. My grandparents did not want to discuss such awful topics, but Mom insisted they know her wishes if that did come to pass. So they listened to her. Mom told them she wanted to be cremated and didn't want to be buried. The whole idea of being buried scared her. She wanted her ashes to be kept with her family where she would be surrounded by love and where it was warm. Hearing Mom talk about her death and funeral arrangements upset my grandparents terribly. It's not a topic any parent would ever want to have to discuss with their child.

The rest of the night continued in a somber tone. After dinner, Jim arrived. He had this really stressed look and was oddly quiet, aside from voicing how angry he was at our father. He never held back on that, saying often, "If that man ever hurts your mother again, I will . . . well . . . he will be sorry, let's just say that." This latest incident had really rattled everyone.

As I lay in bed that night, I couldn't help but think about everything Mom had endured. Even after my father's continued assaults, even in public, he suffered no consequences. How was it that he could repeatedly hurt us and get away with it? He never seemed to get into any trouble for his actions. Now things felt worse. I never dwelled on what Mom said about dying. I had never thought about death or her dying before. Other people die, old people die. But the attacks did scare me. They really did. These last few months had been very unsettling. What bothered me more was that no one seemed to be able to protect us. I don't recall any protection orders against my father. After so many violent encounters, this definitely would have been an option for my mom. She knew my father wasn't going to stop, she even said as much on several occasions. However, I know he made her feel scared and guilty about everything. His blaming her and hurting her made her feel defeated. She was too afraid to press charges, thinking it would make things worse. I wasn't sure if anything we did would matter anyway. My father always did whatever he wanted. Now that he didn't have control of her, it made him even angrier. Living separate from him had changed some things for us, but nothing had changed about him. He was the same scary man he always was. The only difference now was the attorneys and others were discovering it too.

The last few weeks of February, we didn't have to go to visitation due to the recent attack on Mom. It was a relief not having to see my father. Although, the downside was that I missed seeing Trey.

Early in March, we received very upsetting news. Despite my father's actions, Mom's attorney instructed her to resume the normal visitation. I freaked out. I couldn't understand why. Mom explained it had something to do with showing good faith and showing the judge that she was being reasonable. It just didn't seem fair. To this day, it still doesn't. She was always trying to be reasonable and show good faith. Where were the consequences for my father's horrible actions? On top of it all, Mom would have to beg to see her son. It was so ridiculous. Like I said before, most of the time my father left Trey with Gram and we never got to see him at all. He just loved when he had the control and he took pleasure in being spiteful. Somehow, he ended up with the upper hand. We were always left powerless.

# CHAPTER 16

# March Ends with a Roar

The few visits we had with my father in March were bizarre. He must have known he had lost ground in the custody battle with his atrocious behavior. Now he was trying very hard to win us over with bribes of goodies and movies. Did he really think he was going to convince us he had changed? I didn't understand why he wanted custody anyway. When we were all together living as a family, he was miserable. So why the sudden need to be a father? I think it was a game to him, and he just could not lose.

Despite his forced efforts, he didn't win any points with us. First of all, he had no clue what was suitable for kids our age. I recall two very inappropriate movies we went to see during our visits. One was *Altered States,* which was rated R. It had nudity, horror, and language that was not OK for a child. My sister was only ten years old! When she turned eleven, he took us to see *The Omen III: The Final Conflict* at the movie theater in the mall. The opening of this movie is so gruesome. One of the characters shoots himself in the head with a shotgun, and blood splatters all over the place. When Mom found out she was horrified. And Marylyn had nightmares for days after seeing the movie. In addition to his poor choices in entertainment, my father's true colors would show themselves during visitation as well. We would be at a restaurant and suddenly he would start saying awful things about Mom. He would get angry and start to yell about how she "ruined his life." Then he would abruptly take us back to Mom saying he was so upset he wasn't able to continue our visit. His outbursts were always unsettling. They affirmed my reasons for not wanting to live with him or visit him, and why I said as much during my evaluations for custody. I could only hope the legal system would help make that come true. Life had gotten so much better being away from him. We had the perfect setup in our new little corner of the world. A nice home, a cool dog, wonderful friends, and Jim. All we needed was my little brother to be home and everything would be perfect.

That same month we took a trip with Jim. He drove us to some huge mall that had all these cool craft shops and lots of eateries. It felt like an indoor farmers market. I had never seen a place like this before. He also took us to his grandparents' house for a visit. Their home had lots of land. I remember standing on a hill overlooking the property. That day, Jim showed us how to shoot clay pigeons with a shotgun—another cool new thing we were introduced to that month. None of us had ever shot a shotgun before, or any gun for that matter. Jim was very patient with us. When it was my turn, I was nervous. The shotgun was so huge and heavy, it felt awkward trying to hold it. After he placed the headphones on my head and helped me line up the shot, I pulled the trigger. Bummer, I missed! But it was a great experience regardless. Jim complimented us on our efforts and made it fun. It was wonderful not to feel pressure or be afraid to try something new. It was even nicer not to be berated or called names when I didn't hit the clay. Jim never made me feel scared or stupid. It was nice being around him.

The last time my mom encountered a shotgun it was a frightening experience. She was understandably nervous about being around one, and was reluctant to participate at first. But it was clear my mom was growing stronger by the day, shaking off her old fears and not letting them hold her back. Jim gently coached her, reminding her she was in control. She picked up the shotgun and gave it a try. Jim was really caring as he guided her and made her feel safe. My mom and Jim's relationship was getting deeper, and we were all very glad to see her so happy.

Mom wasn't the only one enjoying a blossoming romance that spring. My relationship with Sam had grown into love by March. Sam was very supportive of my difficult past and he was aware of all the emotional turmoil my family and I were going through. He also stuck by my side through some very tough times. After all the heartache I had been through with Patrick, it was a refreshing change to feel trust again. We spent a lot of time together that month. I craved distraction with my brother gone, and the cold weather made for some fun indoor activities. We would go roller-skating with friends often to pass the time away. Ridge Runner Rink knew us all by name at this point. Other days, I went over Sam's house. We would spend most of the time in his large finished basement either listening to music or watching TV. We just enjoyed spending quality time together. I was calm and comfortable in my relationship with Sam. After all the stress and strain of the past several months, calm was a blessing.

That month, Sam, Katie, Katie's boyfriend, and I all attended the spring dance at school. My first school dance. Sam wore a burgundy shirt with gray dress pants, and of course, his boots. I actually wore a skirt and dressy blouse, which was a phenomenon in itself. I remember Jim surprised me with a pretty corsage, which was so sweet. He even joked around with Sam, telling him, "Young man . . . you better mind your Ps and Qs with this little lady of mine, you hear me." We all laughed. Jim's humor was a refreshing addition to our new life.

We had a great time at the dance. Sam was a good dancer, and he even liked to slow dance. I had never slow danced before, and it felt awkward not knowing what to do. Even though I felt clumsy at first, Sam was a good teacher. Several good songs came on over the course of the evening. Our song, "Keep on Loving You" by REO Speedwagon, was one of them. When we weren't dancing, we were hanging out and laughing with other kids from school. Later on when the dance was about to end, Mom, Jim, and my sister came to the school to pick us up. They walked in as Sam and I were dancing to the last song of the night, and someone took a picture of us. I can see us so clearly in my mind. Our arms were around each other's waists as we looked at the camera, cheek-to-cheek with huge smiles. I kept the picture for years and years. It was definitely a night to remember.

Mom received some good news during that month. The landlord contacted her to say a three-bedroom apartment was now available for us. So we were going to move again, but it would be worth it. Now my father wouldn't be able to use my brother's closet bedroom against Mom in court. (He had made it a huge issue, saying his son was sleeping in a closet even though we had made it into an adorable toddler room for him.) I remember moving some of my stuff, but Mom must have gotten help from Grandpop and Jim while we were at school. I came home one day to find most of the larger stuff had already been moved. The new apartment was more spacious, and now our brother had his own official bedroom. I couldn't wait to have him back home so we could be a whole family again.

As the court date approached, the rebuttals from my father and his attorney continued. Mom would say things out loud in frustration sometimes. One time she said, "He wants custody of his son so bad that he is fighting me tooth and nail." I occasionally wondered why he never put the effort into trying to gain custody of my sister and me. I assume our request to stay with Mom had something to do with it. My brother was too little to be able to say which parent he wanted to live with. So the battle raged on. My father accused Mom of being a bad influence on us. Mom disclosed truths about my father's behavior. Accusations flew back and forth. It was an outright battle, and all my father cared about was winning. My hope was that the court would see everything he had done to us and that he didn't exhibit a loving, paternal nature. Living with him had all kinds of terrible consequences. His track record showed that. His violent actions toward Mom and me alone were grounds for jail time.

Other marital settlement issues had to be dealt with as well. I would hear Mom talking about dividing the marital assets off and on. Her main concern was custody of her children. The other things were secondary. However, fifteen years of marriage earned her the right to some things. Mom didn't want the house. Why would she? All the horrible memories were there. His violent outbursts lived in every corner of the house, and none of us wanted to live there anymore.

Personally, I hoped the judge gave him nothing, but I knew that probably would never happen.

On March 31, 1981, I came home from school, walked through that door, and Trey was back! Seeing him standing there, I felt pure elation. I ran over to give him a huge hug, swooping him up off his feet and swinging him around for a few seconds. He seemed bigger. He had definitely grown in the month he was away from us. As I held him, he giggled with joy and said, "I missed you, Thusie. I missed Mommy, I missed you all." His voice was pure bliss to my ears. I had missed his silly toddler talk. I expressed how I missed him too, and then sat down with him to ask him how he was doing. He began to say things like, "I go to school now, and I missed Mommy and my fire truck." He talked about how he went on a train and saw Gram a lot. He rambled on about lots of things. In his excitement, he paused now and then, distracted by Neeki, who kept jumping all over him, trying to lick his face. He giggled, attempting to fight her off at the same time. I sat there watching him as if I hadn't seen him for a year. His interaction with Neeki was adorable. He had only been around her a few days before being taken away. Watching him play in front of me made me so happy.

My grandparents were there, and we all enjoyed a nice visit as a family. We gathered around to pamper him with attention, and Mom began to explain to us how the day went. She had a radiance in her face

126

that I had not seen in a long time. It was sheer happiness. It was clear the weight of her son being away from her had been lifted. She explained that temporary custody had been awarded to her, and there would be another hearing to finalize everything in May. Her attorney felt very positive that all would go well for us. Then she described the moment my brother was released to her, and how happy he was to see her. Gram had to hand him over in the court hallway. Mom hugged him for quite a while before she even left the courthouse and drove straight home to spend time with him.

That afternoon, we showed Trey his new room. He was so young he may not have realized we were now in a new apartment. He was excited to see that he had a new bed, dresser, and a lot more space than his previous bedroom. Jim came over around dinner time and it was a jubilant reunion for all of us. Our little stinker was back, and this time for good.

*Mom and Trey*

Having my brother back made everything just perfect. All the happiness and freedom we had before suddenly flooded back in. Adding additional happiness, Jim finally moved in. Now we all woke up together and had our meals together. We hung out and laughed together as a family. Life was back on track!

Mom winning primary physical custody was exactly what she needed. She had prevailed in the toughest of times. She had taken a mental and physical beating . . . and won. Mom's attorney had done a fantastic job bringing this nightmare to a positive conclusion. We all celebrated this important moment. We would now all be together, and that was the best outcome we could have hoped for. The light at the end of the tunnel seemed so much brighter.

# CHAPTER 17

# Last Pictures

April had arrived and the only thing we still had to contend with was visitation with my father, whose behavior during our visits in April grew erratic and strange. Occasional visitation was a small price to pay for our happiness, we thought. We refused to let his sullen demeanor darken the life we were now living. Maybe we were being naïve. We didn't know how deep his darkness ran, or how determined he was to pull us down out of the light.

## April 11, 1981

Visitation the weekend after Mom won in court wasn't a long visit. Mom picked us up late Saturday afternoon because my father told her he had a prior engagement. That was fine with us because he was in a bad mood anyway. Most of the time, visiting him was like going to a dentist appointment. This time was no different. He made us feel awkward and uncomfortable, always bad-talking Mom or mumbling mean things. I mean, what did he expect? He was a terrible father and husband. Did he really believe a judge would give him custody after all the awful things he did?

I knew my father was not going to change, but visitation now seemed like a minor bump in the road compared to all the happier things in our lives. Despite his dark cloud, things were turning out to be pretty fantastic. Mom was standing up for herself now. She was winning and not taking any more of his crap. However, there were irritations that we still had to endure from time to time, like when my father would call our apartment to talk to Mom. Most of the time it was an unwelcome phone call. Mom wanted to avoid confrontations with him. So if I answered when he called, Mom would get this disgusted look on her face, start waving her hands above her head and dancing around. She would whisper, *"No, no, no . . . Tell him I'm in the shower or something."* It was funny. She took a lot of showers some weeks. Marylyn and I would giggle at each other knowing she was trying to avoid the call. No one could blame her for not wanting to talk to him.

## April 13, 1981

I was getting ready for school in the morning, and Mom was getting my brother ready too. That's when it dawned on me. Mom was now going to be dropping off Trey at the church day care where our father had him enrolled. I asked Mom again if she felt weird about having her son go to *that* day care. Her attitude about it was more optimistic than before.

"Your brother seems to really like it there," she said. "He talks about it all the time and really likes the teachers. I'm going to keep him there for now." I was surprised by how Mom didn't appear to be bothered by it. I shrugged it off, and I didn't bring it up again.

Since the custody hearing, the daily events in our lives had returned to a pleasant normal. The vibe was relaxing and fun again. The stress had left Mom's face. She was smiling more. The best part was when she pulled me aside and told me how proud she was of me. She expressed what a huge help I had been to her over the previous few months, taking on so many responsibilities since we had moved to Plymouth Meeting. I was so grateful to hear it. I felt important and loved, and that meant the world to me. Our communication had really blossomed. Our old environment had made everything so stressed and tense. I felt distant from my mom then. Now things were coming back together. Mom was beginning to break free of her oppressive past and so was I. Being away from my father had changed the chemistry between us. This newfound strength in both of us was helping us bond. Normal day-to-day things we shared with each other and priceless mother–daughter moments—everything had changed for the better. My fairy princess was back. We had found each other again.

## April 19, 1981

Easter Day, my siblings and I attended church with Mom. It was the same church we went to at Christmas. Afterward, we went back to the apartment. While we were all dressed up in our Easter best, someone—I believe it was Katie—took a few pictures of us. The pictures taken that day are the last pictures of us all together.

*Easter Sunday, April 19, 1981*

## April 25–26, 1981

Visitation that weekend was very odd. Twilight-Zone odd. My father was extremely agitated and barely talked to us. He didn't attempt to convince us he was the injured parent, like he usually did. He was preoccupied, and when I asked him why we were even there to visit, he ignored me and wandered off. Gram stayed that weekend to help care for us, and she spent more time with us than he did. She was snippy and nasty to me a few times that weekend. I wasn't sure if she was upset about the court decision, annoyed that she had to watch us or how my father treated her. I know my father was angry that he lost custody. He kept saying he lost because of all the lies. I couldn't understand what lies he was talking about. All the examples he gave never added up to anything resembling the truth. His version of how things had unfolded was ridiculous.

I would think to myself, *He had it all and threw it all away for years and years being an asshole. Now he's upset that his family is gone. What did he expect?*

As far back as I can remember, I didn't understand my father or how he behaved. He always existed in a world I couldn't comprehend. He claimed his life was ruined when he lost custody of his kids, but he didn't enjoy having us around when we all lived together! Maybe we were more interesting to him when we were small? Maybe when we didn't have personalities it was easier for him to tolerate and interact with us? I could spend a lifetime trying to figure him out and never have any answers.

Later that Saturday afternoon, things got even stranger. Patrick showed up out of the blue. I hadn't seen him since the court hearing in December. I wasn't even sure if he was still talking to my father.

I was in the front yard when I saw Patrick walking toward me. He seemed tense and told me he had to talk to me right away. It was urgent. So we walked up the street. While we walked, he revealed to me that he had been sitting on information about my father for weeks and couldn't hold it in anymore. He told me my father had asked him on April 1 to stop by the house because he had something to tell him. When Patrick arrived, he said my father apologized to him for getting him involved in the spying incident months back. My father then asked Patrick if he would go with him on an errand. Patrick agreed and they drove off in my father's car, then arrived at a gun shop. Patrick asked why they were there, and my father claimed he needed protection from my Grandpop and Jim. My father bought a gun that day.

As he spoke, I interrupted him and said, "What? That's just silly. My Grandpop and Jim aren't dangerous. Why would he buy a gun?" My father had told Patrick that Grandpop said a few times he was going to beat him up with a bat or a golf club. Something like that. I thought to myself that Grandpop had every right to threaten him after his daughter was assaulted on numerous occasions. But who knows why he would think Jim was threatening? I vaguely wondered what had happened to the shotgun he'd used to threaten my mother, but was too shaken up at this new development to care.

"Why are you telling me this?" I asked.

According to Patrick, my father picked up the gun on April 10. Once my father had the gun in his possession he started acting strangely. Then to make things worse, he said my father paid for another gun the day he picked up the first gun. Patrick felt uncomfortable knowing my father had bought another gun. It seemed like overkill for simple self-defense. Patrick thought my father was being weirder than usual, and he didn't like the things he was saying. He was really angry and hateful toward Mom, Jim, and Grandpop. He would rant on and on about his disgust toward them. Patrick ended by saying how much it bothered him that my father was acting this way, and that he felt better after telling me what was going on.

As I listened to Patrick describe my father's recent behavior, I tried to grasp everything being said. It was a lot to take in. While we were in deep conversation, my Gram called out for me to come inside. I quickly told Patrick I would have to talk to him later, especially since Gram was in a bad mood. I made him promise to tell my mom what was going on. He agreed, then walked off as I walked back to the house.

I could see my Gram was furious by the look on her face. She asked me why I was talking to Patrick. I explained innocently that he came by to talk, so I was talking to him. She scolded me and said, "Stay away from him. Your father has enough to deal with. You need to come inside now."

*Geez,* she was in a terrible mood. Like I said, things were tense and weird during this visit.

Sunday morning, we had breakfast with Gram and my father. All seemed OK at first, then suddenly my father got up from the table and left.

I looked at Gram and asked, "Why are we even here? He is in such a bad mood."

She looked at me and said, "Finish your breakfast."

Then my father stormed back into the kitchen and loudly announced, "Everything is over now, don't you get it, it's over. I have no life. She stole it from me." I remember how strange his words sounded. She stole *his* life? *What!*

He was so theatrical. He would try to play on the heartstrings of anyone who had the stupidity to fall for it. His *pity me, pity me* crap was . . . a bunch of crap! This new behavior was just him being a bad loser. Breakfast was ruined. It was going to be another wasted day at my father's house.

About an hour before Mom picked us up, I was in the driveway playing basketball with Teddy, trying to fill the time before she arrived. My siblings ran around in the driveway with us. My father would walk over now and then, pause, look at us as if he was going to say something, and then abruptly walk away. I watched him disappear around the side of the house, then go in and out of the house. He didn't interact with us, he just stared at us occasionally. It was super uncomfortable.

Teddy asked, "Hey, what's up with your father? He's being weird."

I told him, "Dude, I have no idea. I think he's upset about all the court stuff."

Shortly before Mom arrived, Patrick showed up. He came over personally to talk to Mom as promised. I found out he had already called her the day before, and also talked to his parents about how odd my father was behaving. He still felt uncomfortable but said talking to everyone helped.

Finally, Mom arrived to pick us up. Katie was with her. She would often keep Mom company on the ride down. When they pulled up, we couldn't wait to get in the car and get out of there. Patrick walked over to the driver's-side window to talk to Mom. While they were talking, my father came out of the house. At first, he walked toward the car with this urgent look on his face. Before he got to the car, he stopped, stared at all of us, then turned and walked toward the back of the house and out of sight. We all stood there for an awkward second looking at one another. Then we shrugged our shoulders almost simultaneously. Mom called out for us to get going, and I said good-bye to Patrick and Teddy.

On the drive home I told Mom and Katie what a weird weekend it had been. Marylyn shouted out, "Gram was mean to us!"

Then I asked Mom, "Did Patrick talk to you?"

She said yes but didn't want to talk about it just then. I figured as much; my siblings were in the car. I could fill her in when we got back to the apartment. So we changed the topic and headed home.

## April 27, 1981

After I got home from school, I was looking forward to having Mom and Jim listen to a song I wanted to play. However, Jim had gone to visit his parents and wouldn't be back until tomorrow. So once dinner and the dishes were done, I asked Mom if she wanted to hear it. I knew she liked the Beatles, so when I heard the song at Sam's house, I knew Mom would like it too. I borrowed the cassette from Sam and played it for her on the big boom box we had sitting in the kitchen. The song was "A Day in the Life." She sat at the kitchen table and we listened together. In case you're not familiar with the song, it is over five minutes long and concludes with this pronounced grand piano ending, followed by a loop of weird chatter.

It's a great song, and enjoying it with Mom was a memorable moment that I will carry with me forever.

After the song ended, Mom and I were talking about it and enjoying our conversation when the phone rang. I jumped up to answer thinking it was Sam, but it was my father instead. He wanted to talk to Mom. *Ughhhh!* Every time he called it was a total bummer and ruined the mood. We were having such a nice night. I hoped his call didn't screw it up. I asked him to hold on a moment. I covered the mouthpiece and whispered, "Do you want to talk to him?"

Mom paused for a second, sighed, and then said, "Yes, I'll pick it up in the bedroom." I stayed on the phone for a few more seconds while she walked to her room. She picked up the call. I could hear them talking and noted that he sounded calm. Mom was quiet and hesitant with her responses. I was being a bit nosey and stayed on the phone for another few seconds, hoping to hear more.

I did hear him say, "Why can't we start over?"

Mom responded, "Maybe when things calm down and the hurt passes, we can be friends someday."

He said, "I love you, Bunnie."

Mom replied, "I once loved you too, Bee Gee. But we need to heal, and maybe then we can be friends." At that point I hung up the phone, making sure I did it very carefully. Not long after, I heard Mom crying in her room. *Great!* Again, he had ruined another fun night. I was so disappointed. Not wanting to bother her, I decided to get my brother ready for bed. I gave him a bath and got him into his pajamas. Then he ran into Mom's room to say good-night. She put him to bed.

A little later on after I got myself ready for bed, I went to say good-night to her. I asked if she was OK and told her I hated when he would call and upset her. She explained that at times she gets sad that everything ended the way it did. She wished nobody had gotten hurt through this whole ordeal.

"Suzie, I am not perfect, but I deserve to be happy. All I want is to be happy and move on with my life." Then, she looked at me and said, "I want to stop being afraid all the time. We are much happier now, right?"

I responded with a very enthusiastic *yes* and she continued, "I hope I can be happy, but sometimes I feel he will never let me go or leave me alone. He can't seem to move on. He just will not let go of things."

That's when I told her I heard some of what he had said on the phone. I told her he sounded so sad, asking if they could get back together. She could tell that worried me.

She said, "It's hard for me when he begs me to get back together. It makes everything so painful. I want to build a new future. Then as soon as I start to feel good, he calls or shows up and makes me feel guilty for everything." I listened to her intently and gave her a hug.

I assured her, "We are all so much happier now, really we are!" She hugged me and I kissed her good-night. Before I left the room, I said, "Maybe tomorrow will be a better day. She smiled and nodded in agreement. I turned and walked back to my bedroom.

As I lay in bed, I thought of how happy things were for us. The further away we got from the old ways, the better we would be. The changes in our lives were far better than what we had before. We should keep moving in that direction.

*Pictures taken in our new apartment in March 1981. These pictures of Mom goofing around and making funny faces with us are priceless. A moment in time when the happiness was evident on our faces. They are a time capsule of joy.*

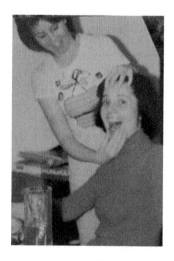

# CHAPTER 18

# The Day Everything Changed

April 28, 1981. We woke up and got ready for school. My sister and I prepared for the day, while my brother ate cereal in the kitchen. Mom got him ready after she finished getting dressed, same as any other day. I ate some breakfast, then popped into Mom's bedroom to give her a kiss good-bye before heading out the door.

It was a nice sunny day. The bus ride was normal with typical teen conversation between Katie, Sam, and me. I went to my morning classes, and around 11:30 a.m. the phone in the classroom started ringing. My teacher answered it, wrote out a note, and gave it to me as a pass to go to the office.

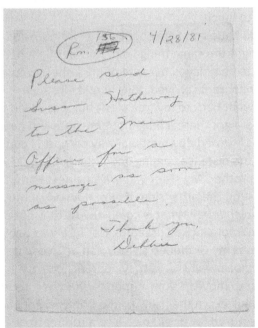

*I still have the note from that day. I keep it in my mom's jewelry box.*

As I walked down the hall toward the office, I couldn't help but feel nervous. I hadn't done anything wrong as far as I knew. I walked up to the reception desk and before I even said anything, the principal came over to me. He said, "Hello, Susan. Your grandparents called, and they're coming to get you from school today. I'm not sure what time they'll be here. Do not take the bus home. Do you understand?"

I nodded yes.

He repeated, "Remember, your grandparents want you to stay at school and not to leave. They will come into the school to get you."

I nodded again. Then he handed me a hall pass and instructed me to go to my free classroom for the day. I must have looked perplexed, because he quickly assured me, "You're not in any trouble."

"OK." But I was thinking, *What is going on? Why are my grandparents coming to get me? Man, what did my father do now?* I assumed that my grandparents had to pick me up since my mom would be delayed getting home. Something must have happened. I kept the note, placing it in my pocket, and walked to my free class. At least I got to hang out there for the day, which was cool. In this class I was able to listen to music, play a game, or do artwork. From what I remember, I listened to a few records and then I went to lunch.

At lunch, I told Katie and Sam about the weird note and my visit to the office. They thought the same thing I did. Another fight had happened and Mom was going to be delayed because of my father. I was sure that was it. When my grandparents arrived, they would fill me in.

After lunch I went back to my free class, but was called to the office again shortly after I got there. I pulled out my note and headed down to the office. Just as I turned down the hallway corridor, I could see my grandparents in the distance coming down the hallway. My Grandmom was holding my brother. My sister was walking next to my Grandpop, and there was a priest on the other side of him. *How odd,* I thought. *What the heck is a priest doing here? What is going on?* As they got closer, I could see that my Grandmom looked dreadful. Her face was beet red and blotchy, and so was my Grandpop's. They had been crying. Panic began to set in, and my stomach felt sick as they approached.

Things started to move in slow motion for me. As I stood there watching them walk down the hallway, the principal appeared and stood beside me. He gestured for us all to go into a room across from the office. Inside was a small conference room. We all walked in, and the principal turned and walked out, shutting the door behind him. We sat down in chairs that were scattered in no special order. My chair faced the door.

My grandparents and the priest were all in front of me. I felt a whirlwind of emotions, and I could sense something was very wrong. Panic, worry, and confusion were at the forefront of my mind. I blurted out, "What's going on? Where's Mom? What's wrong?" Immediately, Grandmom and Grandpop began to sob. I became even more alarmed, asking again, "What's wrong?" My sister started to say the same thing. We were both getting very upset. The priest started to speak.

"Your mom is in a better place now."

I responded, "What are you talking about? Where is she?" I could see the priest was looking at my Grandpop, seeking approval for what he was about to say. Instinctively I knew he was there to support my grandparents. Then the priest spoke.

"Everything is going to be all right."

Then my Grandpop said, "Our Bunnie is dead. Your father killed her. He shot her, and she died this morning."

The priest said, "Your mother died today, but she is at peace now. She is safe now."

I heard them both, and I heard my sister and grandparents start to cry. Then I remember feeling a rush of panic, or maybe horror. How do I describe the feeling of hearing my mom was dead? Are there even words to describe the out-of-body experience that began to overtake me? The shock was overwhelming. Suffocating and unreal. And yet, I could still hear everyone crying around me and knew it was true. I could not process all of my emotions. My sister was crying. My brother heard everyone crying and he began crying too. Disbelief. Confusion. This could not be happening. It was unbelievable. I was stunned. I wanted answers.

"What happened?" I demanded to know. "Where is she?" Questions and emotions slammed into each other and I couldn't make sense of anything that was coming out of my mouth. I didn't know how to collect myself and be empathetic at the same time. I was upset but I was angry too. *Is this what grief is?* I wanted to know where she was immediately. Where did it happen? It seemed like forever being in that moment. The sounds of sobbing, the crushing feeling in my chest. I began to find it hard to breathe. My emotions were smothering me. I couldn't process clearly what was being said or what had happened. Overwhelmed, I turned to my grandparents for guidance. I asked them directly, "What happened?"

In a monotone voice, Grandpop tried to tell me what had unfolded earlier that day. He explained my father shot Mom several times at the day care that morning, and she died at the hospital. At that moment, further questions were too difficult to ask. We sat there suffocating from the shock and loss. For me, it felt like I had fallen in a hole. The darkness began to envelop me as the light from above dimmed away.

# CHAPTER 19

# Nothing Will Ever Be the Same

I don't remember leaving the conference room or even leaving the school that day. I do remember being in my grandparents' car trying to find a space in my head to survive. Sitting there in the car, I couldn't remember what my mom looked like. I tried to picture her smile. I had just seen her that morning. She had said good-bye to me and my sister. I wanted to hear the sound of her voice. Hear her laugh. I couldn't believe she was not there anymore. I felt so alone, and my stomach was queasy. This sick, empty, lonely feeling was overwhelming. I didn't know how to handle this. My feelings were jumping all over the place. From sadness to anger, then fear. My mind wrestled with one question: *How could this be happening?*

It wasn't fair. Everything was getting better for us. Our lives were finally happy, and we had plans for the future. Mom was happy. We were bonding like never before. We had a new outlook on life. We had Jim. *Oh no, Jim! What about Jim? Where is he? Does he know what happened?* Thoughts raced through my head. *The dog! What about our dog!* I must have thought about a million different things before we pulled into our apartment complex. I was relieved to be there. For a brief moment, I felt a calmness come over me. This is our home, the place we all felt safe and comfortable. As we entered the apartment, I was surprised and relieved that Jim was there. He gave us hugs and we cried together. I found out later that he had been called to the hospital and was questioned by the police. He then came to the apartment to help with the dog and wait for us to arrive.

We were told we would be staying at our grandparents' house, and were instructed to gather some clothes and any other necessities. I robotically obeyed the request and went to grab what I needed. My body seemed so heavy as I stumbled around the apartment. This crushing feeling weighed me down as I walked around the place we called home. It was like having a fever. I felt drained and foggy.

When I walked into the hallway, Mom's bedroom was the first door I came to. I stopped in the doorway gazing into her room. I saw her bed and her hairbrush on her dresser. All the pain and grief gushed into my head all over again. I felt enormous dread and uncertainty. Tears rolled down my cheeks as I crossed over the threshold. As I entered her room, I could already smell her essence in the air. I walked over to her bed and sat down. Picking up her pillow, I pressed it to my face and breathed in. I could smell her, and for a brief moment I felt calm, as if she were there with me.

Suddenly, my Grandmom appeared in the doorway and interrupted my moment of comfort. I put the pillow back, wiped away my tears, and got up off the bed. I walked past her as she too entered the room, I assume for the same reasons I had. Trying to find something to grasp onto. Hoping Mom's personal things would comfort her in some way. She was overwhelmed with grief too. I walked into my bedroom and tried to gather what I thought I would need. Everything seemed bleak. I can't remember what I took and what I left. Honestly, it didn't matter anyway.

I picked out a few things for my brother, asking him what toys and stuffed animals he wanted to bring with him. His innocent mind was so confused by all the trauma he had endured that day. He looked at me with exasperation, wanting his toys to stay in his room. He didn't want to take anything. He just wanted his mommy. My sister and grandparents came into the room, and together we tried to gather a few things for him, making the situation as calm as we could. We were all trying so hard to be strong.

Everyone met in the living room. Before we left, we gave Jim more hugs and kisses. I remember he whispered, "Keep your chin up, darling. I love you, sweetie." I started to cry again and hugged him harder. As I turned to walk out of the apartment, I was filled with terrible anxiety. Walking away from my home and Mom's essence. Away from Jim and our dog. Away from the new life we had grown to love. Our joy, our freedom, our new future. It was gone. Gone the moment Mom died. Gone because of my father.

It was a very quiet drive all the way to our grandparents' house. When we arrived, I walked into the house and sat down in a chair in the living room. I felt as if I was melting into the chair, not knowing what to do. Hours seemed to pass as I sat in that chair. I kept looking at my siblings as they walked by, wondering what they were thinking about. My mind wandered off in all kinds of directions. *Do my siblings understand what's happened? What did my brother see? What are we going to do? Where was Mom now? Is my father in jail?* The overwhelming panic filled my head to exhaustion. My mind splintered into thousands of thoughts and questions, with barely any answers.

Occasionally in the background, I heard people's voices or a knock at the door. Friends and neighbors came in to say how sorry they were for our loss. Some arrived with food and tried to comfort my Grandmom and Grandpop. My grandparents were shattered, and I felt heartbroken for them. The look on their faces showed pain each time they recognized someone who had arrived, that person being another memory linked to their daughter. I guess me sitting there frozen, watching, was evidence of my pure shock. I didn't really greet anyone, I just sat there. Every time someone came over to speak to me, I looked at them and saw their lips moving, but didn't remember what they said.

Later that evening, Katie and Sam came to pay their respects and offer comfort. A lot of the time we just sat there, looking around, looking at each other, looking for an answer. Nobody could make sense of what had happened. The overwhelming grief and shock replaced normal function. What could anyone say that would make anything any better? Nothing. No one could help us. We weren't going to wake up from this nightmare.

That night, my brother woke up crying. He wanted his mommy and he needed comforting. This behavior went on for days and weeks. Whenever he heard sirens, or the township fire horn going off, he would start to cry frantically. He was never like that before. He had always loved fire engines and police cars, and now he was terrified when he heard them. We all tried to comfort him as best we could when he got upset. My sister was horrendously affected too. She was heartbroken and scared, lost in her own thoughts. She wanted to know what was going to happen to us. I remember during those terrible first days, we both had the same thoughts most of the time. Wanting to be with Jim. Wanting to be back in our apartment. Wanting to see our dog. But most of all, we wanted our mom.

Twenty-four hours after we had arrived at my grandparents' house, the TV news and newspapers revealed more details of what had happened. (The news had been running the story the day she died, but I don't remember seeing anything until the day after.) From the article in the newspaper, I learned more details of my mother's murder. It was worse than I could have ever imagined.

*News clipping from the day after*

The *Philadelphia Bulletin* had the story on the front page. There was a picture of my parents and the headline read, "THEY WERE LOVERS ON STAGE, NOW HE'S HELD IN HER DEATH." The article gave times, locations, and vivid details of what had occurred the previous morning. I learned how she died, the brutality of how he killed her. How she had a can of mace gripped in her hand. Reading that, I knew she had been scared. Then I read how a witness saw her running away as a man was shooting at her. The witness said my mother fell to the ground, then the man walked closer and shot her several more times. I stood there frozen in horror, paper in hand, staring at the article. Tears fell and blotted the paper as I cried. My mom ran for her life. My father hunted her down and made sure she died. He shot her over and over to make sure she would never walk away from it. And through that horrific act, he took everything from me. *Everything.*

Everything I ever cared about was gone because of him.

I put the article down on my Grandmom's coffee table and sat back in the chair, my head heavy with despair. I questioned everything. *Why, why did my father always win? Why did he always destroy everything? I had hope and Mom had happiness. Now we have emptiness.* I sat thinking in that chair consumed with my thoughts for so long that I didn't realize what was going on around me. Someone had turned on the TV in the living room. Suddenly I was jolted back into the moment. The local news

146

station began to broadcast the murder of my mother. I sat there frozen watching the broadcast. Just like the article, the information was horrific to hear.

*A tragic murder unfolded yesterday at approximately 8:45 a.m. as a young mother died while dropping off her son at day care on Remington Road in Wynnewood, Pennsylvania. The Church of the Holy Apostles offers a Montessori day school at that location. Mrs. Hathaway had just exited the school when her estranged husband shot her six times as she returned to her car. Mrs. Hathaway was pronounced dead at 9:25 a.m. at Haverford Community Hospital. An autopsy revealed that she had been shot four times in the head and once in the neck, and other bullets grazed her. The weapon was a .32 caliber. She died instantly. Mr. Hathaway was arrested several blocks from the scene. Witnesses describe the incident as brutal, hearing the gunshots, seeing her run, and hearing her screaming. There were several witnesses including other mothers with children attending the day care. Later the police were approached by the teacher from the day care who revealed to them that the son of the victim was still inside the school. He was later released to family. Mr. Hathaway is currently being held at the Delaware County Prison.*

After reading and seeing the news that morning, I approached my grandparents and asked them to tell me how they found out about Mom's death. We assembled in the living room and they sat in their usual spots on the couch. I sat across from them in the same familiar chair. Shockingly, my Grandmom was the first to start talking. It was as if she needed to talk about it, desperately trying to process what was happening too. I listened attentively. In brief, here's how the details of that day unfolded:

My Grandmom received a call mid-morning that Mom was at the Haverford Hospital. They didn't tell her anything, only that they should come as soon as they were able. The hospital was about forty-five minutes away from their house. Upon arrival they noticed it was a mental hospital. At first they thought their daughter had succumbed to my father's torment and had a mental breakdown. When they arrived, the receptionist at the front desk told them they were at the wrong hospital. She instructed them to go over to the Haverford Community Hospital (later named Mercy Haverford ER). They got back in their car and headed over to that location. Again, they spoke to the desk clerk, giving their names and my mom's name. The clerk pointed over to the officer who was waiting for them. The officer greeted my grandparents and began to tell them what had happened. It was then they found out Mom had died earlier that morning. The officer explained as delicately as he could that their daughter had died from numerous gunshot wounds, and that her husband had been taken into custody for the crime. He concluded by telling them the incident all happened at their grandson's day care location.

My Grandpop then told me he had to identify Mom. Grandmom explained she was so devastated that she couldn't bring herself to even go into the room. I remember her saying she regretted not saying good-bye to her daughter at the hospital that day. In my mind, it was best she remembers her daughter alive, happy, and beautiful rather than how she looked on that day. I can't even imagine what it was like for my Grandpop to endure such an unbelievably horrible moment. It still breaks my heart that he had to see his daughter in that state. No parent should have to witness that.

The police had to question each of them. At some point during all the chaos, they were notified that their grandson had been in the care of an on-scene officer at the crime scene. I was shocked and saddened to hear my brother had sat in a police car for two hours. My poor baby brother! He had been there the entire time until he was released to our Gram. When my grandparents were finished at the hospital and police station, they arranged to meet up with Gram to pick up my brother. After that, they asked a priest to accompany them to help them break the devastating news to all of us.

When Grandmom was finished sharing the events of that day, I looked over at my Grandpop. He never said anything more. He had sat there listening and crying during Grandmom's explanation of that day. Looking at him, I couldn't help but feel even more grief. I had my answers, but I had no comfort. Life itself would never be the same for any of us.

Later that day, my Uncle Mike, my mom's brother, arrived. He did his best to try and comfort his parents during this extremely difficult time. I sat in my usual chair, observing how he took charge of helping my grandparents find paperwork and assisting them with important decisions regarding Mom's funeral arrangements. I could hear conversations taking place but wasn't fully engaged in what was being said. Sometimes Mom's name was mentioned, and each time I would feel this piercing pain in my chest. Another day of confusion and sadness.

I always remember my grandparents' house being so quiet. Kind of an uncomfortable quiet. I wished there was a radio on or something filtering the background air. But the last two days, that was not the case. The only constant sound was the phone and the doorbell ringing. Friends and family continued to visit, each trying to console my family. I remember getting a call from Teddy. He didn't know what to say to me. It was an awkward call and I felt weird trying to talk to him. I was in a fog and couldn't think straight. I don't even remember what we talked about. Patrick and his parents called too, each trying to pass on condolences. All of the calls were uncomfortable. No one knew what to say. Everyone was trying to be supportive, but nobody knew how to react to such horror. Finding the right words was a struggle, especially when they too were trying to cope with this loss and shock. Katie and Sam came to my grandparents' house several times that week. I know they were trying to be supportive, and it wasn't that I was ungrateful. I just didn't feel like seeing anyone. It was hard being around people. I wanted to hide or run away from all the pain. But I couldn't. I was trapped in this awful reality and with every breath I took, the air was getting thinner.

The preparations for Mom's funeral were a mashed-up blur of days. I only recall bits of conversation. Uncle Mike took over everything related to the funeral arrangements. He had to go to the funeral home and witness his sister in the shocking condition she was in. I can only imagine how devastating this was for him. My grandparents instructed him on what outfit we thought would be nice and a few other details. However, they were so grief-stricken they couldn't go with him or do anything more. Overhearing some of the arrangements they were discussing brought me back to the memory of Mom telling us what she wanted if anything ever happened to her. Mom was very clear about wanting to be cremated, and wanting her ashes kept with her family. She did not want to be buried. It frightened her. She said, "I don't want to be alone in the dark, in the ground." Those were her wishes. However, things became a mess between what my grandparents wanted, what my mom wanted, and what the church would allow.

I know my grandparents tried to fulfill their daughter's wishes as best they could. They appealed to their church for a full funeral service with cremation, and their church had to consult with the Philadelphia Diocese to approve their requests. When the reply came back, it was not as expected. They would allow a cremation after a Catholic mass. However, her ashes would have to be buried in a Catholic cemetery. They said they would not permit ashes to be kept with the family. The Catholic rules were clear. Her ashes had to be buried. So my grandparents arranged for burial in the family plot.

When I found out, I was very upset. A few unfavorable words may have come out of my mouth in response. As far as I was concerned, who the heck were they to say no to my mom's wishes? My grandparents and I even had a heated exchange in the living room when I found out that she had to be buried. I mouthed off to both of them saying, "That's not what she wanted! She doesn't want to be buried, she told you it scared her!" I was making things worse, but I was upset and beyond consoling. During this emotional time, no one was going to punish me for being upset. Everyone's emotions were elevated, and mine were just overflowing. But to this day, the topic of my mom's burial upsets me beyond belief. Religion never should have stepped in front of my mother's wishes. No matter what the *rules* are.

I have never resolved my anger over the lack of empathy by the church toward my mother not wanting to be buried. I harbor great exasperation and regret that she is not where she wanted to be. At the time, I was young, and I didn't have enough clout to change anything.

# Chapter 20

# A Funeral, Good-byes, and Grief

When I was a child, Mom's warmth and sympathy had helped me through the loss of my beloved cat, Pumpkin. Pumpkin died in the summer of 1978, purely by accident. He got out of the house during a party my parents were having. I looked for him for two full days. On the third day, Teddy heard him meowing under his house porch. Mom called animal control to see if they could help us get him out. By the time the tech arrived and removed Pumpkin from under there, he had already passed away. I was overwhelmed with grief. My Pumpkin was gone, my best buddy and the sweetest animal I had ever known. My heart was broken. The tech wrapped Pumpkin in a cloth and let us carry him home. I sat on the stoop in front of my house and cried. Mom joined me and she was crying too. She put her hand on my shoulder and said, "Let's find a place in the backyard for him. A place you think would be nice." I carried Pumpkin to the backyard, and chose a spot under an odd-looking tree. It had a strange branch shaped like a U, jetting sideways and then straight up. There I buried my precious little friend. For Christmas that year, Mom made me an ornament with a cat sitting in a stocking. She had Pumpkin's name engraved along with the date.

*Pumpkin and me on Halloween*

This was my earliest recollection of death and grief, and my mom helped me through it every step of the way. Who was going to help me now?

# May 1, 1981

The day of my mother's funeral. I dressed in the same skirt and top that I had worn on Easter. Just nine days earlier when I had put on that outfit, my mom was alive. Now, I stood in my grandparents' house wearing the same thing for her funeral. It was like being in a terrible nightmare. *When will I wake up? When? Please, please let me wake up!* As the moment elapsed into reality, I grabbed the photo of all of us on Easter morning and a letter I wrote to Mom from my dresser. Then I headed downstairs to wait for the rest of the family. A few minutes later, we all climbed into the black limousine waiting outside. All except my brother. Someone had offered to watch him for the day. He was too young to attend the services.

It was a short ride around the block to the church. The drive didn't offer much time for reflection. As I sat there, I clutched the letter and picture in my hand. All these years later, I don't remember what I wrote to my mom. It makes me sad that I can't remember that.

When we arrived at Queen of Peace Church and got out of the car, I saw Jim in the parking lot. He was wearing a suit and had black shades on. I didn't get a chance to talk to him as we were quickly guided toward the church's side entrance. My grandparents, sister, uncles, and aunts entered at the side of the church together. Just a few steps inside, there was a small entry room that led into the main part of the church. The casket was in that room up against the wall on the left side. When I laid my eyes on it, I found it hard to breathe. It felt as if the air had vanished from the room. As I struggled to catch my breath and calm the panic that was building inside me, I was startled by the funeral director's loud voice as he greeted my grandparents with his sympathies. He asked them, did they want him to open the lid now? My grandparents both nodded yes. We all stood there like stone figures. The lid was to be lifted so we would have the opportunity to see Mom before the service.

Just seconds before the lid was raised, I noticed this large crucifix attached to the top of the casket. Later, I learned it was a casket cross, used to decorate the lid. I still have it in my possession today. It sits next to my bed, by my nightstand. It's the only religious thing I have ever kept. I keep it because it was my mom's. I will always keep it with me, just because it was hers.

When the lid was fully open, I got nervous. I wasn't sure if I was ready to see her. Gazing at her beautiful face again might make it harder for me to let go. But the reason for seeing her was for closure, to say our good-byes to the woman we loved so much. I tried to soothe myself by thinking that maybe seeing her again would help me find some peace.

Then, that moment of heartbreak immediately turned to disbelief. There was a sharp inward breath from everyone standing near the casket. It was startling, and that is an understatement. At first, I was unsure if it was my mom lying there. The only thing I recognized were her clothes. As a family, we had picked out a white ruffled blouse with her burgundy velvet suit jacket and skirt. We had also chosen a special brooch from her jewelry box to adorn her jacket. Her hair was in a style similar to what she used to wear. However, my mother's once beautiful appearance was severely altered by her brutal death, and the trauma she had sustained was evident. You could see they had tried to cover her wounds cosmetically, but despite their efforts there was an obvious dip in her forehead. Her neck had a noticeable dent and the bruising was visible. Her makeup was dreadful: a horrid blue eyeshadow and obnoxious red lipstick were applied to her face. The bold makeup application made her look like a mannequin. She would never have worn those colors. Her appearance was beyond what anyone would have expected.

What we all needed was some comfort after this overwhelming tragedy. Instead, this solemn moment had become another nightmare. My sister was traumatized by the gruesome visual and became visibly shaken. The image of her mother was too shocking for her and she began to cry. I felt heartbroken for her and cried too. I couldn't even protect her from this. I looked at my grandparents who were visibly decimated. I could see they were suffering terribly. Naïvely, I believed I was going to see my mom in peaceful slumber—her stunning loveliness lighting up the room like Sleeping Beauty. Instead, we received more nightmarish memories that none of us needed. She didn't look peaceful, and the beautiful glow she had in life was gone. I felt no one should view my mom in this state.

In a low whisper my grandmother asked the funeral director to close the casket for the service. We all looked at one another in agreement.

Before the lid was closed, we individually said our good-byes. When it was my turn to approach, I again felt all the weight of the world had landed on my shoulders. I took a few steps, reached into the casket, and placed my letter and picture next to my mom's waist. I took a brief look at her face, and then focused on her outfit to calm myself. I whispered, "I love you, Mom," and with my finger, I gently touched her hand. I took a step backward and moved aside so my grandparents could say their good-byes. I watched them touch her hand and give her a kiss. The director then closed the lid, and we all turned to proceed into the church. As we walked toward the pews, the sound of our shoes echoed loudly. Each of us genuflected, then we slid down to our sections of the pew and waited to receive the mourners.

Our family sat in the front middle pew of the church. My Grandmom was on the end and I was next to her. Before the church opened the doors to allow people in, my Uncle Mike walked up to the casket. A kneeling platform had been placed in front of it. He knelt down and folded his hands in prayer. Then, he completely broke down in tears. He had kept himself together while making the funeral arrangements and supporting my grandparents, but it was evident he had bottled up all his grief. At that moment, he couldn't hold it in anymore. It was difficult to see my uncle so sad. I had never seen him cry before. The death of his only sibling was a terrible loss to him. After he collected himself, he rose up and sat in the pew next to my aunt. I bowed my head again and thought about how hard Mom's death was on everyone. My head throbbed from all the sorrow.

Soon, people began to walk up and convey their condolences, saying how sorry they were for the loss of our mother/Bunnie. There were faces I knew and some I didn't. I looked up and saw Jim again. He looked very handsome in his suit, but his face was stressed and sad. He was trying so hard to be strong under the circumstances. After paying his respects, he disappeared in the pews behind us. Behind Jim came Sam and Katie. They both were very emotional, and it was distressing for me to have to accept their condolences. The whole funeral atmosphere was overwhelming and suffocating. I wished Jim, Katie, and Sam could have sat with us. We were like family, and they adored my mom. We could have comforted one another during the services. Instead, they all sat together a few rows behind us.

I often wish my grandparents had been able to see how kind Jim was to Mom and us. He was a sweet man. He loved my mother and he loved us too. Unfortunately, my grandparents were in no frame of mind to be thinking clearly. So Jim was sadly in the shadows most of the time before and after Mom's death.

As the procession continued, other familiar faces arrived: extended family, neighbors near and far, Mom's close friends old and new, her singing colleagues. So many, many people. All of them loved her. Some moments, I looked behind me and could see the line of people that ran all the way out the door. The church was very large, seating up to a thousand parishioners. Even as the mass was about to start, there was still a line of people out the door and the church was filled to capacity. People lined up along the back of the church, standing any place there was room to stand. It was heartwarming to see all the people who stayed to pay their respects to my mother and family. She was truly loved by so many people.

When the mass began, I felt myself drifting away to someplace in my mind. I recognized this feeling. It was the darkness creeping back in. Once again I was lost, alone, and afraid. I felt so empty inside. *What is wrong with me?* I should have been full of tears and sadness. But I had no tears. The only thing I felt was the fear of the unknown.

Once the long mass ended, we slowly filed out of the church and into our cars. The North Hills Country Club would host the luncheon. While there, my sister and I were able to spend more time with Jim. We missed him so much. During our brief time together, he gave us positive pep talks, telling us to keep our chins up and always remember he is thinking of us no matter where he is. He held my brother on his lap for a while and told me he would stay in touch as best he could. Then midway through the lunch Jim said he had to leave. I asked him why and he simply said it was best that he allow our family to be together. My siblings and I said good-bye to Jim. I felt so broken watching him leave. There was tension in the room that day. My grandparents found it difficult seeing Jim. Somehow his presence was painful. At that moment, everything was painful. After Jim left, I kept hoping that somehow he would stay in our lives. We needed him and he needed us.

The ride home from the funeral lunch was quiet and seemed longer than normal. It had been an emotionally draining day. I remember going up to my room and sitting on the bed, staring at the white wall across from me. *How do I get through this? How do I still breathe, walk, or think?*

I just existed. Sitting there, I only recall thinking that tomorrow would be another painful day. Tomorrow we had to go to the cemetery and bury Mom's ashes.

# May 2, 1981

The next day, we drove to the Holy Sepulchre Cemetery. Walked out to the site and stood around a small area of ground that had been dug up. Our immediate family and close friends were in attendance. The funeral director presented a bronze, cube-shaped urn. Mom's ashes would be placed next to our grandparents' burial plots. While we waited a few minutes for everyone to arrive, I glanced around at all the other tombstones. I also noticed a large tree near the grave site. Even though I was surrounded by those closest to me, I felt alone. I looked at the hole in the ground where my mother's ashes would rest. I suddenly felt cold and queasy knowing she would have to stay there. Overwhelming sorrow and anger simultaneously overtook me. I couldn't tell which emotion was strongest.

My train of thought was broken when the priest began to speak. Asking everyone to gather around, he began to say a few prayers. I stared at the urn that sat on a cover near the hole. They would bury it after we left the site. For a few moments before heading back to the car, everyone took a moment to reflect and place a flower at her urn. As I stood there, I didn't know what to do. A part of me wanted to run away screaming. The other part of me wanted to lie on the ground next to my mom and never leave. I missed her, and I didn't want her to be alone. My heart was breaking with every breath I took and every tear that streamed down my face. In my grief, I glanced up and saw my grandparents slowly walk away holding hands, heading back to the car together. I looked back down at Mom's urn and took a deep breath. Slowly taking small steps backward, I finally turned around and began to walk toward the car.

While sitting in the car, I looked out my window as we drove away from the site. My eyes were blurred by tears as I watched the numerous tombstones rapidly pass by. My heart was heavy with despair. I didn't want to leave her there all alone. I had no choice.

In the days following my mother's death, I awoke from horrible dreams every night. I would wake up and for a few seconds I could feel the terror so fresh in my thoughts I would be petrified. These dreams made it hard to fall back to sleep or function during the day. My grandparents noticed how depressed and anxious I was. The next thing I knew, I was under the care of a psychiatrist and given antianxiety medication to help me cope. Grandmom held onto my prescription and gave me the pills as prescribed. With all the traumatic events that had happened in my life growing up, and the additional trauma of my mother's murder, I was going to need some help. Medication and therapy were the beginning of a long road of treatment for me.

Despite my best efforts, each day and night my mind was spinning out of control. I would wake up, in a room that was not mine. The surroundings were a mixture of my grandparents' things and other odds and ends. My emotions swirled around in my head and I felt despair taking over. I was being swallowed up by it all, and felt so lost.

Even with medication, getting out of bed each day was tough. The constant reminders of my mother's absence were always present. Equally tough was watching my siblings suffer. My brother was still waking up crying, asking for Mom and wanting to know where she was. Each of us tried to comfort him and attempted to say something positive. It was difficult to find the right way to tell him Mom was gone. We had to be creative in what we said; he was only three. I heard my grandparents tell him soothing things like, "She loves you and is watching over you from heaven," and, "Mommy is with the angels now." He seemed to accept that story, and because it worked to help him feel better, we stuck to it. Consistency was soothing for him. Gosh knows he hadn't had any of that in the last few months. He still needed comforting when he heard a siren or fire horn. Holding him until the sound was over helped a lot. It was evident how traumatized he was by what he had endured that terrible day. This new behavior from my brother was horrible to witness. I felt awful for him and helpless. How does a child that age process it all? He had to find a way to cope. How does a toddler do that?

My sister was not the same either. She didn't laugh or pester me like before. My once stubborn and outgoing sister was now quiet and sad. When she did talk, she asked lots of questions. Most of them I was afraid to answer. What is going to happen to Jim? Our dog? Our things at the apartment? What about our school? The house in Merion? She was just as worried, sad, and confused as I was. I wasn't sure of the answers myself. It all felt hopeless. What was happening to our family was unfair. I was so angry at my father for making all of us suffer.

In quiet moments while my siblings were playing in the backyard or occupied with my grandparents, I had nothing to do but think. As I sat in my room alone, my thoughts would turn to doubt, and I would question why. Why did I ever let the happiness sink in? I should have known my father would ruin everything. Why did I think for one minute he would let us live in peace? How stupid I was, believing we could ever be happy.

I would think about my grandparents, my siblings, and what our lives were going to be like now with Mom gone. I felt sad for my grandparents, losing their only daughter and now having to care for us. How was that going to work? Grandpop was seventy, and Grandmom was sixty. They were about to retire. Were they too old to take care of us? Would we be taken away? Or worse, put into foster care?

Panic set in. My unanswered questions took control, and I began to overanalyze everything. I didn't want to live with strangers. If I had a choice, I would want to stay with my family. Then I started to think about the awkward living conditions at my grandparents' house. How uncomfortable and bored we had been during the two weeks Mom was on vacation in the summer. Now, it was my new home. I wasn't sure if I should be grateful or upset. I distinctly remember there were no kids our age to play with on this block. I remember vividly on hot, humid days doing nothing but melting into the grass while watching the laundry dry on the clothesline. This sudden jolt of reality was alarming to me. I was grateful to have a place with family, but uncomfortable at all the differences between this home and the one we had left.

There were notable oddities in the way my grandparents lived. They were so old-fashioned and very religious. We weren't raised with religion. I only went to church when we visited them, or on the occasional Easter and Christmas with Mom. My Grandmom didn't like the way I dressed, and she didn't like the music I listened to. My rambling thoughts were making me panic even more. I had to stop overthinking everything, take a deep breath, and try to reflect on what I did have. For a teen, that was hard in a normal environment. But with the disaster of a life I had now, I was having a tough time trying to think positively each minute of the day. The one thing I was grateful for was that my grandparents and my siblings were all near me. We had each other, and that was a lot more than nothing.

# Chapter 21

# **Closet of Memories**

A week had gone by since the funeral and each day seemed to take forever to end. Grandpop had returned to the apartment a few more times, bringing back more and more things each trip. All of Mom's belongings were kept together down in the basement of my grandparents' house. Along one side of the room were her clothes, shoes, and personal effects. I realized that my Grandpop had moved us four times since October. It was hard to believe we had moved that many times in six months. He must have been so exhausted emotionally and physically from that alone.

I went down several days a week to look at Mom's stuff. Surrounded by her belongings, I felt comforted. Being near items that used to belong to Mom would give me a brief feeling of happiness. Just like I had with her pillow in her apartment bedroom, I would smell her clothes and remember how she smelled. I needed to feel she was still here. I wanted to seal up her smell in my memory and never let it fade. Those few seconds of comfort were all I had, then sadness crept back in. I would try so hard to focus on her face in my mind, finding it difficult to remember what she looked like without a picture. I couldn't understand why my mind was being so cruel to me. Staring at the long rack of clothes in the basement brought back childhood memories of my mom's dressing room in the Merion house. Closing my eyes, I fought to bring the memories into focus . . .

Next to my parents' bedroom there was a smaller room that had a sofa bed and my mom's makeup vanity. Mom used it as her dressing room. I remember a few occasions when I was sick as a child, I stayed in that room. I had a few tough bouts with some nasty childhood sickness. When the doctor came to our house to evaluate me, Mom would sit beside me and listen attentively as he described my ailments. During my recovery, she would bring me water and give me my medicine. Attempting to lift my spirits, she would sing to me. Every time I was sick, I always remember Mom being there.

That same room held other memories of my childhood too, such as when I would sit on the sofa bed and watch her do her hair and makeup. I thought it was incredible how she could roll her hair in all those curlers and actually go to sleep in them. The next day, she would still be walking around with those curlers in. Then prior to performing in a show, she would tease her hair out and magically get it all done up just perfect. She wore her hair in a lot of different styles. Sometimes she just wore it down with a nice wave from the curlers, or she would style it in a mix between a 1960s beehive and sweeping updo. All were very classic, and no matter what style she did, she always looked lovely. For shows she would wear a lot of makeup during a performance. She knew how to make her eyes bolder, almost Egyptian-looking. For an everyday look she toned it down. Even in the casual look she wore around the house, she always managed to appear stunning.

*Mom glowed with beauty inside and out*

As I watched her do her hair or get dolled up for a performance, I admired her for not just her sense of style, but her confidence. Since I was never very girly, or confident, my mom would try to help me along. When I was around age six, she would do my hair in pigtails or a ponytail. Occasionally for holidays or special occasions, she would roll my hair in curlers. Sleeping in them was super uncomfortable. However, the next day, she would take the curlers out and fix my hair into a really cute style.

I never grew tired of watching her perform her everyday rituals. Mom was so pretty and the things she did intrigued me. I was captivated with how skillfully she made herself up for what appeared to me to be glamorous events. Maybe it was because I was much simpler in my attire as a young girl and teen. Through the years her dressing room had other uses. Later when my sister and brother arrived, the sofa was switched out for a comfy chair, and Mom would use that room for breastfeeding. Less glamorous, maybe—but no less beautiful.

I remember sitting on her bed lots of times while Mom got dressed for a night out or rehearsal. She kept several jewelry boxes on her dresser. I loved when she would place them on the bed and let me look through and play with her jewelry. I would try things on, and play pretend with them. I especially loved the pieces shaped like bunny rabbits. (Her nickname, Bunnie, had inspired bunny jewelry and bunny figurines all over our house.) Mom's bedroom closet was quite entertaining as well, full of shoes, boots, purses, and all kinds of nice clothes. It was fun to watch her flit around the bedroom in her fuzzy pink robe, try on her different outfits, and figure out what she was going to wear that night. When I was old enough to notice, I saw while she was changing that she had an enormous scar on her arm. It ran from her shoulder, along her upper arm, and back into her armpit. When I asked her about it, she sat down and explained what happened. When she was two years old, she put her hand into an old-fashioned Wringer washing machine. It nearly tore her arm off. She got a skin graft and had to go through a lot of physical therapy to regain use of her arm again. The scar left her feeling self-conscious and protective. For years, she would only wear shirts with long sleeves. When she was in school, she kept it hidden. In the summertime she even wore a cover-up over her bathing suit. However, as she got older, she tried to make peace with her scar and not let it bother her as much. She didn't want it to control her all the time. It was a part of who she was. She wasn't one to let anything hold her back.

*Me age four with Mom*

Now in my adulthood when I look at her pink fuzzy robe that hangs in my closet, her jewelry box, and any of the bunny keepsakes scattered around my home, they bring me some comfort. I cherish the memory of my mom—my very own glamorous fairy princess that I have always looked up to.

# Chapter 22

# Slipping Away

Father's Day weekend, we all took a trip to Virginia to visit Uncle Mike. He and his family lived there. We didn't see him very often, generally only on holidays or family milestone events. I didn't know him well enough to see any similarities between him and my mom. However, I remembered that when he was around Mom, she laughed and joked with him a lot. As I got older, I learned they were only fourteen months apart.

The ride was long, and the visit was normal enough. We stayed for the day, and all seemed fine until it was time to leave. As we said our good-byes, my grandparents told me my siblings were staying for a longer visit. It was summer, so it didn't seem too odd to me. My brother could play with his cousin, who was about a year younger than he was, and my sister would be with him. My comfort with the situation changed drastically once we got in the car.

On the drive home, my grandparents revealed to me that my siblings were going to be staying with my uncle and his family . . . for good.

I had trouble understanding, asking how long they were staying exactly, refusing to believe that my siblings and I were being separated. But it was true. The adults had all agreed it was the best solution for everyone. My heart crumbled hearing this, my thoughts turned into confusion, worry, and panic. *How exactly is this a good idea?* It was another gut punch to my sanity. I asked more and more questions, and then realized this was probably the reason they hadn't told us anything to begin with. They didn't want us to get upset, cause a scene, or be allowed too much time to dwell on it. In my mind, they had tricked us. Ripped the Band-Aid off. Made it quick and got it over with. Who was this easier for? Not me, and not my siblings.

I was horrified at this new turn of events. I needed my brother and sister. I didn't have anything else to keep me together. They were my connection to Mom, to my past, to everything! Nearly every memory I have from my life had them in it. I couldn't understand or accept this decision. My grandparents further explained why they had settled on this arrangement. Their age was one of them. I recalled then how my

Grandpop was seventy and my Grandmom was sixty. They felt that a younger family structure was a more appropriate solution for my siblings' upbringing. As for me, I was older, a little more independent, and they felt I could manage. I was stunned and sad, sobbing in the backseat during the long drive back to my grandparents' house. I was more alone now than ever before. Once again my life would change, and not for the better.

Other losses ate at me as I sat in the car.

After Mom's murder, leaving the apartment behind felt like another death to mourn. It was our last link to that happiness we once had, including the memories of Jim. I guess I thought he would always be there. How naïve I was to think he would be able to see us grow up. With Mom gone, our connection to Jim was ending too. All in less than two months, I had lost everything that meant anything to me.

Prior to my siblings leaving, a few attempted celebrations had made us all realize holidays from now on wouldn't be anything like before. On Mother's Day, my sister and I had made a card for Grandmom in an attempt to fill the void of Mom not being there. Grandmom's birthday was the very next day. Both days were somber because of Mom's absence. May 24 was my fifteenth birthday and I didn't care. When my brother turned four seven days later, we had a cake for him and made a fuss. He really needed something to cheer up his little world. But he was still waking up with nightmares and would still ask for Mom. When he did, it was heart-wrenching.

Friends were also falling away from me one by one. In mid-May we had a visit from Teddy and his family. Teddy and I sat on the porch steps for a while, just talking about things going on in the old neighborhood. We finally came around to talking about what was on our minds—the elephant in the room, so-to-speak. We couldn't ignore it anymore. I lived far away and wasn't returning to Merion. These last few months had changed everything so quickly, we never had the chance to adjust. Now things were worse. I had tried to keep in touch by calling him, but that was an epic failure. Living across the street from one another for all those years enriched our friendship. We could always talk to each other in person. Now the distance had strained everything. Our afternoon visit was enjoyable, but at the same time it was a reminder of another comfort in my life coming to an end.

Ever since Mom died, Patrick had been keeping in touch with me. He would call a few times a week and we would reminisce about the past.

Talking about good times and knowing he cared about my mom was comforting for me. I was desperately trying to hold onto anything connected to Mom, even the broken relationship with Patrick.

Then at the end of May, Patrick and his parents came over to my grandparents' house. It was an uncomfortable gathering; no one seemed happy. Patrick's mom started the conversation. They were putting the kibosh on our connection. Simply put, she made it clear that with the recent trauma, they felt that everyone needed to move on and heal. That was it. She flat-out told us to move on. Patrick's mom and my Grandmom both seemed to have a firm stance on the matter. I recall how surprisingly upset I was. After everything I had been through with Patrick and the history we had, I felt another huge loss. It felt like a repeat of emotions from when we broke up earlier in the year. I cried for most of the day. He was my first love and he was strongly connected to so much of my past. I carried a deep hurt inside for a very long time.

Time at my old school had also come to a close. School had been a positive diversion in my life. It allowed me to see Katie and Sam and try to function like a "normal" teen. I wanted to soak in my remaining days, and desperately tried to hang onto every moment. As the school year came to an end, I appreciated how many students and teachers treated me with kindness in those final weeks. On the last day of school many people signed my yearbook knowing I wouldn't be back in the fall. I was touched by how each of them wrote words of encouragement for my future. Come September, I would have to go to a new school closer to my grandparents' house. My third school in less than a year.

So, during that long ride back from my uncle's without my sister and brother, that last straw of loss hit me like a ton of bricks.

I began to overthink everything. *Why can't we all be together? Why did my Uncle not want me? Was it because I was too old? Maybe they didn't like me?* Even though my grandparents had explained why, I still couldn't process why it would be best for us to be raised this way. *Hadn't we all been through enough?* Though it may have been a little selfish, I felt angry at everything I was going through. Also, I was sickened at the thought of how my siblings must have felt at that moment. *They must be freaking out and feeling alone and helpless.* I could not see my grandparents' side, blinded by my frustration and self-pity at all I had lost. I was only fifteen, and I felt like I had been through a whole lifetime of pain. Yet, I was too young to be grateful for the roof over my head, or to understand the hard decisions my grandparents had to make. All I knew at that moment in my life was that life sucked. And each day, it sucked even more.

The following day was awful. My thoughts were consumed with questions and sorrow. I was having a difficult time trying to emotionally process this bombshell. How do I react? My whole life has changed in so many ways so quickly I can't keep up. I had lost both parents in one day, and now my siblings. I didn't even say a proper goodbye to them. None of us had any time to catch our breath after losing our mother. Now we were being pulled apart. All in less than two months, I had lost everything that meant anything to me.

The next several days without my siblings were torture. I woke up at night with horrible nightmares. Each of them took the wind out of me, leaving me feeling heartbroken. The ones I remember the most were so vivid. I could hear my brother calling for me. I was running but could never reach him. Then I was in a car trying to ask people to help me find my sister and brother. I had these dreams over and over. Dreams of my siblings being lost, as I desperately tried to find them. I searched and searched, even hitchhiked. Finally, when I found them, I couldn't get to them. They were fading, fading away until they were invisible. I could hear them calling for me, always out of reach.

My dreams would turn into living nightmares each time I awoke, realizing they were really gone, and were hundreds of miles away from me. I wanted to melt away into my bed, to disappear into the air and not feel this shitty life anymore.

I was so unhappy, and everything felt hopeless. I thought about letting go of all this pain. Not staying in this world anymore would be easier. I was so done with it all. Dying seemed simpler. I thought about it way too much, hoping I would get hit by a car or get fatally sick. I thought about taking all my medication if I could get it from my grandmother. I could go to sleep and never wake up—it seemed to be the answer. Then I wouldn't have this miserable life or this pain and loneliness anymore. These were my thoughts every night while I lay in bed. Every time I was alone, and even at times when I was not alone, it consumed my thoughts.

So why did I go on? At the same time I was thinking about killing myself, I would remember my siblings and grandparents. I would feel guilty and then afraid of how it would cause them more pain. Afraid that if I died, they would hate me for hurting them. What would happen to my brother and sister if I died? Losing someone else would be horrible for them and my grandparents. They would be completely alone, and how could I put them all through another funeral? I thought about Jim. How he always told me to keep my chin up. I would let him down too if I did something to harm myself.

Despite how horrible everything was for me, I also thought about my mom and how she didn't have a choice. She wanted to live, but my father took that away from her. I thought about what she had said to me that day in the car. How she tried to leave him. How she tried to do the best she could. She was hurting and trying to survive. I had to do the same thing. I had to keep going. I didn't want my mom to be disappointed in me.

Even with my suicidal thoughts, my conscience was loud and relentless. It forced me to remember the family I still had. Living or dying, my life hurt. It was a constant, painful struggle to exist each day. But I was trying to find strength.

A few days later, I went to my Grandpop for help. I told him I was having a hard time with all my sadness, how I found it difficult to live each day and didn't want to live anymore. I could see that what I revealed to him broke his heart. He was instantly emotional, and I felt horrible. He stood there looking at me with his soft blue eyes. Then he dropped his head, shaking it. In a cracked voice he began to say something, but I couldn't make out what it was. At that point I was even more upset. I didn't want to hurt him. I just wanted help. I needed someone to talk to. I asked him if he could take me to my doctor. He looked up at me and softly told me to go sit in the sun porch. He would be in shortly. So, I did as he asked.

It was a few minutes before he joined me there. He came in and sat down in one of the odd, bouncing metal chairs we kept on the porch. As we sat there together in silence for a few moments, I observed how Grandpop always looked so comfy. On this occasion, he wore tan twill dress pants—a staple in his wardrobe—and a dress shirt underneath a cardigan button-down sweater. He said, "Suzie, you need to count your blessings. You have to count the ones you have." He went on to say, "I know how hard it has been on you. The loss of our Bunnie has been tough on everyone, but you have to remember your mom would want you to spend more time being thankful for this beautiful day."

Then he got up, walked over to me, and placed his hands on my shoulders. "You are loved." I could hear the crackle in his voice again.

Then, he turned and walked out of the porch. I sat there for a long while. I continued to feel guilty for upsetting him. I didn't want to do that, I only wanted the pain to stop. I'm not sure what hurt more, upsetting my Grandpop or the guilt that I had for not being stronger for my mom and siblings. I stayed on the porch thinking about what he had said.

My Grandpop's solemn demeanor was a recent development. He had changed. He used to always be so cheery. I had always found his personality captivating, and I recall how much he loved and treasured my mom. Growing up, when he came over to visit us, I might say, "Hi, Grandpop. It's so good to see you," and his response would be, "It's good to be seen." Or if you asked how he was doing, he would respond, "I woke up today, so that is a good start." He also made memorable toasts and would speak in Polish saying "*Nostrovia*" or "*Salute,*" meaning, "Cheers" or "To good health." After everything that had happened, he was not the same person I remembered.

That night, my Grandpop's words remained with me for a long time. For some reason, he had a way of making you think about things. Maybe it was how he simplified everything. He always said stuff with such pride and kindness, but also this new seriousness that made me pay attention. Oddly, I felt better. His words made sense and he wasn't angry with me. It was as if he knew how much I was struggling, and he was trying his best to give me strength by saying what he said. He made me think, and that helped me.

I realized I didn't want to upset him anymore. I wanted to try and do better.

The next morning, my grandmother told me I had an appointment with the doctor. During my visit, I let out the deep sorrow of missing my siblings. I became unhinged in his office, crying and yelling. Everything had piled up and I was drowning in more sorrow than I could physically handle. I told him everything I was feeling. How my thoughts had beaten me down. How I went to my Grandpop for help, and how talking to him had made me feel both better and guilty. The doctor was supportive and agreed that having someone I could vent to was extremely important. Although, he still asked me if I had or would try to harm myself. I explained how I felt and was honest. Since I had not tried anything, I didn't have to go to a treatment center that day. However, due to the serious concerns regarding my welfare, the doctor asked me to see him two more times that week. My grandparents were put on notice that if I said anything more about wanting to take my own life, I would need to be admitted to the hospital. He adjusted my medication, and I had an additional appointment a few days later. In both meetings, I agreed that during tough times I needed to keep remembering who needed me. That was the key to keeping me focused. I promised I would do my best to take things day by day.

Even with the meds, there were days I felt I was losing the battle. There were days I could feel the unhappiness and anxiety creeping back in. I had to emotionally smack myself in the face, a lot. I continued to be honest and express my feelings with my doctor. It did help, and so did the medication adjustments along the way. I was working hard to try and not let anyone down. Including my mom. I would often talk to myself, saying things like, *Mom would want me to stay strong. I have to stay positive for her and my siblings. I have to keep fighting. They're all counting on me.*

I was making some progress. But the constant blows to my life added more stress on my relationships with Katie and Sam. I was not myself and emotionally worse than when I met them. They were understanding during all the weeks of struggles. I hadn't been thinking clearly during those weeks after Mom's death. Sam stood by me but my emotions were even more challenging now. My depression and the added loss of my siblings had really wiped me out. Our relationship was strained and the distance between us festered.

In addition to feeling that everything was slipping away from me, something else popped up. Something frightening. We learned in June that my father was out on bail.

# Chapter 23

# Various Forms of Escape

I really don't think anyone can fully understand the fear our entire family endured because of this man. The change in my grandparents since my father's recent violence was striking, especially my Grandmom. For as long as I had known her, my Grandmom had always been strong, loving, and fearless. Fueled by her deep faith and a difficult past, she had been a force to be reckoned with.

I recall hearing about her past from my mom and Uncle Mike on different occasions. Grandmom had two siblings: an older sister, Marie, who passed away when I was younger, and a brother named Bill, her youngest sibling. When Uncle Mike was born, my Grandmom lived in Tuskegee, Alabama. Her former husband, Howard, had abandoned them early in the marriage, leaving my Grandmom no choice but to move back to Philadelphia to be near family. That is where she gave birth to my mom. Mike and Bunnie were fourteen months apart and Grandmom raised them as a single parent, on her own, until they were preteens. This was virtually unheard of in the 1940s and '50s. The way I remember Grandmom, she had natural red hair peppered with some gray, blue eyes, and a robust frame. She was very pretty. Her incredibly strong-willed personality stands out in my mind, but she was a classy lady through and through. The rules of etiquette were entwined in her soul. She never wore white after Labor Day and always had on a dress or skirt. I never saw her in pants. Though she had been a nurse at Abington Hospital for several years, her true passions were her church and her love of flowers. She was extremely talented in floral arranging, which she did professionally for weddings and events, and also for her church.

In 1957, my grandparents, Kay and Ted, met through mutual friends. When they married, Uncle Mike and Mom were thirteen and twelve. Grandpop later adopted them, and they all moved to Ardsley, Pennsylvania. There they settled into a nice suburban life. Mom said her upbringing wasn't always easy, but her stepfather was a good man. Grandpop used his firm but loving family values and strong faith to work through any trials he faced raising my mom and her brother. The hurt left behind from their biological father who abandoned them was something they all had to deal with. Mom once explained to me when I was a teenager that this topic was sensitive, and her parents didn't talk about it often. Each of them had to deal with their emotions and move on as best they could.

But losing their daughter was beyond anything they could move on from. The fear and paranoia my grandparents were experiencing and the trauma they had been through changed them into shells of their former selves. It changed all of us. And now we were all walking on eggshells after receiving the terrifying update that my father had been released on bail. The tension and anxiety were elevated for everyone. My emotions were all over the place, and I was scared. *Who knows what he'll do? What if he comes to the house and tries to kill all of us?*

Both my grandparents were afraid with me. My father had caused so much damage. Now he was out of prison and awaiting his trial. *Walking around free.* We were not free. Just as my mom was not free even after she left him. Instead, we were all on edge. My Grandmom had already been so freaked out, and she was hurled into further panic after hearing this news. It was so bad, my Grandpop had to put steel plates behind Grandmom's bed and along the window wall of their bedroom. She was sure it would protect them if he came to their house in the middle of the night while they were in bed sleeping and tried to shoot them through the wall. She even called the local police asking that they patrol our street more often.

And the hits just kept coming. A few days later, my grandparents were in the kitchen talking as I walked in, oblivious of the tense discussion they were having. They both looked at me with alarm on their faces. I was worried. *What happened? Are my siblings OK? Did my father do something?* I looked at them with immediate concern. "What's wrong?" I blurted out. Then my Grandmom held out her hand. She was holding a green paper. My Grandpop began to explain.

"Suzie, this is for you." I took the paper and read it. I had received a subpoena.

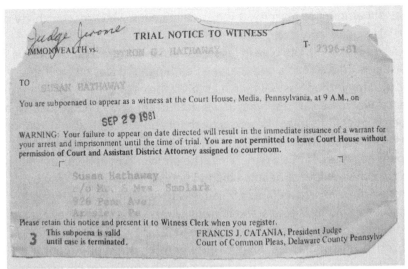

*My subpoena*

I didn't know what a subpoena was exactly. Grandpop explained that it was a summons. I had been called to appear in court as a witness in my own mother's murder trial. My reaction was immediate terror. What did this mean? I looked at them for answers. My Grandpop explained that I would have to testify at the trial.

*Holy crap!* In a few months, I would have to face my father in court. I felt overwhelmed with so many emotions. Alarm, fear, dread . . . pick one. Any of them would fit. The pit in my stomach kept getting bigger and bigger. Of course, I dwelled on it and that made it worse. I would have to tell the jury what happened to me and things I saw. I hardly slept that night and was exhausted the next day. I couldn't stop thinking about how soon I'd be in a courtroom, facing my father.

A day or two later, Patrick's parents called my grandparents. Patrick had also received a subpoena. I assumed his parents were as alarmed about the situation as we were. It appeared Patrick and I were in the same boat.

A few weeks later, I had to meet with the prosecuting attorney to go over the case and review the facts. He told us my father had pleaded not guilty by reason of diminished capacity. *Whatever the heck that means.*

Well, according to the Merriam-Webster dictionary, it's an abnormal mental condition that renders a person unable to form the specific intent necessary for the commission of a crime (as first-degree murder) but that

173

does not amount to insanity. It is also called diminished responsibility or partial insanity.

After explaining the plea in layman's terms, the prosecutor and his assisting staff also explained that the death penalty was off the table because my father was claiming mental disturbances. Then, we went over what it would be like testifying. It was important that I understood what types of questions might be asked by them and the defense. Everyone was very patient and sympathetic of my panicked state, but the whole experience was seriously unnerving. The anticipation of being in a huge courtroom with lots of people I didn't know, and my father close by, terrified me. I expressed how afraid I was to see him again. The prosecutor said he would stand in front of me if that made me feel better, and suggested keeping my focus on the judge if I wanted. After my concerns were addressed, I had to answer more questions about the night my father strangled Mom. I had to describe the hockey stick incident. How he had behaved toward me and my siblings in the past and before Mom died. I told them things I heard and saw before and during my parents' separation. I was asked about my relationship with Patrick and what I knew about the spying and tape recordings. I had to explain to them how I found out about the gun, and what I heard on the phone the night before my mom died. I told them everything I knew while they took notes. After I was finished, my grandparents spoke for a while. I waited in another room until they were done. Before we left, the prosecutor explained we would meet again with the attorneys closer to the trial. Then he told me that I just had to tell the truth and not to worry. Though one of the lawyers assured me they would try very hard to spare me as much duress as possible, it wasn't very comforting. I was still petrified.

By July, I recall what a miserable teenager I was. I would wake up to a new day and continue to worry about my father being out free until trial. Despite my best efforts to stay focused and keep my mom and siblings in my mind, I continued to struggle. I felt I just existed day to day with no joy. The roller coaster of a life I had and all the recent horrors made it difficult to get out of bed. At some point each day or while I slept at night, thoughts would creep in and eat away at me. I had to remind myself often that I had a place to live, with people I knew. Then I would think about how selfish I was being. Trying to get through each day was exhausting. I would worry about my siblings, and then I was depressed all over again about losing Mom.

If I had too much time to think, all I would do was that. My siblings were always on my mind. Even though they were together, I felt in my gut this sudden change was hard on them too. Living with people you didn't know very well would be tough on anyone. I thought about how confused they must be and wondered often how they were doing. Was my brother still waking up with nightmares? Was Marylyn happy that she had at least one sibling with her? I had to remind myself that my brother and sister were much younger than me and required so much more attention. I would try and convince myself they were in a better place, hoping that they were doing OK and trying to keep in mind they may need me someday. I had to hang on even though I was hurting inside and missed them so badly.

I missed the sound of their voices, their laughter when playing. I never thought I would miss arguing with my sister, giving her a hug, or having her around to talk to. But I did, terribly. Helping my brother get dressed. Putting him to bed, reading him a book, or watching over him. There was no one around messing with my stuff or bothering me all the time with questions. It felt lonely. The quiet and emptiness everywhere was deafening. I hated that they were so far away. Virginia was not around the corner, and the distance was awful. My relationship with them was cut down to phone calls, and honestly, talking on the phone didn't help. I would try and speak to them as often as I could, but sometimes it was easier not to call. The more I talked to them, the more I missed them. And sometimes talking was a struggle. My brother was still hard to communicate with on the phone, and my sister seemed quiet and different. When we did speak on the phone, I would try to picture them in my head and it scared me that I would forget what they looked like. Weird how the mind plays that trick on you. First with my mom, and now my siblings.

That summer, there was no looking into the future or looking forward to anything. I clearly remember just living for each day, trying to get through it. Most days were thick and heavy, almost suffocating like a hot, humid summer day. But it wasn't the weather that was making me feel that way. It was my life. How did I function with all the stress and uncertainty?

I'll let you in on the secret . . . I just did it.

I did it all the time, every day. I kept on breathing and I kept on living. I had to. Mom would have wanted me to. Even though nothing was the same anymore, I had to keep going. Everyone I loved was on my mind and would not shut up. The conscience ghosts in my brain constantly reminded me of what I had to do, whispering to me each day and night that I had to stay strong.

Positive distractions became a necessity in my life. I felt as if every week presented another disastrous challenge. Seeing friends and getaways helped, so my grandparents tried to offer me lots of freedom. (They probably needed a break from me too. Anything to salvage their sanity was a good thing.) Katie and I saw each other as much as possible. I was able to spend a lot of weekends away with her, and that was a huge relief. The busier I was, the less I dwelled on things. If I was not away at the shore or visiting someone else, I was with Katie. We did so much together: sleepovers, babysitting, hanging out at the mall, or sometimes she came to stay with me. With little to do at my house, we often took advantage of my Grandmom's pool membership to escape the boredom. Katie knew how hard life was on me, so she kept me busy. She even helped set up a reunion with Jim.

Katie, Sam, and I all went bowling together and Jim met us there. It felt like old times, even if it was just for a few hours. We laughed, enjoyed the game, and even paused to cry a moment or two. Being together again brought a range of emotions. Life had ripped Jim away from us and my siblings. Although we were able to hang out and enjoy this reunion together, the heaviness of loss still permeated the air. When the time came to say good-bye, it felt like a piece of me was tearing away. It was a bittersweet reunion, and I would not see Jim again until several years later.

In addition to weekend stays with Katie, I was invited to visit with Mom's friend Mrs. Robin for a weekend. Mrs. Robin and mom performed together in a number of shows and became good friends. I was happy to visit with her. She brought me along to a wedding she was attending. I also had the opportunity to see how my dog, Monique, was doing. Mrs. Robin was kind enough to take care of our dog after the tragedy, and later her daughter adopted her. During the visit we watched some cool movies and visited with her family. I enjoyed being around people who knew Mom. Mrs. Robin was so warm and caring, and she comforted me when I broke down during a very emotional moment while staying with them. The death of my mother and all the other added losses were so deeply painful. Even in fun times I felt guilty and would cry uncontrollably. I was lucky to have Mom's friend in my life in such trying times. My mom's memories, family, and friends were the glue I needed to mend my sadness.

As I tried to take one day at a time that summer, I recall a few enjoyable moments spent with Sam. Despite the distance with me living in Ardsley full-time, we still managed to see each other often. One weekend Sam came to the Cape May shore house. I remember a nice, peaceful moment when we stood on the second-story porch of the house. Across the street someone was playing their radio rather loudly. It was a Tom Petty song called "The Waiting." We stood there listening to it, and I felt peaceful standing there with him. For a moment, all the worries of the world were gone.

However, I had begun to take notice of a few stresses that plagued our relationship that summer. Sam had started to change a little. I had caught him on a few occasions with a wandering eye. The trust I had for him began to slip. Maybe I had not realized how much distance was growing between us. We fought more often, and I sensed an unusual detachment from him. Suddenly, he was busy a lot and not around to take my calls. He had other things to do on the weekends, which was not normal. So with Katie's help, one weekend we took a ride over to his house after he told me he was not available to go out. His mom told us he was at our favorite roller-skating rink. We went to the rink and I discovered he was seeing someone else on the side. Things became very heated and ugly, and we broke up. It was a nasty split. I was shocked and hurt that he had found another girlfriend. These emotions swirled around in my mind for days. A mixture of rage and heartbreak.

The following weekend, I went to his house to retrieve my mother's school ring. I had given it to him with love. Now that we were over, I wanted it back. The encounter was horrible. I said awful things to him, and he said unpleasant things back. I recall that, during the yelling, he told me he was sorry about the loss of my mom and how he loved her too. He explained he didn't want to hurt me, but things between us were not the same. He then gave the ring back and told me he tried to be there for me. We were different people now, and he was sorry. I was not in the mood to hear him. Nothing he said made me feel better. Nothing was the same anymore. I was so angry, I didn't believe him and called him a liar and a cheat. After that day, we never spoke again. The anger and disappointment I had over losing Sam stayed with me for a long time.

A few days later I was happily pulled out of my misery when a classmate from my old neighborhood called me out of the blue. I hadn't seen my middle school friend Jodie since the funeral and I missed being around her. When she invited me to visit, I was relieved to go on another getaway back to my old stomping ground. She was always like a big sister to me. She gave me suggestions for fashion and makeup and would make me feel confident. Most of the time I couldn't be bothered trying to look nice. I never felt like I was pretty, so it seemed stupid to me. However, Jodie would always try to boost my confidence. During the visit, I even reconnected with Rick, another former middle school classmate. Rick and Jodie were happy memories for me to look back on that difficult summer. In that time in my life, any degree of happiness was a gift.

After I came home from my mini vacation visiting Jodie, the happiness began to fade. I was so lonely at my grandparents' house. I didn't have anyone to brag to. No one to share my fun times with. In the past, I could always tell my sister about things. Now it was too quiet, and I felt alone. I missed my brother and sister, I missed having them in my life. When I was occupied, it didn't seem so bad. But now . . . I had to desperately try to use my Grandpop's wisdom and the advice from my therapist to hang on. Even with the meds and the visits twice a week to my doctor, my anxiety kept getting the better of me. I didn't want anyone to know I was still stumbling. I felt I was such a failure. I couldn't even hold my own for a few days without breaking down. When I was alone and not constantly occupied with something to do, my frustration and sadness would overwhelm me.

In my desperation, I found a new outlet to soothe my pain. I started cutting small lines into my thigh, high up so no one could see them. Small nicks, using a pin. I liked the control, and the pain pulled my focus away from my sorrow. This was my new distraction. My method to my madness. It was my private escape. Until a few weeks later.

My grandmother drove me to a new doctor for a physical checkup, which was required by the new school I would soon be attending. I had never been to this practice before and wondered what the visit would involve. I was already on edge. What was going to happen if the doctor saw the marks on my thigh? I squirmed in my seat the entire ride to the appointment. Sitting in the waiting room, I stared at a magazine trying to avoid my guilty conscience. A few minutes later, my name was called. I followed the nurse to the exam room. She took me in and took my weight and height. Then she instructed me to undress leaving on my undergarments, and handed me a paper gown. *Crap! I am totally going to get in so much trouble if the doctor sees my cuts.*

As the doctor began the physical, I hoped that he would not need to undo the gown. I sat there feeling really nervous. Minutes later, sure enough, he saw my cuts. He looked at them and then looked at me. He had this odd concern on his face and then asked, "Did you do these?"

I looked at him like a deer in headlights, then took a huge gulp and answered honestly, "Yes."

He then looked at the nurse and said, "I will be right back."

He left me there with the nurse. *Where is he going?* I thought. As he stepped out of the room, I sat there staring at the nurse and never said a word. Moments later, my Grandmom came into the room with the doctor. By the look on her face, she was not happy. She looked at me with squinted eyes and disgust on her face. She said, "What are those? What are you doing to your leg?" I didn't have an answer for her. I sat there frozen and embarrassed.

The doctor interrupted the tense moment and said, "They're not infected, but I wanted everyone to know that this needs to be addressed." He said I needed to discuss this with my therapist. Grandmom agreed, looked at me with that stern stare, and then returned to the waiting room closing the door behind her. I was so humiliated and upset at the same time. The doctor sat back down on his exam chair as I looked down at the floor. He started to explain how he didn't want me to get an infection, and he gave me some gel to put on the cuts. He told me I had to stop hurting myself. After that embarrassing reveal, my appointment was over. I got dressed and met my Grandmom in the waiting room.

Grandmom had some very harsh words for me on the ride home. "What in the world–?" she started to say, then stopped mid-speech. She was so upset that I was not following the therapist's advice. She asked if I was taking my medication.

I answered her, "Yes, I'm taking the meds."

"Then why are you disfiguring your body? Your behavior is harmful and selfish. *You are acting just like your father.*"

At that moment, I think all the air in the car was sucked out and I was completely stunned. Then I got angry. *How dare she compare me to my father! He was NOT who I wanted to be. Ever!* I defended myself, refuting her claims and saying it had nothing to do with my father. I missed my mom and my siblings. I was upset and frustrated with everything. She was quiet at first, then she said, "This is not how you solve your problems." We didn't speak anymore the rest of the ride home. I was fuming in the car and nothing she said sank in until later.

The more I thought about what she said, the more it haunted me. I sulked and reviewed the whole situation in my head all night, until I realized, I could only be angry at myself. No way did I want to be anything like my father! But now, that was what she thought of me. I was sure my Grandpop would be disappointed in me too. Perfect. More guilt for me to harbor. I was so good at making poor choices. However, my latest actions were a pivotal change that would take place in my thought process later. My Grandmom's words may have been harsh, but they were effective.

The very next day, I had an appointment with my therapist. Grandmom spoke to him before I even went into his office to make sure he knew what was going on. Then it was my turn. We had an interesting discussion about my cutting and how I used it as a way to keep my thoughts of suicide and misery at bay. Then I told him what my Grandmom said to me in the car. He was rather shocked at her statement. He even commented that it was wrong for her to compare me to my father. Before I left his office, he said he would be adjusting my medication.

Meanwhile, I began to practice self-control regarding my cutting. I'd be lying if I said it was easy to stop. It wasn't easy. But I had Grandmom's harsh words as a strong driving force. They lingered in my head, giving me the desire to take control. I wanted to be like my mom and nothing like my father. I worked harder to do better, with thoughts of Mom to guide me.

# Chapter 24

# **The Sighting**

Up until the end of August, after spending a weekend at the shore, we hadn't heard any news about my father. Nothing since being notified about his release and receiving the subpoena. However, a day or two later, the attorney called and told us the trial date had been changed. We would not be going to trial in September as we were originally told. The new date was December 7. To be honest, I was comforted by this news. The longer I didn't have to face my father and all the pain of the past, the more relieved I was.

It's strange when the road of life twists and turns unexpectedly.

My Uncle Bill, my Grandmother's brother, had recently moved in with us. He was staying in the spare bedroom down the hall. During his stay he arranged to take me into the city for lunch one day, a nice distraction from the recent stresses. I had only been to the city once or twice before, so I was pretty excited to take the train downtown and walk the streets of Philadelphia. Uncle Bill was very familiar with the city having lived there for many years. He knew his way around and also knew the best places to eat. As we roamed the streets just chatting and occasionally pausing to look at a shop, something insane happened.

We suddenly passed my father on the sidewalk.

Everyone's eyes locked that split second when we recognized each other. *Holy crap!* It was like seeing a grizzly bear standing in front of you. There is that immediate shock, and then fear and panic. My uncle and I never broke stride, and just kept on walking. Yet it felt like a slow-motion moment. Realizing what had just happened we quickly looked for the closest shop door and darted in. I was having a hard time catching my breath. I paced back and forth, not knowing how to handle the shock of what had just happened. My uncle looked at me and asked if I was OK. Then he said, "What are the chances of that happening? Him being on the *same street* at the *same time* we are in Philly! *Jeezus!*" He was just as stunned and freaked out as I was. We stayed in that shop for a good while. It was a small café and I could smell coffee and baked goods. Then we decided to take our chances and head to the restaurant where my uncle had originally intended for us to go for lunch.

I don't remember the name of the restaurant but I do remember it was a nice place. It had an upscale décor, nice tablecloths, and linen napkins. I was far too shaken to take in much else. As we waited to be served, we had the opportunity to catch our breath and chat. We spent some time talking about how crazy it was that we had seen my father. My uncle was understandably concerned and kept asking if I was all right. I reassured him I was fine. But inside, I was freaked out. I merely picked at my lunch. I'm sure my uncle knew what had stolen my appetite, but we continued with some small talk, avoiding the real issue. Then we decided to head back to the train to get home. On the train, I thought about how my grandparents were going to react when they heard what had happened.

When we arrived back at the house, my uncle filled them in on our encounter earlier that day. Sure enough, it was a difficult conversation. I could see the panic on their faces as we told them. Grandmom looked at my Grandpop and blurted out that she wanted the police to know right away. She also wanted to call the prosecuting attorney. She was sure he was stalking us. All I kept thinking was how bizarre it was that we ran into him. Was it by chance? We were in a crowded city several weeks after he was released from jail. The situation was unnerving, and sure enough it prompted my grandparents to call the police and attorneys. I heard them on the phone asking for a protection order, fearing my father would show up at other locations. They wanted to be sure he wouldn't come anywhere near their home, church, or my school. I would hear chatter from them over the next few days involving other legal matters. Most of the time they didn't include me in those conversations, wanting to shield me from it as much as possible. Later I learned they had purchased a gun for safety, going as far as to take lessons at a gun range. My father being released had flung so much fear into their lives, and it wasn't over. Soon we all would be seeing him again at the trial.

# Chapter 25

# Lessons in Faith, Cruelty, and Kindness

One Sunday after church, we went to see the gravestone that was newly positioned at my mom's grave site. Despite my disgust toward her being buried, I did appreciate the love and care my grandparents had put into her headstone. The words they chose were perfect and the stone was really beautiful. It was a small, flat, rose-colored granite grave cover with a light-gray section in the center. In that center area was a beautiful inscription in remembrance of Mom's beauty and her most precious talent: YOUR BEAUTY IS EVIDENT TO ALL WHO LOVE YOU. KEEP ON SINGING.

After that day, we would occasionally visit the grave after church on Sunday or on holidays. Grandmom would clean off the stone and place flowers there. Each time I was there, I never felt comfortable. I couldn't help it. For so many reasons, I hated that she was there. Mom should be alive and not in a cemetery surrounded by all these other deceased people. It felt stark and void of any warmth. To me it was a lonely place and it made me sad. Being there sucked all the breath out of me. It made things real. I knew she was gone, but being at her burial place made it worse. When I was older, the only time I saw or visited her grave was when I attended another funeral.

Many years later, after my grandparents had passed, I visited one more time with my brother. I wanted to try and make peace with my feelings about that place, to give it another try. As I stood at her grave on that sunny, breezy day, I tried to remind myself that Mom is not alone, that being buried there she is surrounded by her family members who rest with her. But the comfort I felt was brief. It was clear to me that my feelings and opinions hadn't faded, and still affect me to this day. She shouldn't have been ripped away from all of us so tragically in the first place. She shouldn't be buried. It's not what she wanted. My disapproval burns inside. However, I've worked hard to embrace my hurt and frustration and redirect it into a more positive action. I try to remember how she lives within me and is not in the dark. After all, she is the reason I try so hard to be positive as an adult. In remembrance of her, I keep trying. She continues to give me the strength to rise above and carry on.

It took me years to find that strength in myself. Back when everything changed, when the wounds of Mom's death and separation from my siblings were still fresh, I struggled to see anything in a positive light. All that anger and sadness leached out and affected those around me, especially my grandparents. They were dealing with the same loss, and also had the added responsibility of taking care of me. Some days when I roamed around my grandparents' house or watched them as they did their normal routines, I would stress about how they were feeling and what they were going through. I felt awkward at times living with them. I didn't fit in. I could never be like their daughter. Even though I was their daughter's child, I was so different. I didn't look like her or even have any of her talents. I would think about how their lives had changed so immensely. Now they had me to raise, and I was a mess.

Things only got worse when I began school again. I started my new school year with more pressure than ever before. Being the new kid again added to my dread. It didn't help that this school was enormous compared to my previous school. My bus stop was at the community center located a few streets over from the house. At the bus stop that first day I chose to stand alone, indifferent to the other kids.

The school was nicknamed the "fish tank" school. As I wandered around the building the first few days, I understood why. It had lots of open glass windows and really long hallways. I was quiet in class the first few days. It was my way of protecting myself. To the few kids who asked if I had just moved to the area, I gave the needed information but nothing more. Right out of the gate, I quickly noticed things at this school were very different from my last school. It had a much larger student body than the Plymouth Meeting school. I also found out fast that the display of compassion and welcoming I had experienced overwhelmingly from students in my previous school were not a part of the equation here. These kids were brutal, and when they found out who I was, it got even more interesting. It took barely two weeks into the school year for the gossip about me to start buzzing. Somehow people found out who I was. The reactions were divided between either gawking at me or steering clear of me. I struggled to stop myself from walking out of school each day.

One day in the cafeteria, a girl I never met before walked up to me and said, "Hey, your dad is a killer!" Everyone around me stopped in their tracks. I just stood there, caught off guard and stunned.

I looked at her and thought, *Wow, she really just blurted that out in front of, like, a hundred other kids.* It took a second or two for me to catch up with the moment as I tried to process her intentions. Was she trying to make a statement? Or start a fight? My reaction was shock and then embarrassment, but I quickly recovered. As I stared at her, anger welled up inside me. After a few more awkward seconds, the silence became heated anger, and I even surprised myself with my response.

"Yep, and you know what? The apple might not fall far from the tree." Then I took a step toward her to confirm I was ready for a challenge if necessary.

Just as I stepped forward, a kid blurted out a super-loud, "Damn!" Then I could hear other gasps and comments from the kids standing around me. I was already sweating from the feverish pumping of anger and adrenaline, thinking I was going to have a fight on my hands. Then, the girl stepped back sort of startled and put her hands up in a protective manner. I realized this stupid girl didn't know what to say. She just gawked at me with a dumb, blank look on her face. So I side-stepped and walked past her toward the back of the cafeteria and outside into the courtyard. I stayed out there for a while, going over in my head everything that had just happened. *Could my life get any worse?* I couldn't escape my father no matter where I was. I hated my life.

After that day, it seemed the entire school knew I wasn't going to put up with any shit. Things calmed down a bit, and a few kids in my classes did say nicer things to me such as, "Hey, sorry for what happened to your family." My train-wreck life made it difficult for me to trust anyone or be around happy, well-adjusted kids. I isolated myself a lot of the time. Nothing about my life could be explained in a simple conversation, so my defense mechanism was staying quiet for my own protection. This new school made me realize I didn't play well with others. I began to make a few friends with a couple of kids who were outcasts like me, but I didn't trust anyone else. Especially a lot of the girls. They were the ones who bullied me the most. I'm not sure if the other girls were afraid of me, or if it was because I was unfriendly? All I remember is that they were mean and would say awful things as I walked by. I could hear their piercing Valley-Girl-style chitter chatter.

"Oh, my *gawd,* she is so weird."

They would flock together in the halls, giggling and staring at me. Sometimes I would stop and stare back at them, wondering why they felt the need to pick on me. I didn't bother anyone. I didn't get in their faces. After a few seconds of my stare, they would quickly scoot off down the hallway like androids. I just wanted to freak out! I couldn't stand them. They made my life even more of a living hell.

I couldn't seem to get a break. This constant bullying was eating me apart, and my frustration quickly turned into bitterness. If someone gave me a hard time, I fought back. So most people probably remember me as a weird girl with an attitude. On the outside, I was more aggressive than ever with a no-filter demeanor. Inwardly I was a complete mess. I had no self-esteem, and I think my horrible prior home life was to blame for my tendency to be socially awkward. Even with my meds and therapy, I was moody and irritated. If I didn't agree with something, I just said so. I even mouthed off to my teachers, which prompted a frequent, "Ms. Hathaway, you have a detention."

"Whatever, I don't care," was my typical response. As you can imagine, I racked up quite a few detentions with that attitude. Then I got some more when I was caught smoking in the school hallway. When they called my grandparents to let them know about my concerning behavior, let's just say, they were not happy with me. And that's an understatement.

When I got home that day, my Grandpop came to my room for one of his firm talks. He sat down across from me, starting off the conversation with, "You have upset your Grandmom." Then he said, "Your mom is watching you from above. She can see how you're acting out. You need to count your blessings and try to make your mom proud of you."

That's when I stupidly blurted out, "Well she's dead, so she can't see me. And if she were here, she would see how bogus my school is.

Everyone stares at me and says horrible things about me. I hate my school and I hate that I'm separated from my brother and sister!"

My feelings about losing my siblings and all the changes in my life had turned into anger. After I lashed out to my Grandpop, his face got this very sad look and I could tell he was getting emotional. Then he collected himself in order to be stern with his response. He told me again that I need to have faith and need to remember that Bunnie is looking over me even though it may not feel like she is. Then he affirmed some rules, telling me if I can't abide by the rules, he will have to put me into foster care. Now *that* got my attention. I looked at him wide-eyed with shock. His words frightened me. I didn't want that to ever happen and I promptly apologized to him. I promised him that I would work hard to be better. Before he left my room, he added his own feelings about my siblings and our separation. He told me how heartbroken he was for having to split up his grandchildren, explaining that everyone was doing the best they could. Then, he rose up off my bed and left the room. I sat there in my room for a long while as I digested the alternative I was given.

I was trying to be a normal kid, but how could I do that? My life was never normal. I was damaged goods before my mom even died, and that's how my mind processed life most days. I was either sad or angry. It was a defeated feeling that I just couldn't seem to shake. Even with my Grandpop's wise words, how I reacted to things was a direct result of my messed-up life. I was a kid who had lots of anger, sadness, and frustration. Regardless, I never wanted to hurt them. I would try to control myself, but I kept screwing it up. I acted on impulse often and then when I was in trouble, it was too late to fix the destruction. It was a serious challenge for me to stay on the path of good behavior, especially in school. At times, my grandparents would have to resort to tough tactics to gain my attention. They called me out on my bad behavior or if I was out of line, and again I would try hard to be better. I feel they truly wanted me to be strong and get through this horrible ordeal. They too were along for the ride. There was no easy path; it was going to be a day-to-day process that would last a long time.

In my grandparents' eyes, religion was the solution to everything. So when October arrived, they announced that I would be starting CCD religious education class, also known as Catechism. Having been raised with very little religion growing up, it all felt new to me. Outside of visits with my grandparents in the past, I really didn't go to church. When I did go, I abided by all the rules and traditions of their Catholic faith, but it wasn't voluntary.

One day a week after school, I'd spend an hour being taught lessons of the Catholic faith by Father O'Neil at Queen of Peace Church. He was a stout, pleasant man with salt-and-pepper hair, bright blue eyes, and black-framed glasses. His jolly, round face and happy smile complemented his nice personality. He reminded me of Frosty the Snowman, and I would chuckle inside each time I saw him. He would teach me all the information I needed to prepare for the required sacraments: Confession, Communion, and Confirmation. (I had already been baptized as a child. My grandmother had insisted on it.) Father O'Neil would review with me the history of Jesus and God. I really tried hard to wrap my head around all he taught me. However, most of the information was confusing to me and difficult to accept. During these classes I had many questions. My questions were driven by my frustration with the concept of a god who seemed uncaring. I listened as Father O'Neill explained how God sent his son to be crucified by hateful people, and I was blown away by that. In addition, he explained how Jesus rose up from the dead, met with others, and then later went back to sit next to his father in heaven. It was all too unbelievable for me. I was baffled. Why would anyone follow this confusing religion? What is the point of it all? Not to mention that the entire belief system is based on scriptures written thousands of years ago and from a time of great bias. There is fantastical imagery of angels, saints, devils, and demons. I could not comprehend or believe in all of this magical, whimsical stuff. I often disagreed with the teachings and felt discouraged.

My own additional complaints were, even if you follow all the rules like my grandparents did, go to service consistently, pray and live a faithful life, then why would God allow horrible people to destroy everything you held dear? I wasn't able to grasp this kind of cruel reality.

Father O'Neil's explanations were rational to him, but didn't help to clarify anything for me. I would question him often, saying, "So your God turns away from horrible things that happen in the world because he gave us free will? Why do we follow him then? What's the point? If he saw or knew my mother's murder was going to happen, why didn't he help my mom? She didn't deserve to be hunted down and murdered by my father. Where was God? Was he watching this? Why would he let a mother of three children die brutally for no reason? Why did God let him hurt me and my family? Why didn't he just let my father die when he took all those pills? Why didn't God just let him turn the gun on himself? Why would anyone want to worship that kind of god?"

I was overcome with frustration, but Father O'Neil was patient with me. He struggled and desperately tried to help me find understanding and faith in the teachings. Salvation will be found in the end, he explained. He was a good person and strong in his faith. I listened to what he had to say, but at that time in my life, I was young and angry and did not agree with any of it. Religion was not showing me justification for all the sacrifices we had to make by following it. It was not going to work for me no matter how hard Father O'Neil tried to educate me.

After months of sessions, I chose to keep my opinion to myself. I completed my classes, respected my grandparents' wishes, and received my sacraments. I even continued to attend church for the next four years while living with my grandparents, choosing to keep an open mind in the hopes I would feel something, *anything,* to help me accept the Catholic teachings. But it never comforted me in the way it comforted my grandparents. Through the years I decided instead to believe what made me feel comfortable: that people are responsible for themselves and their actions. That there isn't an invisible spirit watching over all that goes on. That God, the devil, and heaven are either symbols to help guide people who found comfort in faith, or excuses that bad people can take advantage of. I believe for the most part that religion tries to foster goodness. I'm in full support of that. However, I don't like the obligation they require of worshiping a god. I don't like the hypocrisy that comes from the Bible and its unrealistic motivation in certain areas. Some of the things done in the name of God are horrifying. So instead, I wanted to follow my inner light. My love for my mother and family are my inspiration. I try to practice the ideal that we all bleed red and should all be treated lovingly. I believe in the magic of kindness and living life fairly. I feel people need to focus more on being a good person, to practice kindness to themselves and others. Regardless of gender, color, or sexual preference. This should happen all the time while we are alive on this earth. It's what we do in this life, and how we treat others in the here and now that is important. In my thinking, you have one life, so make it count. And when you're gone, you're gone. Your memories of what you did for others will be your everlasting memorial. If more people practiced kindness our world would be less violent, competitive, prejudicial, hypocritical, and angry. More kids could walk through the halls in school without fear of being bullied. Fewer people would have to suffer loss at the hand of another. Being a good individual should be everyone's goal. Being a good person is a choice anyone can make, regardless of race and religious belief. We should be worshiping being kind to one another. That is my faith.

# Chapter 26

# The Trial: Part I

*After my mother's death, reading the newspaper coverage and watching the TV reports gave us only a general idea of what took place that day. But nothing could have prepared us for the brutality of the trial. The witness testimony and detailed descriptions they each gave were so vivid. Add to that the evidence bags, charts, photos, and never-ending sorrow of it all. Years after the trial, none of it has ever left me.*

## Day 1—December 7, 1981

I barely slept the night before, tossing and turning, thinking about seeing my father again, worrying about what I would have to say on the stand. I was dreading this day and now it was here. I tried to eat some toast and took my medication. My grandparents were really quiet all morning, and the air had a thickness to it. We got into the car and headed down to the Delaware County Courthouse in Media, Pennsylvania. It was a good half-hour drive.

The court building was a sight to see. Huge ionic pillars surrounded the steps making it look like a miniature Philadelphia Art Museum. Inside there was a long hallway leading to the courtroom. Near the courtroom door I saw Patrick in the hallway with his father. Patrick was there to testify about his knowledge of the guns my father had purchased a week before the murder, and other incidents he had witnessed. We glanced at each other and did a sloppy, timid wave to one another. He looked as terrified as I was. Moments later, the prosecuting attorney met us in the hallway and directed all of us to another room down the hall. I could feel the overwhelming anxiousness building inside, unsure if I could pull myself together to even testify. My testimony was intended to help show my father's history of violence. I had firsthand knowledge of what he had done to me, Mom, and our family all those months and years prior to Mom's murder. In addition, my overhearing some of the conversation between Mom and my father the night before her murder was important somehow.

My grandparents, Patrick's dad, and the prosecuting team stepped away into another room to meet briefly behind closed doors. Waiting in that room allowed me to think too much and put me into a state of panic. Then the door opened, and my eyes almost popped out of my head from nervousness. The prosecutor's assistant walked in and called Patrick and me into the office where my grandparents and his dad were waiting. That is when they gave us the good news.

"Your testimony will not be needed."

I gasped so loudly that the entire room looked at me. The prosecutor explained that the witness testimony, evidence, and documentation were solid, and he felt there was no need to put Patrick and me through any additional stress. I was so grateful that I would not have to sit up there and feel my father's eyes burning on me as I testified against him. That day at that moment, Patrick and I both took a deep breath of relief.

Then it was time for us to go into the courtroom. My grandparents guided me to the door, and we all walked in. I followed my grandparents and took my seat beside them in one of the rows toward the front. I looked around the room in awe. The seats were pew benches, rows of them. The room had a very high ceiling and an aisle separating both sides. The judge's bench seat was raised up behind a large wooden desk. Behind his seat were wood-paneled walls that went all the way to the ceiling, and above his seat higher on the wall was lettering that read, IN GOD WE TRUST. It dawned on me that the courtroom felt familiar, like being in a church. As I looked around, I saw that the witness box was on my right. In the front of the room, below where the judge sat, was the court reporter. The prosecution sat on the right-hand side in front of our family.

To my left was a table where my father and his attorney were seated.

My stomach grew queasy as soon as I saw him. The fear I felt after passing him by chance that day in Philly returned, but it was amplified. Even before he murdered my mom, seeing him always gave me that shiver in my spine. Now it was worse; he was downright terrifying. Where I was seated made me feel uncomfortably exposed. Sometimes out of the corner of my eye I could see his head or body shift and I knew he had turned to look at me. I did my best not to lock eyes with him but wasn't always successful. Each time his eyes met mine, it was unpleasant and filled me with anxiety. When I felt him looking at me, I stared forward or shifted slightly in my seat so that he was not in view.

Moments later the bailiff announced for all to stand as the judge made his way to his seat. There was some legal talk, and then the judge asked for the jury to be brought in. After the jurors were sworn in, the judge asked to move forward with the opening statements: brief explanations of how the prosecution and the defense believed the events unfolded the day my mother was murdered. The prosecution would argue this was a case of intentional, willful, premeditated, and deliberate murder. Whereas my father's attorney would present extensive psychiatric testimony to prove that, as a result of intoxication and mental disturbances, his client had a diminished capacity and was unable to form the specific intent to commit first-degree murder.

The prosecution went first, providing a review of the months that led up to the day of Mom's murder: the bitter custody battle and other violent assaults. Then he went on to briefly describe what happened that morning. He spoke very clearly about what the facts were and how each witness would reveal what they saw or evidence that was collected. Hearing the prosecution detail how my mother died in this abbreviated method was devastating to hear. The events that took place that morning were horrifying, painful, and far worse than I had ever imagined.

The defense attorney told the judge he refrained from giving an opening statement. There was whispering and chatter in the courtroom. *How odd,* I thought. It seemed strange that he declined. I'm sure there was some legal reason for it, but what did it matter? Each witness would soon testify to what they saw, and my life would change again forever. I would never be able to unhear what I heard.

The judge asked the prosecution to call the first witness to the stand. It had begun.

## Mrs. Green

The first witness called was the teacher at the day care, Mrs. Green. She was asked to describe what happened that morning. These are her words detailing the moments after Mom dropped off my brother.

"I heard knocking on the door and the voice of an anxious woman on the other side. It was Mrs. Fin. She is the mother of one of the students. She had just dropped off her daughter moments after Mrs. Hathaway had left. I could tell Mrs. Fin was panicked. As soon as I opened the door, she told me to call the police. She explained that a man was shooting at a woman near her car and her son was still in the car. Mrs. Fin went on to say she could hear a woman scream out, 'Oh God, he has a gun!' and then saw her start to run away from the man. The man was shooting at her. Mrs. Fin was frantic about her infant son and also worried for the woman. At this point we were standing inside the door and we heard the popping sounds and screaming, and so did the children. I called the police. A minute or so went by and the popping sound stopped. So I open the door to peer out. Again, another shot rang out and I could see a woman on the ground, partially hidden by a bush, lying on the front lawn of the house next door. The man was standing above her doing something. I shut the door."

The prosecution asked Mrs. Green to describe the door. "Well, the door is a large metal door and it does not have any windows. So I have to open it to see out. Either I would look out or Mrs. Fin and I would both look out. A few more minutes went by and Mrs. Fin was desperate to leave. She wanted to try and get to the upper area of the church and go out that door to get to her son. So I opened the door again, looking for the man. This time I saw him kneeling over the woman, who was not moving. Suddenly, more shots rang out. I closed the door again. Mrs. Fin was frantic and planning her escape. We waited a few more seconds, hoping the man was gone. She then decided to go find the other door so she could leave. I decided to open the door one last time. Peering out cautiously, I was able to see the woman still lying in the grass. She was about fifteen feet away. I did not see the man. I stepped out of the door, moving slowly along the stone path. I still didn't see the man. I looked over at the woman and could see so much blood."

The prosecution interrupted, asking Mrs. Green if she went over to the woman. Mrs. Green answered, "I did not go over to her. I went back into school and stayed with the children." As she talked about the children, my mind wandered off.

*My little brother was in that day care while this was happening. He was in there! My father didn't care about anyone who was there. He didn't care that his son was less than twenty-five feet from where he was committing this horrific act. His son's mother lay dying on the grass outside his classroom, and he didn't care.*

There were so many levels of anger and disbelief in my thoughts about what he did that day, and the years and years of malicious behavior leading up to this final violent act. Now it was all being played out in full detail for everyone to hear.

When the teacher's testimony concluded, the judge told the jury that the court would be adjourned for the day. We stayed seated until the jury and judge left the room. That is when I noticed my Gram. She was seated behind my father and had been blocked from my view by other people attending the trial. My eyes followed her as she exited her seat and began to walk out of the courtroom. We never spoke. I was interrupted by my grandparents as they whispered to me to move quickly, ushering me out of my seat. We all left the courtroom and headed straight for our car to avoid a run-in with my father. The ride home was quiet. Later that night, I sat in a hot bath and tried to dissolve all the pain away.

## Day 2—December 8, 1981

Each witness had a different perspective of the events that unfolded that day. On the second day of the trial, we heard from another witness, Mrs. Fin. Her daughter attended the day care, and her son was in the car during the incident.

## Mrs. Fin

"I arrived at the day care and pulled up behind another car. The path to the day care is right there. I left my year-old son, Matthew, in his car seat in the back of the car, then walked my daughter down the path into the day care. I walked past a woman who had just come out of the door. I dropped off my daughter and returned to the path to walk to my car. As I walked down the path, I saw a woman and a man behind my car in the street. Suddenly, while walking I saw the man pull out a gun and heard the woman scream out, 'Oh God, he has a gun!' The woman began to turn to run away. At that moment, I panicked because my son was in the car and I feared for the woman who was running away. I turned and ran back to the day care door. I could hear the gunshots. I frantically knocked for them to let me in. When Mrs. Green opened the door, I told her to call the police. I explained what was happening and then we all started to hear more screaming and the popping sounds. Mrs. Green was on the phone and we were frightened. All of a sudden, it was quiet. Mrs. Green and I opened the door and we looked out to see what was happening. More shots rang out and we shut the door. There was no window in the door, so we had to open it to see what was happening. I was frantic. I wanted to get to my son but was afraid the man was still outside. We opened the door several more times in between the firing. The last time I saw Mrs. Green open the door, it was quiet again. I asked Connie—she is the teacher's aide—to help me get to the other exit. By the time I reached the upper entrance of the church, this was the front door of the church, I did not see anyone around my car. I ran to my car and got in my car. My son was OK. I then realized in all the panic, I forgot to get my daughter. I moved my car to the church parking lot and ran back into the church day care classroom to retrieve my daughter. I got back to my car and could see an officer attending to the woman. I then drove home and called the police from my house, explaining what I saw that day."

Before Mrs. Fin left the witness box, the prosecutor asked her if she recognized the shooter. She said, "Yes, I do. It's the defendant sitting next to his attorney."

There were a few similar questions from the defense, but nothing more than rehashing what Mrs. Fin had already said. Both attorneys agreed they had no further questions for the witness.

## Mrs. Key

The third witness was a woman named Mrs. Key. She lived on the corner of the street that faces the church. From her house, she could view the front of the church at an angle. Mrs. Key described what she saw and heard that morning.

"I heard screams and popping sounds around 8:45 a.m. and thought it was unusual, but I remembered it was trash day. I thought maybe that's what the sound was. So I gathered up the trash and went outside my front door. Then I continued to hear screams and more popping sounds. I looked in the direction of these sounds and saw a man standing over a woman with what I thought was a gun. Then I heard more popping sounds, and then it stopped. I ran to my neighbor's house to see if she was seeing any of this. I thought together we could call the police. I knocked on her door but got no answer. So I ran back into my house and called my neighbor. She answered and explained she was afraid to answer her door. I asked her if she saw what was going on outside, and she answered yes. So I asked her if she would call the police also. I continued to keep an eye on what was going on from inside my home. I could see the man was now walking in the street toward a car. He tried to get in the car but couldn't. Then he walked farther down the street to a second car parked on the street. He got in that car and drove away slowly."

The prosecution interrupted, asking her whether she got a good look at the man. She said yes. Then he asked if she could describe him. Mrs. Key said, "He was wearing a nice suit, had curly hair, and glasses." Then the prosecutor asked her if he was in the courtroom that day. She said yes, then pointed to my father. The prosecution had no further questions. The defense then began to question this witness. He asked her more questions about the cars and where they were parked, wanting her to describe her view of the church and the area around it. Then she was dismissed, and they moved on to the next witness.

## Cable Worker

The fourth witness was a young man in his mid-twenties, a TV cable technician. That day he was driving down a side street that faces the church to finish a cable job. From that vantage point, he saw a portion of what was going on that morning.

"I was coming down Dover Road in my work van. I was slowly approaching the intersection where the church was and kept hearing what I believed were gunshots. I slowed to a crawl and began to notice where the sound was coming from. I have a working knowledge of guns having been raised as a hunter as a kid and young adult. I felt confident it was a gun sound. At that point I saw a man walking, and a woman was running away from the man. More shots were fired. She fell to the ground and I saw the man walk over to her. The man stood above her for a moment and another shot rang out. Then the man knelt down and was doing something. I wasn't sure what it was. At this point I had slowly turned my van onto Remington Road and continued to drive slowly. I saw the man touch the woman and I noticed the man was doing something next to the woman. My van slowly inched to the scene and I continued right past them. I tried to view more but had to continue slowly since I didn't want the man with the gun to notice me. I drove down the street and turned around as soon as I could. By the time I had, the man had gotten in his car and literally drove past me as I came back up the street."

The prosecution asked the cable technician if he recognized the man in the courtroom. He said, "Yes, he is sitting next to his attorney in a blue suit, white shirt, and red tie." No further questions from the prosecution.

The defense, however, did ask the cable worker a few questions. Most of them were to clarify his testimony regarding the streets he drove on and his viewpoint: more rehashing of what he had already said. The cable worker was a strong witness and didn't take any flak from my father's attorney. He had a stern attitude, but he was polite. The defense finished his questioning, and the witness was dismissed.

## Mrs. Cill

The fifth witness was Mrs. Cill, who lived directly across the street from the church. From her bedroom window, she could see the cars parked on the street, the house next to the church, the lawn, and the church walkway.

*Walkway to the day care—on the left is the lawn where my mother died*

After she described her location and vantage point, the prosecutor asked her to talk about what she witnessed after the sound of screams and gunshots prompted her to go to her bedroom window. Mrs. Cill began to speak, but her voice was very low.

"I heard screaming and–"

The judge interrupted her and asked her to please speak up. She apologized and continued on, raising her voice.

"I heard screaming and popping sounds and went to my bedroom window to look out. I saw a woman running away from the cars parked in front of the church pathway. The woman kept looking back as she ran away from a man who was walking slowly after her. I could see he was holding a gun and shooting it as he walked after her. I could not believe what I was seeing. Then I saw the woman turn around and she raised her hands up to cover her face. She put her head down, and then I heard another shot. I watched the woman fall to the ground. She landed on her back and her feet were facing the street."

Mrs. Cill paused to collect herself. It was evident to all she was still traumatized by what she had seen that day. Her sadness affected me and my grandparents as well. Tears ran down my face and our sniffles could be heard by everyone around us.

The prosecutor expressed that she could take her time. After a few seconds she continued. "I ran to grab my phone from the nightstand and pulled it to the window. I called the police and stayed on the phone with them as I watched out my window. I told them everything I saw moment by moment. The police asked me if the woman on the ground was moving. I told him no, she was not moving, and she hadn't moved since she fell. The police asked me where the man was. I told them the man was still standing by the woman. She's lying on the front lawn of my neighbor's house. Their house is next to the church. It was about ten feet from the walkway of the church. Then I could see the man was fumbling with something. Then he crouched down next to her or was kneeling next to her. Some time passed, maybe a few minutes. Then all of a sudden, I saw him put the gun right up to her head. More gunshots rang out and I jumped . . ."

Mrs. Cill paused again. She was crying, and her voice was wavering. Then she said, "I saw everything that morning. I saw what happened to that woman. It was horrible." The prosecutor grabbed a tissue for her and gave her a moment to calm down. The judge broke in and allowed her a moment to collect herself.

During this brief pause, I sat there frozen after having listened to the moment-by-moment details of my mother's murder. More tears ran down my cheeks. I felt so raw with emotion. Hearing each detail painted such a horrific picture. My skin felt like it was being stripped off my body. It was excruciating trying to process all that I had heard, but it was more than I could absorb. My grandparents were crying, and I could hear the sounds of sniffles and moans all throughout the courtroom. Every word of testimony was painful, and all of our hearts were breaking.

The judge broke into my thoughts as he asked the witness if she was able to go on. She answered yes, and the prosecutor asked her to please continue and to pick up after the man fired the last shot.

"OK, well, the man stood up and slowly walked back to the cars on the street. He tried to get into the car parked by the church pathway, but he couldn't get in. Then he walked up farther to another car up the street and got in that car. Then he drove away."

The prosecutor asked her if that man she saw was in the courtroom that day. Mrs. Cill pointed to my father, describing his clothes. The prosecution thanked her for her testimony, and he returned to his seat.

A few seconds went by before the judge's voice made me jump. He abruptly asked if my father's attorney wanted to cross-examine Mrs. Cill. The defense attorney stood up and answered, "No, your honor," and sat back down. Everyone's heads turned and then there was more whispered chatter. The fact that my father's attorney did not question this witness made a huge impact on me and everyone in the courtroom that day. I thought to myself, *What would he ask her if he did question her? What could he possibly ask that would be helpful to my father's case? Nothing! Nothing could change the horrifying description of what this witness just told the courtroom. In my mind, her testimony was the most critical.*

As the seconds ticked by, the chatter became noisier, and the judge loudly announced to break for lunch. It was a good time to get out of that courtroom and breathe in some much-needed fresh air. We all needed the break badly after that emotional morning. I followed my grandparents out of the courtroom, and we all went to a local restaurant for lunch. No one was up for eating and the atmosphere was very somber.

## Officer Bernard

Upon our return from lunch, the prosecution called the next witness. His name was Officer Bernard. He was on the scene that morning and was asked to explain what happened.

"A radio message came in while I was on patrol. There was an incident taking place at the Holy Apostles Church location on Remington Road in Haverford Township indicating shots fired, and someone was shot. Upon arrival at the scene, I could see my sergeant had pulled into the location just ahead of me. He was waving and pointing to the grass. I saw what appeared to be a body lying on the grass in front of a home next to the church walkway location. I grabbed my first aid kit and approached the body. I noted seeing several head injuries right away. I could see the victim was a white female, approximately thirty years of age. She was lying face up and I tried to take her pulse. I was only able to find a faint pulse in the carotid artery. I could see she was bleeding profusely from her head wounds and I administered first aid. I tried to stop the bleeding with some compresses. Then I removed her glasses and saw her eyelids were turning blue and were swelling. This indicated a lack of oxygen. So I tilted her head back and to the side, to better her airway. At that point I heard gurgling sounds coming from her and could clearly see she had a massive left-side head wound. There was another wound directly in the center of the forehead. I continued to evaluate her wounds and the scene around me. Her hands were clenched at her side. The right hand had a mace container in it. It was the kind that sprays."

The prosecution asked the officer, "Was the spray used?

"Yes, later it was determined she had indeed sprayed the mace." The prosecutor asked Officer Bernard to continue. "OK, I then saw in her left hand were keys and she had a purse under her right shoulder. Alongside her body were shell casings on the grass."

"Did the woman ever speak to you?" asked the prosecutor.

"No, she was unable to speak."

"Did you see anything more around the body?"

"Yes, there were several more casings, and at the time I thought the victim was shot with an automatic weapon. I thought this mainly because there were so many shell casings at the scene. However, later I found out the weapon was a revolver."

The prosecutor asked the officer to explain why he originally thought an automatic weapon was used. Officer Bernard explained that the number of casings meant the shooter had emptied the gun casings and reloaded the gun to fire more rounds. "With a revolver, the way you get the casings out of the gun is to either drop them out, shake them out, or physically pull them out. Then you must reload the gun manually again. This takes a few seconds or minutes to do, depending on the person."

The prosecution walked over to a table and picked up a bag. He held up a few bags of evidence collected at the scene. As he referenced each exhibit item number, Officer Bernard explained what they were. He rattled off the items: a .32 caliber gun, bullets or slugs pulled from the victim, casings found at the scene, the victim's keys, her glasses, and the mace can. Then the prosecution asked Officer Bernard what he did next.

"Well, the ambulance had arrived, and I accompanied the victim in the ambulance. The paramedics urgently worked on her, trying again and again to see if they could get any further vital signs. They still only had a faint pulse from her carotid artery. Due to her visible wound, I was unsure but feared she was not likely to make it. The wounds she had sustained were quite extensive. Regardless, the paramedics kept trying to do all they could for her. Upon arrival at the hospital, I waited while the doctor assessed her. After the final medical assessment was made, the doctor announced she had expired around 9:20 a.m."

The sound of sniffling again was very evident in the courtroom. There was a pause as both the prosecutor and the witness took a second before more questions were asked. I sat there drowning in grief. The pain in my heart from what he had described and then the announcement of her time of death . . . I wanted to just melt into the bench where I was seated. I really didn't want to hear any more about what happened. My head and heart were pounding from overwhelming sorrow.

The judge asked if the prosecution was going to continue. The prosecutor apologized and expressed that he would continue. Officer Bernard picked up his testimony at the point after he learned the victim had passed.

"I then left the hospital and went back to the scene to assist my sergeant. He was still gathering the evidence. Together we covered the area and found six shells at the location of the body and four more on the grass along the way to the body. We also found casings in the street, a projectile near a tree and loose bullets near the body location. All the evidence had been bagged and coded to be taken to the station for evidence retention."

There was a brief pause as the prosecution walked over to the evidence table again. The attorney picked up what appeared to be a photo. He walked over and held up the photo to Officer Bernard, asking him one last question. "Do you recognize the person in this picture?"

Officer Bernard looked at the picture. He then looked back at the prosecutor and said, "No, I don't know who that is."

Then the prosecutor walked over to the jury and showed them the photograph. I could see the photo now. My heart sank as I realized it was a picture of my mom. This realization defined so much for me. It was seared into my brain forever. Officer Bernard couldn't identify the person he tried to help that day. My beautiful Mom had been injured so badly she was unrecognizable. It was gut-wrenching. I could hear my own sobs echoing in the courtroom, along with my grandparents'. The overwhelming heartbreak went on and on with each person's testimony. I didn't think I could feel any more grief but clearly, I was wrong.

When the judge asked if the defense wanted to cross-examine the witness, again my father's attorney had nothing to ask. The testimony from Officer Bernard was damning, and the picture of my mother sent a very clear message.

# Officer Joe

The prosecution moved on and called the next witness. We would now hear from Officer Joe. He was the one who pulled my father over that day while he drove away from the scene. Most of the testimony was about the color of the car, and how Officer Joe and one other officer struggled to get my father to pull over.

He explained, "We had our guns drawn as we approached the car. The defendant was in the car and just sat there. I could hear his music playing. I opened the door and removed the defendant from the car, at which time I heard the defendant say, 'Don't worry, I won't hurt anyone else.' He said that statement twice. I proceeded to handcuff the defendant and read him his rights. Then I began a pat-down. My partner kept his gun drawn on the defendant as I did this. I found a gun in the man's right coat pocket. Upon removal of the gun from the pocket, I saw what appeared to be blood and hair on the barrel of the gun. The defendant was placed into the police car and driven back to police headquarters. While at the station, we did a more thorough search of the defendant. During this search I noticed he was well dressed, wearing a suit and dress shoes. In his pants pocket I found a handful of live .32 caliber ammunition. In his wallet I found the application for another firearm. The document was for a .22 automatic handgun. I also read his license and was now aware of who the defendant was. I then had him sit down in a chair. I continued to look further through his jacket and belongings. I found a few pieces of candy and additional ammunition."

The prosecution asked the officer, "Has the defendant said anything during all of this?"

Offer Joe said, "No, he didn't say anything more than what he said when we took him out of the car. However, I noticed the defendant began to slump in the chair and looked as if he was falling asleep or passing out. He didn't fall out of the chair, but for precautionary reasons he was taken to the ER in an ambulance. We had him checked out in case he ingested something or was on drugs. We stayed with Mr. Hathaway the entire time. He appeared to be unconscious upon arrival at the ER. We carried him in and placed him on the ER table. Then an ER physician began to examine him. Mr. Hathaway woke up and the doctor performed a few tests, looking at his eyes. And then the doctor brought Mr. Hathaway's arms above his head and then let them drop. Then he moved his arms from his side upward, and again they dropped to his side."

The prosecutor asked Officer Joe if he stayed with my father the whole time. Officer Joe answered that he had, and added that after the doctor was finished with his evaluation, he said he couldn't find anything physically wrong with him.

From my seat I could see my father shifting, he grew increasingly agitated during this line of questioning. He could be seen leaning over frequently, whispering into his attorney's ear some comment or another. It seemed he was unhappy with the officer's assessment of his condition, never addressing his claim to be under the influence of alcohol. He kept pestering his attorney to say something. Suddenly, his attorney shouted,

"Objection!"

I was startled as my father's attorney practically screamed out his disapproval of Officer Joe's last comment on my father's behalf. The defense explained the officer could not say what the doctor said. Only the doctor could testify to his medical assessment. So the judge explained this to the officer and asked for the response to continue.

"OK, well then we transported Mr. Hathaway back to the police headquarters. He was placed into a cell wearing his undershirt and underwear. All his other clothes had been removed and bagged for evidence. He was left in the holding cell and we observed that he fell asleep for several hours. When he woke up, he was told he could make a phone call. A little while later, an attorney arrived. He spoke with his council, and we were notified a blood test was ordered."

For the defense, Officer Joe answered additional questions regarding the arrest, paperwork, and protocol. The cross-examination went on for a while, mostly repeating information we had heard earlier from other witnesses. After all questions were answered, the judge advised we would adjourn for the day.

I was so relieved finally to be able to leave that courtroom. The day's testimony was brutal and completely drained me. I firmly believe there is such a thing as too much to process. How many times can our fresh wounds be ripped open? Again, the car ride home was silent, and the dinner table was quiet. Even though I did have some questions, I held back from asking them. My grandparents were hurting enough, and I didn't want to make things worse.

## Day 3—December 9, 1981

The third day of the trial, we heard testimony from a number of physicians and psychiatrists, including the ER physician, the medical examiner, and various psychologists who evaluated my father. My head was left spinning from all the medical jargon, but pieces of their testimony stick out in my head.

## ER Doctor

The ER physician took the stand first. He described his examination of my father the day of the murder, stating that during the exam he noticed Mr. Hathaway was groggy and felt further review of his vitals was needed. He noted that my father had an unstable gait but no signs of trauma. There were no cuts or bruises, no signs of catatonic behavior. He was compliant with all the doctor's requests and didn't show any signs of confusion. His thoughts were that my father had been drinking.

The prosecution then asked if any blood was drawn during the visit, and the doctor said no. When it was the defense's turn, he asked why no blood was drawn at the hospital. The ER doctor responded that he saw no reason for a blood draw. He felt Mr. Hathaway was compliant, he did not show signs of shock, and it was not required. After the cross-examination from the defense, the ER doctor was dismissed.

## Medical Examiner

The medical examiner who had performed the autopsy on Mom was asked to describe his findings and the evidence pulled from her body. I remember quite a bit of what he said that day. I know that may sound morbid, but there was a profound reason I needed to hear the facts. I needed to know: *Was my mom in pain during it all?* I already knew she was terrified. She ran away from my father in fear. But I *had* to know whether there was terrible pain when she was hit by the bullets. And after she fell to the ground, was she awake? Was she alert at any moment when my father was kneeling next to her? I wanted to hear so badly that she never knew what was going on. Especially when he shot her several more times. My Grandmom wanted to know this too. I think we all needed to know for our comfort and our sanity. It was a nagging, gut-wrenching feeling of uncertainty that we just had to have answered.

The medical examiner began to explain his findings in horrifying detail.

"The first two bullets that hit Mrs. Hathaway would not have been fatal. The first bullet grazed her left breast, and she would likely have been unaware of the pain from the panic. The second bullet entered her neck on the left side and exited out the right front side of her neck. This wound would have been more serious and would have caused her to fall and incur blood loss. She would have needed medical care from this injury, and she would have been unconscious. The close-range shot to the forehead also did not kill her."

*What! How can that be?* I was shocked, and I immediately looked at my grandparents who also appeared perplexed at this disclosure. We listened to the explanation with intense interest.

The prosecution asked him to explain. He continued, "This bullet had flattened itself up against the skull of her forehead. This portion of the skull is very hard and resilient. The bullet did not penetrate her skull. It appeared this shot had been fired six to twelve inches away from her. I believe Mr. Hathaway would have been either standing in front of or over her when this shot was fired."

The prosecution broke in asking, "So if the shooting had ended there, Mrs. Hathaway could have survived her injuries?"

The medical examiner answered, "It is very possible, yes."

The prosecution asked him to continue. "The remaining three bullets, however, were fired at even closer range. These bullets entered into the left side of her head above the ear. The muzzle of the gun would have been pressed up against her head and fired."

The prosecutor interrupted again and asked if he could explain to the court how he knew this.

The medical examiner explained, "Gunpowder residue and burns were found on her scalp. This would clearly indicate that the barrel of the gun had been placed up against her head and then fired. Those bullets traveled through, but not out, causing her brain to stop functioning almost immediately. Those last three bullets were fatal."

I sat there in anguish, pinching my arm so hard just to try and keep from throwing up. Tears ran down my cheeks as I listened to the examiner describe my mother's injuries. The pain sucked the very breath from my lungs, as did the realization that if my father had stopped, if he had walked away sooner, my mother may have survived. No matter how difficult it was, I knew I had to listen to it all. I had to know the answer to my question.

The prosecutor then approached the witness and asked him to point out on a diagram where these bullets had hit my mom. As the medical examiner pointed to the areas on the diagram where each bullet had hit her, I could hear myself crying again. My nose was running, and my heart was pounding in my ears. I felt nauseous.

Then the medical examiner was asked to explain why Officer Bernard heard gurgle sounds and the reason behind the involuntary movements he observed. The witness explained, "The brain injury and lack of oxygen to her body was why. As the brain became aware it was injured, it began to react. These signs are physical signs that a person is close to death."

My grandparents were crying too. The brutality of Mom's death was sickening to hear. I kept thinking to myself, *How could he do that to her? Seeing her face and knowing she was the mother of his children!* I struggled with so many emotions that were all mixed together. And then, the answer we had been waiting for.

The prosecutor asked, "Would she have spoken?"

"No, she would not have been speaking. I am medically certain Mrs. Hathaway was unconscious from the gunshot neck injury and blood loss. She would not have been awake during the four close-range shots that followed."

As those words spilled from his mouth, I realized he had just confirmed what I had wanted to know. After all these months of waiting for some small comfort, if there was any comfort to be found in anything at all, receiving that small bit of information gave me peace. While I recognized my mom suffered terrible fear trying to escape her attack, I was somehow relieved knowing she was not awake or aware during those last brutal moments. Quickly my momentary peace faded when I saw how this testimony affected my grandparents. They were visibly shaken having to listen to how their beloved daughter was murdered. My Grandpop reached out to hold my grandmother's hand, trying to comfort her as he had done several times during the trial. I could only think that they too were somehow relieved to know their daughter was unconscious as my father ended her life. I often caught myself thinking if there is any justice in this world, he will be given what he deserves tenfold. Soon my relief subsided, and I felt numb. Was that a normal feeling? Was I ever going to be *normal* after hearing all the horror of how my mom died? These questions and more pulsed in my head like a bad headache as the questioning of the witness continued.

As the defense attorney moved on with his questions, I kept dwelling on the final minutes before my mom died and what the witnesses had described. Sick to my stomach, feeling worse sitting in that courtroom than the day I was told she died, I forgot for a moment where I was. All the sound around me went away as my tears continued to fall. It was like I was under water. Everything around me was muffled. Suddenly, I became conscious of my Grandpop shaking my arm and looking at me with a concerned expression on his face. Then I began to hear his voice, asking if I was OK. The judge had called for a break for lunch.

## Psychiatrists

The medical testimony regarding my father's behavior and psychological capacity was extensive. Psychiatrists who had evaluated my father after the crime, as well as my father's own psychiatrist, were questioned either about my father's history prior to the crime or his behavior the day of the crime. Some of them spoke about my father's hostile actions leading up to the death of my mom, stating how he showed an increased level of frustration, anger, and rage. They spoke about his relationship with his mother, the history of violence in his marriage, and how my father was known to have a violent temper. Each of these doctors was aware and acknowledged there had been several violent attacks on Mom prior to the murder, as well as brutal attacks on me and my sister, all of which were documented in the custody hearings.

There were also questions and explanation regarding my father's attempted suicide, which was documented in medical records. He did take a number of pills. He did call his wife and mother to tell them what he had done. He was taken to the hospital and treated. But although he was depressed about the separation, custody battle, and pending divorce, they argued he was also very methodical and functional. These doctors, testifying for the prosecution, pointed out that although he was very distraught over his wife's infidelity and pending divorce at that time, he had not made any other attempts on his life—even when he was in possession of a gun. While he had the weapon in his possession for more than a week prior to the murder, he did not shoot himself during that time. He also did not turn the gun on himself after he used it to commit the crime. There were questions back and forth, and arguments as to why this had not occurred. I could see my father stir in his chair again, noticeably whispering to his attorney.

Another of the psychiatrists, one called by the defense, explained that my father's past suicide attempt was medication by choice, and a far less gruesome death. He tried to convey that my father had no intention of using the gun on himself or anyone. He wanted it for protection. I became incredibly frustrated with this doctor, thinking to myself how ridiculous it was to suggest my father was afraid of guns. He had no problems threatening my mother with a rifle a few months earlier. If he was so distraught and afraid of the gun, why did he purchase two guns then?

The psychiatrists on both sides had strong testimony, but as far as I was concerned, none of them confirmed my father was mentally impaired by diminished capacity. And his defense was based on that assumption.

One of the psychiatrists in particular illustrated my father's mental state so clearly that I still remember the things he said all these years later. He explained, "In my medical opinion, Mr. Hathaway did not have a mental breakdown, but instead he was in a state of rage from immense frustration. Let's be very clear, Mr. Hathaway did not shoot his estranged wife with a banana. He did not go up to a tree and try to talk to a tree or shoot a tree. As evidence has been presented, he dressed in a suit, drank alcohol prior to the crime, was able to drive himself to the day care location, brought with him a loaded gun, with lots of ammo in his car. He knew his wife would be there dropping off their son. He argued with her. He pulled out the gun and continued to follow Mrs. Hathaway while shooting at her. We heard testimony that his terrified wife sprayed him with mace. That did not stop him. She continued to run away from him, but Mr. Hathaway continued to go after her. He pursued her and he continued to shoot at her. Then when his wife was on the ground, he had the ability to reload the pistol and shoot her several more times. He was able to get up, walk away, find his car, and drive away."

While there were several interruptions by the defense during this doctor's testimony, in my opinion he made it clear that my father was not convincing anyone he was crazy. It was evident to me that he felt my father was a calculated and dangerous individual. He and others saw right through my father for what he really was. An angry, frustrated, vengeful man. Hearing all the testimony from these medical experts on my father's psyche made me feel vindicated in some way. Having been his victim for so long, it was comforting to hear affirmation that he was dangerous. And everyone in that courtroom knew it too.

## Expert Witness

The defense introduced an expert witness to present the information about my father's blood alcohol concentration (BAC). This doctor confirmed that a blood draw was completed eight hours after the murder. The result showed my father had a BAC between .16 and .28 percent and would have been quite inebriated at the time of the blood test. The defense wanted further clarification on how my father was able to accomplish so much if he was so inebriated. The review of the facts showed he was highly functional during the crime. He did not show signs of impairment until he was seen by the officers slumping over in his chair, upon which he was transferred by ambulance to the ER and assessed as functional and possibly had been drinking. The witness responded that he couldn't form a specific mental assessment of my father's condition prior to the time of the blood test because it was taken eight hours later. He proposed that the alcohol was consumed not the night before but rather that morning and may not have affected his function until after his arrest.

During all of this very detailed testimony, there was constant interruption by both the defense and the prosecution. But ultimately, the answers were given, the facts were presented, and each doctor was excused.

## Day 4—December 10, 1981

We entered the courtroom and took our usual places as testimony resumed. That day we would hear from a few close friends of my parents who were brought in as character witnesses.

211

# Mrs. Robin

I remember Mrs. Robin fondly. She was my mom's friend who had adopted our dog, Monique, after the tragedy, and who I had visited earlier in the summer. Mrs. Robin had performed with both of my parents but formed a close relationship with Mom outside of performing. Her testimony was primarily about her relationship with Mom, and how Mom had discussed her marital problems during their conversations. The incidents she heard about from Mom confirmed the attacks that had been documented.

# Mr. Brown

Mr. Brown was a friend of both my parents, and I vaguely remembered seeing him at our house and in shows. He testified about how long he had known them and his knowledge of their recent marital problems based on their interactions, and what my father had disclosed to him.

# Mrs. Pearl

Mrs. Pearl was Teddy's mom, our neighbor and a friend of my mother for many years. She also divulged conversations and interactions with my mom that substantiated years of marital problems. There was a little rebuttal back and forth between the prosecution and the defense regarding Mrs. Pearl and the other character witnesses. Once all questions had been answered, one by one they were dismissed.

Then the judge asked the defense to call the next witness. After some delay, the defense attorney announced my father would now testify.

# Chapter 27

# **The Trial: Part II**

A hiss of whispers arose around the courtroom. I watched my father rise out of his seat and walk to the witness stand to testify on his own behalf. I heard my Grandpop mumble something as my father sat down in the witness box, but I couldn't make out what it was. It was eerie to see the man who had been the object of fear throughout my childhood up there being sworn in. I cast my eyes toward the jury box to avoid directly looking at him. From time to time I would look up, and it seemed like he was always looking at me. Occasionally he managed to lock eyes with me, and I became afraid. I finally decided to just keep my head down. This way I could hear what was being said but not feel scared. It sickened me how he was trying to appear so sad on the stand. The pained expression on his face turned my stomach, and hearing his voice sent goosebumps up the back of my neck. I felt a warm, sick feeling come over me whenever he spoke about me or my mom, especially when he used her name, *Bunnie*. It was painful to hear that name roll off his lips. He had no right to even speak her name. As he sat up there using his soft-spoken, apologetic voice, I couldn't help but feel disgusted. I just wanted him to stand up and admit what he did.

*Stand up in that box and just stop all this whimpering. We deserve to hear the truth!*

The stress of the trial was affecting me inwardly and outwardly, my emotions raging from day after day of horror. Now seeing him up there, hearing him tell his distorted version of reality, lying about what really happened while I grew up, put my brain on overload. The whole ordeal was causing me so much anxiety, I couldn't reign in my emotions any longer, despite what courtroom decorum required. Soon, tears were rolling down my cheeks and I was hysterical again. My Uncle Bill, who was sitting next to me that day, saw how upset I was. He tapped me on the shoulder and whispered, "Let's go out to the hallway," signaling for me to leave with him. I excused myself to my grandparents, and he escorted me out of the courtroom into the hall. My uncle then suggested I go take a moment to myself, and maybe use the ladies' room. He was right. I needed a break. I could splash some water over my face, take a few deep breaths, and collect myself. I might feel better not hearing my father talk for a bit. So I walked to the bathroom door a few feet away. Unfortunately, I didn't find the peace I was looking for, but something else entirely.

Just as I reached the door, a lady walked in ahead of me. Before I even had a moment to get to the sink, the reporter pounced. "Hey, you are Susan, Susan Hathaway, the daughter of Mr. Hathaway? Are you going to testify? Ms. Hathaway, are you going to testify about what your dad did to your mother? Do you have anything to say?" It happened so fast, it was difficult to react to her or the situation. So caught off guard by her questions and her forcefulness, I just stood there like a statue as she continued to barrage me with questions.

Just then, out of a stall appeared a lady who immediately ascended on the reporter. She got right in her face saying, "How dare you attack this child in the ladies' room. She is just a *child*. You have no right speaking to her. Get away from her, get out of this room immediately." I stood there quiet as the two women engaged in this quarrel. When the reporter went to say something, this lady stopped her again. "Don't you speak to this child again," she said sternly, affirming her authority. Then the reporter turned and left out the bathroom door. I stood glued to the floor in the same spot, even as I watched her leave the room.

The kind lady, my savior, turned around to look at me. She put her hand on my shoulder and said, "Sweetie, are you OK?"

"Yes, thank you."

"You ignore them. If they ask you any questions, just keep on walking and remember, people know you are only a child. You should not have to go through what you are going through, ever!" She rubbed my shoulder, gave me this sweet smile and said, "Stay strong, sweetie, OK?" She asked me once again if I was all right, and then she turned away and left the bathroom.

Still stunned, I blinked a few times, then quickly ran into a stall. Afterward, I went to the sink, washed my hands, and patted my face with water. Grabbing a paper towel, I wiped my face and gazed into the mirror. There, staring back at me, was me. But it was this freaked-out version of me. My face was red and blotchy. I looked as horrible as I felt. Just as I was ready to turn and leave, someone knocked on the door of the bathroom. I nearly jumped out of my skin! I could hear my uncle say from the hallway, "You OK in there?" I left the bathroom and began to explain what had happened. He told me he would talk to a few people about reminding the press that I was a minor and not to harass me. I asked him if he had seen the nice woman who helped me, but he hadn't seen her. I never found out who she was, but she was a good person. Her kindness offered me a minute of comfort in a very difficult time.

Upon reentering the courtroom, I saw that my father was still on the stand. I took a huge, deep breath and held it as I scooted back into my seat. Moments later, the judge announced a break for lunch. *Great timing.* I was happy to leave the courtroom again. We all left together and headed out of the courthouse, ignoring the press who had gathered outside.

After lunch, we headed back into the courtroom where my father was back in the box testifying. I sat there calmly and listened as he and the attorneys went back and forth over all kinds of topics. I was feeling more relaxed (credit to my Grandmom for having me take my medication at lunch). Even though I felt calmer, hearing him tell his version of the truth was infuriating and disturbing. How could he honestly believe he was a good husband and father? According to him, his marriage was perfect prior to the affair. When he started talking about how he was torn apart by the affair and by being painted as an abusive parent during the custody battle, he started to cry, and I got irritated. *What a liar he is. How can he still think this way after all he's done?*

The prosecutor was prepared with ample documentation to the contrary, and he questioned my father about the custody reports that outlined his abuse. That was when my ears perked up. I really wanted to hear him respond to these questions.

The prosecutor read from a document that described the hockey stick incident: "Mr. Hathaway, your wife and daughter testified that you screamed out loud, in front of them and your other children, while beating your eldest daughter in the kitchen and later with a hockey stick in her bedroom, 'I will make sure you never walk again.' Is that what you said?"

The defense interrupted for relevance, and the judge allowed the questioning to continue. My father responded with more bull crap, saying, "Yes, Suzie had lied to us, and my wife and I felt she needed to be taught a lesson. I was wrong to have taken it so far."

Immediately I was filled with heated fury at this lie. Mom had nothing to do with what he did! That liar would say anything to blame my mom.

There was a lot of disruption by the defense and arguing over this line of questioning. But the prosecution explained he was trying to show a pattern of abuse prior to the murder. Questioning resumed.

Next, my father had to answer for the abuse to my mom prior to our family leaving home in October of 1980, how he held a shotgun on Mom, how he attacked her and strangled her. His responses were more fabricated nonsense. He tried to say my mom would antagonize him and bully him on purpose to make him angry. When he was asked about stalking my mom while they were separated, taping her private conversations, and using his daughter's boyfriend, who was a minor, to assist him, his response was laughable. He tried to say that he was only concerned for his children's safety since my mom was involved with a younger man who was doing drugs.

*More lies!* I wanted to scream.

He admitted to taking my brother to Florida for a trip and asserted he had the right to do so. Then he expressed why he felt it necessary to keep his son from his mother, explaining again how the man Mom was involved with made our home no place for his children.

Then came questions about the assault in February at the bank, which several witnesses and a police report had documented. With each question, my father would spew more blubbering and lies. He tried to suggest that he was so emotionally depressed and heartbroken over the marriage problems that he couldn't think straight. He acted out on impulse because he loved his wife so much. He cried, grumbled, and appealed to the jury to understand his desperation.

I rolled my eyes.

Objection after objection during all this questioning made it a full day of testimony that left us all emotionally drained. I was beyond relieved when the judge announced we would adjourn for the day and start fresh in the morning.

On the ride home that day, for the first time in days, my grandparents actually talked. One topic of discussion surprised me. My grandparents said they weren't aware of several things mentioned in court that day. I hadn't realized that details on the abuse to our family had never been addressed fully by my mother, and they were shocked. Grandpop even commented on the subject. In a low, choked-up voice he said, "You and your mother were very strong, very strong." He shook his head as he talked, and I could tell by the sound of his voice how upset he was. My

Grandpop didn't elaborate on things very much. He was a man of few words. Only occasionally when he wanted to make his point, he expressed his thoughts and that was the end of it. This was one of those times.

## Day 5 – December 11, 1981

My father took the stand again for the remainder of the morning. The day's testimony would be his recounting of the evening prior to and the day of the murder. His pitiful attempts to act like he cared, his empty moans of despair, were so fake to me that I didn't feel one ounce of pity for him. I saw right through his lies, and I hoped the jury did as well. Yesterday into that morning, a definite shift had taken place inside of me. My father's groveling on the stand made me feel less afraid. I was more offended than fearful at this act he was putting on. His emotional efforts to get away with what he did were disturbing. He was actually trying to act like he was the victim, behaving like a devastated husband who was ripped apart by the loss of his wife and children. He was desperate and trying to blame her for why his life was turned upside down. He wanted the entire courtroom to believe he was a shattered man who lost his mind. As he saw it, he had been put through harsh criticism, and blamed Mom and her family for bullying him.

My eyes were rolling inside my skull. Listening to him was at the same time shocking and totally unsurprising. I became enraged with a new power that was building inside. I had had enough of him sitting up there acting as if he was the innocent person. It was then that I wanted to testify. I wanted to get up there on the stand and tell them exactly who he was and what he was capable of doing.

*My father is the man who would put poison out on our front yard to punish neighborhood dogs who might wander across our lawn. The man who erected a seven-foot fence and coated it with engine grease to stain the clothes of anyone who dared to cut down our driveway on the way to the train station (and who laughed gleefully when he saw someone fall for his trap). The man who, after learning I had told Teddy that we kept soda and liquor in the basement, shoved me so hard into a door frame that I sliced my hand open. The man who slammed me into a dresser and hit me across the head when I was stupid enough to open the window to get a better look at a beautiful first snowfall one winter morning. The man who*

217

*terrorized my family for years, holding us captive by fear. I was only fifteen years old, but I was old enough to know and remember what he did to us. And I wanted him to pay for it.*

For now, all I could do was watch him dig his own hole.

He was asked to describe the night before the murder, and his vague memory of the events was a little too convenient. He remembered he called Mom the night before, I answered the phone, and then Mom came on the line. He told her he missed her and wanted her back. It crushed him that she said she didn't love him anymore and only wanted to be friends. He went on to describe how after this conversation, he decided he didn't want to live anymore and was going to prepare for his suicide. He explained that he went up to the attic of his home, found his wedding suit, and put it on. Then he proceeded to drink a bottle of champagne and was up all night drinking, trying to muster up the courage to kill himself. Later that morning he decided he wanted to drive over to the day care. He needed to say good-bye to his wife. His explanation made no sense, and my blood was boiling.

*Why not leave the gun at home then? If he had to say good-bye to her? Why? Why would he need to bring the gun?* I'll tell you why, because it was all bull crap. He planned it all and was up all night plotting, not drinking.

In my eyes, here is where my father's story got even more ridiculous. He remembered speaking to her standing at the car, and then seeing her lying on the ground bleeding. He described how grief-stricken he was seeing her lying there hurt. The additional details he added were odd, like how he noticed her hair was short now. How he loved her long hair and now it had been cut into a shorter style. How he touched her hair and believed she was in pain, and how he wanted to put her out of her pain.

In my head I was screaming, *He can remember so many details and yet, he can't remember who shot her?*

He described being so sad, and then being in the car. His face was hurting. He didn't know why until later at the police station when he found out his wife had sprayed him with mace. He didn't know why she would do that. Then he recalls the police standing at his car. The questions went on and on, back and forth over much of the same testimony. I had zoned out during some of it, thinking about how he was using that phony broken-man voice again. It was déjà vu. That same pathetic, apologetic voice he would use after hitting me.

*Suzie, why do you purposely push me and make me so angry? Why can't you just listen the first time I tell you?* Blah, blah, blah.

I felt sick to my stomach again and wasn't sure if the nausea would ever leave me. The more I replayed in my head what he claimed he remembered about that day, the more upset I became. I was screaming in my mind, what a liar! He abused us for years and the fear he instilled in our lives was suffocating. Mom had dealt with his torture even longer. He had imprisoned her, belittled her, physically hurt her, stalked her, and tried to kill her before. He enrolled his son at that specific church day care, knowing full well what it represented. I know in my gut he did that on purpose. That location was a reminder, and it fueled his rage each time he dropped off his son. His actions were planned and final this time. He brought a deadly weapon to where he knew she would be. Then in the end she was running for her life. He shot her until he ran out of bullets, and then when he ran out, he reloaded the gun and shot her four more times at point-blank range. That imagery crushes my heart. What kind of person does that? He said he recalled her bleeding. Well, if you saw someone bleeding on the ground, wouldn't you run to get help? Or scream out *fire!* to get attention? He did none of those things. He was fifteen feet from the day care door, and less than five feet from the door of the house on the lawn where she lay bleeding. He never tried to get help for her and had no intention of trying to save her. He made damn sure Mom would never be with anyone but him. This is what he wanted— to make sure Mom, her parents, and her boyfriend wouldn't win in the end.

He was a possessive, narcissistic, hateful, cold-blooded killer.

In the background of my thoughts, I could hear all the discussion, rebuttals, and debates between the attorneys. The sound was a constant broken-record repeat of many of the same questions, just in different ways or asking for different details. Testimony went on for hours in between all the objections. Finally, his testimony was over. The judge asked if they had any more witnesses or evidence to present. Both sides said no, and a wave of whispering again spread across the courtroom.

The judge asked the attorneys to begin their closing arguments. Each attorney summarized what they had presented over the previous five days, giving their side of what the witness testimony and evidence produced. After they were finished, each sat down. The judge began to speak to the jury about their responsibility. I clearly remember he used the word *malice*. I had never heard the word before and was interested to find out what it meant.

"Members of the jury, there is a term called *malice,* which is intentional homicide whereby the conduct was *willful, deliberate,* or *premeditated.*" After citing an example of another legal case to illustrate his point, he asked the jury to think about this word and understand how it relates to the case. He dismissed them for deliberation. Then the judge left the bench and the entire courtroom began to file out. I could hear all the conversations around me. People were whispering and discussing the case. There were more people in the courtroom today than on previous days, so it took us longer than usual to file out of the room. It was 1:30 p.m.

Sitting around a table at the same restaurant we had gone to every day that week, we all waited with bated breath for the final answers. What was the jury's decision going to be? At lunch that day, our prosecutor joined us. My grandparents asked him what he thought. He said he felt there was a good chance if we waited for a few hours, a verdict would come in. However, if the jury needed more time to consider evidence, he suggested we all go home and await the verdict there. My Grandmom asked if he thought the jury would deliberate long. His response was he felt the trial went very well and he had the feeling they wouldn't need to deliberate very long. Everyone knew that Mr. Hathaway was guilty of murder. However, he was not sure what sentence they would give. He only hoped they came back with first-degree murder. In Pennsylvania, that meant life in prison and no chance of parole.

At 3:05 p.m., merely an hour and a half since we arrived at the restaurant, we had all been sitting and just waiting when a legal assistant came right up to our table and whispered something into the prosecutor's ear. He looked at my Grandmom and said, "They're back." We all looked at each other with surprised faces.

Walking back together to the courthouse, I kept wondering, *What does it mean that the jury came back so fast? Is that good?* I hung onto hope that it meant they saw right through all the lies and understood what an evil man my father was.

As we got closer, I could see on the stairs of the courthouse there were more reporters than ever before. My heart was racing as we shuffled past them, each of them yelling out random questions that we were not interested in answering. The only question on our minds was the one about to be answered by the judge and jury.

Walking into the courtroom, I noticed that the room was filled with a lot more people than any days prior. Some lined the walls on the sides of the room and others filled in the space behind the last rows of seats. It was 3:45 p.m. The judge entered and sat in his chair. Then he called for the jury to come in. After they were seated, he said to them, "I understand you have arrived at a verdict. Will you please have your foreperson rise."

The clerk began to read, "Byron G. Hathaway, the defendant, do you find him guilty or not guilty, charging him with murder in the first degree?"

The foreman: "Guilty."

At that moment, there was this huge gasp and then whispering. I heard the doors behind us open and shuffling going on. I suspect it was the media leaving. We all had our arms around each other and each of us breathed heavily and began to cry. There was this brief moment of relief and satisfaction knowing he was found guilty of first-degree murder.

We had won!

Suddenly, as quickly as that emotion arrived, it left. And in its place grew enormous sadness and grief. It was not a winning moment. The catharsis lasted only seconds, because at that moment I realized, Mom was still gone.

The judge asked for silence, tapping his gavel.

The clerk asked the jury a second question regarding charges for possession of firearms without a license.

The foreman: "Guilty also."

Then my father's attorney asked that each member of the jury be polled to say their verdict aloud. The judge explained that when the clerk called them by seat number, they must stand and state their verdict. Each juror stood up when called, and each juror said, "Yes." Not one of them disagreed with the verdict. The jury had spoken. My father was guilty of first-degree murder.

The judge thanked the jurors and dismissed them. Then he asked my father's attorney to present his client. They both walked up to the podium. The judge read out the sentence.

"In the Delaware County, state of Pennsylvania, Byron G. Hathaway, Jr. is sentenced to life imprisonment without parole and is remanded to the

Delaware County prison." My father looked at his attorney, then turned sideways trying to look over in my direction. No looking away this time. This time I stared right at him. He mouthed something to me, but I didn't know what he said. Nor did I care. As he was handcuffed and led out of the courtroom, he once again turned his head back trying to look at me. I watched him as they carted him away in cuffs. It was something I needed to see. I never took my eyes off him as he disappeared out of sight. There was a split-second feeling of warm calm and relief that came over me, like when the sun comes out from behind a cloud and warms you. It was fleeting, but a relief nonetheless. He would never hurt me or my family again and there was some finality to that, but I still felt hopeless.

A few moments passed, and we began to make our way out of the courtroom. Drained of every bit of emotion from the shock of it all, we filed out like robots into the hallway. Flashes were going off constantly. The media was upon us, shouting out all kinds of questions and commentary. It was total chaos! As my family huddled together trying to get to our car, I kept thinking, *When is that feeling of relief going to hit me? Why is this pit in my stomach still there?* It kept tugging at me and did not go away.

Before the verdict was announced, I craved justice, wanting and needing closure to this nightmare. For months I waited and hoped for this enormous burden of pain to be lifted. Then when the moment of truth arrived, I anticipated the sensation of closure, for this elation and positiveness to rain down on me, but it didn't come. Nothing happened. It was a split-second sigh of relief knowing he would remain in prison for life, but nothing had really changed. Mom was dead. No verdict was going to magically bring her back. She was gone forever. All that I had was the reality staring back at me. Mom was gone, and my father would live out the rest of his life in a cell. Both my parents were never coming home.

# Chapter 28

# Facing My Boogeyman

By spring of 1992, eleven years after the trial, my life had changed a lot. My marriage had ended, and so had a hard-won custody battle for my two children. After months of court hearings and the kindness of my family and friends who stood up for me during the custody battle, it was finally over. Visitation was set, emotions subsided, and we all eased into our new lives and schedule. Having a relatively happy new life, I thought I was heading toward a better place. However, after the dust settled, it didn't feel that way. This dark cloud still hovered over me, following me with each step I took. I had a new address, a new love in my life, and new freedoms. But something was always nagging at me. This anxiety and fear loomed over me and caused me to feel like a failure no matter how hard I tried to make better choices or learn from my mistakes. I was angry with myself for letting my dark past overtake the beautiful light of my mom's memory.

I desperately tried to suppress the pain my father had left me with. But even though he wasn't in my life anymore, he was still disruptive to me on many levels. Even though I had managed to make it through a number of external struggles, such as my marriage, I had failed to do anything to better myself on the inside. That scared little girl was still within me and I couldn't seem to let go of her. Anxiety and fear were ingrained in my very identity, and I wasn't sure who I was without them. As I waged this internal battle, I became even more frustrated that I wasn't passing on my mother's legacy with strength and pride. I was dishonoring all the lessons my grandparents had fought to instill in me. How can I be a strong mother for my children if I am still a frightened little girl? Finally, I decided I was not going to let my father control me or my life anymore. I had to do something. I owed myself, my children, and my mom that much. *But how? How could I be as strong as my mom?* I thought about that question a lot. Then the realization popped into my head. It was a horrifying yet honest thought, and in that moment, I understood what I had to do. I would have to confront my fear and face my father. It was the only way to gain control of my life and be strong.

That summer, frightened but determined, I made the arrangements to go see him, with some guidance from my Gram. She gave me some instructions and I made the calls.

After my father's incarceration, my Gram had sent birthday cards to me at my grandparents' house while I lived there, attempting as best she could to stay in touch. I didn't see her while living with my grandparents. But a few months into living on my own, I reached out to my father's mom and began to mend as many wounds as we could in our delicate situation. My Gram was not to blame for the horrible events that took place, but her life was also changed permanently as a result of her son's actions. I accepted her back into my life. She even helped name my first child.

When I called to inquire about visitation, I learned it was only permitted if the inmate approved you. After a few weeks went by, I received approval and planned an early two-hour drive to the prison.

On the drive, I thought about all that had happened since I watched my father being led out of the courtroom, in handcuffs, eleven years ago.

I wish I could say that after the trial, the dark cloud lifted and I found the feeling of closure I had been waiting for, but it never came. Instead, I continued to struggle, feeling alone and bitter, grappling with depression, panic attacks, and PTSD. I was reckless and got into trouble in school and even with the police. I was often angry and felt sorry for myself, thinking only about what I didn't have and what had been taken from me. Typical, stupid teenage rebellion . . . and then some. My grandparents were true saints having survived me and all my teen troubles. Life for me was a battle back and forth trying to be grateful for having my grandparents but feeling miserable about everything else.

In the summer of 1982, my uncle and his wife separated, and Trey suddenly came back to live with me at our grandparents' house. It was a very strange feeling having him back in my life. The separation had caused an odd distance between us. He was then five years old, and we both had changed. He wasn't the toddler I remembered. I missed so much of his development in the time we had been apart, I was detached and awkward around him. Caution was another motivator. How was I supposed to go from having him ripped away from my life, to opening up my heart again?

The following year, my sister returned, and the emotional estrangement was much of the same. Marylyn had suffered her own struggles while living in her temporary home. She arrived hurt and broken. After years of separation, we were back together again and trying to cope. The hardest part was that the pain we had all suffered had not been suffered together. We had grieved alone in different homes with different emotional strains, and that lack of sibling togetherness had left each of us injured psychologically. I didn't know how to relate to my siblings the same way I had before, and they too struggled with similar emotional barriers. Most of the time we suffered independently. I buried myself in my own personal distractions, and only allowed my heart to open a little.

Six months before my graduation from high school, my Grandpop had an important talk with me. He told me that after I graduated, he wanted me to stand on my own two feet, find my own place, and build my future. He reminded me that my mother was looking down on me, and I needed to be there for my sister and brother. I was the oldest, and he and Grandmom would not be around forever. In his firm but loving way, he explained that I had to show them how grown-up I could be. I felt afraid and burdened with all he was saying to me. How was I going to do all that? I was overwhelmed. However, like every other time, somehow my fear turned into a challenge to overcome. I worked hard to get myself together, wanting my mom and grandparents to be proud of me. I needed to show them I could do it. So I secured a full-time job and worked hard to become even more independent.

Moving out on my own one week after graduating high school was scary for me. Instead of feeling excited and optimistic like a typical eighteen-year-old with newfound independence, I was having even more panic episodes. Simply passing someone who reminded me of my father gave me panic attacks. If I worked with a man who resembled or had characteristics of my father, it would put me into a bad place mentally. If an older male hovered over my shoulder for anything, I would become uncomfortable and feel sick to my stomach. I couldn't get on an elevator with a man alone. A debilitating terror would come over me at the thought of being trapped in a small space with a man. In spite of being on medication for my anxiety and my constant effort to keep strong, I continued to deal with emotional obstacles. Fears constantly creeped in, even in my sleep in the form of chronic nightmares. In one of my recurring dreams, I was trapped in my father's studio and was trying to get out. I could hear my mom screaming and my siblings crying. But I still couldn't get the door open. I would pull and pull, and nothing would happen. I bashed my body into the door over and over. When the door finally broke open, it turned into a fog and the door was gone. I frantically looked for my mother and siblings, but no one was there. In another dream, my mom was driving, and my siblings and I were passengers. Suddenly, the car went off the bridge and we were falling, screaming, and we couldn't get out of the car. We kept falling and falling. I would wake up crying, feeling distraught and alone. These dreams were the most vivid, horrible reminders of my past, and they plagued me even in my waking hours.

As I fought desperately to be strong and normal, my anxiety was constant. My fears and insecurities were a huge burden. Despite my continued efforts with therapy and medication, it seemed to never resolve anything fully. I still felt this hold over me, an internal captor that never let me go for long. All the emotional setbacks were smothering me, causing further stress at my job and relationships. My lack of self-worth was draining. I truly wanted to make my mom and grandparents proud of me, but felt like I was losing the battle. I was so disappointed with myself most of the time that I didn't tell others how I felt. It was too embarrassing to admit my father still plagued my life. The only way to fight off the doom and gloom was to think of my mom and all I had to live up to. So I constantly thought of her and my grandparents. My Grandmom's words haunted me: *You are acting just like your father.* I tried so very hard to be more like Mom and never be like my father. It was a battle of wills within myself and despite how hard I fought it, it followed me well into my young adult years.

When I discovered I was pregnant two years after marrying my long-time boyfriend, I looked to my inner conscience for answers, asking my mom to guide me. In the beginning, I was panicky at the thought of being a parent. I never had a normal upbringing, and the first few weeks I was afraid all the time. I tried to hide my fears in company, not wanting people to think I was weird for being afraid to have children. Experiencing all these new emotions made me think back to when my mom was pregnant with my brother. During Mom's pregnancy, she was confined to bed rest for the last several months. I remember going into her bedroom and hanging out with her while she lay in bed. Mom didn't have any shyness about showing her belly while pregnant. Whenever the baby was moving around, she would show me her tummy and I held my hand on it whenever it kicked. Feeling this little baby push and poke out a foot or hand at any given moment was the most amazing and strange thing I had ever experienced! I also remembered hearing about her struggle giving birth. Trey was born breech and Mom didn't have a C-section. His birth was very tough on them both, and very rare from what I understand. When they both came home, I had the opportunity to hold him and became Mom's big helper. Breastfeeding was hard for her. She allowed me to witness this natural method of feeding a baby, though she had a condition that made it difficult and extremely painful. Regardless, she didn't give up and managed through it. She was a tough lady. During my own pregnancy, those memories gave me the motivation to stay strong when I was scared.

Thoughts of my mom often gave me strength to push away the dark thoughts of my father. The memory of my own childhood experiences haunted me so much, I vowed I would never treat my children like my father had treated me. *Ever.* It made me even more determined not to repeat the past. The cycle of abuse would end with me. My fear became my awareness. At that time in my life I was employed as a nanny, already caring for two children. In this way, I was already breaking the cycle of child abuse by being a loving caregiver. I realized that if I could be loving and kind in my care for other children, I could do the same for my own child. My mother's memories and my grandparents' morals kept me strong for my daughter's birth, and the birth of my son eighteen months later. Caring for them gave my life purpose.

*Left, my daughter and me; Right, my son and me*

In the winter of 1991, my health took a left turn when I was suddenly stricken with medullary sponge kidney (MSK), a congenital disorder I had no idea I had. This resulted in a complicated surgery that left me in the hospital for eighteen days. Once home, my anxieties returned, and years of communication breakdowns in my marriage were causing serious strain. My husband and I had been growing further apart emotionally for a long time. I felt I had honestly tried to make things work but after I had exhausted all compromises, I gave up trying. My marriage ended for many reasons, but primarily because I had given up and emotionally moved on. It was a difficult divorce and custody battle to the very end. During those emotional months, the fears from the past crept in. I watched myself going through what my mother had gone through all those years ago. I felt afraid and helpless, fighting for my children in court and trying to hang onto my sanity at the same time. Happy memories of my mother, and music, helped soothe my pain and get me through these toughest times. For comfort, I often found myself circling back to my favorite songs that Mom liked. "The Forest" by The Cure was a beautiful escape. Mom said she liked it when I played it for her before she died. Escaping into it, life would seem simpler for a few moments.

*It's been a long road,* I thought as my car drove closer and closer to the prison. The Cure album *Wish* played from the car's cassette player, calming my thoughts.

Upon entering the prison's visiting station, I had to go through the security procedures, which were unsettling. I presented my ID and approval document, then put all my personal items into a locker. They patted me down and then I walked through a screening machine. The prison setting was overwhelming, and my surroundings made me feel uneasy. While I sat in the screening room waiting to be called to go to the visitation area, my fear of being near my father again weighed heavily on my mind. My thoughts reeled as I went over and over in my head what he did to Mom, to me, and to our whole family. My heart ached as I thought about how my siblings and I were separated and forced to face the trauma of losing our mother alone. The pain he caused was set in stone and there had been no relief.

I considered leaving. As I waited for my turn in the prison visitation room, I kept having arguments with myself. *You just drove two hours to get here. You have to do this. You have to face him. This fear has to stop.*

"Susan Hathaway!"

Out of the blue, the guard called my name and I almost jumped out of my skin. I stood up and walked to the door. Security waved a metal detector wand over me and then I had to go through another electronic screening arch. I followed a few other visitors outside through another door and along a paved walkway that ran along the side of the building. On my right were high double fences topped with thick barbed wire. To my left was a large courtyard area surrounded by brick buildings and walkways. Ahead of me was another building with glass windows and a sign that said VISITOR AREA.

Once inside, I was surprised by how large the room was. There were several tables, each one surrounded by a few chairs. Along the front far corner wall were some vending machines. I was shocked at how closely this place resembled a school cafeteria. It was an open space arranged so that a prisoner could sit at one end of the table and the visitor across from them. The table acted as the only divide, permitting only a slight separation from the inmate. My heart was pounding. I kept telling myself I was safe. There was no way he could do anything in that environment. Even though I was very unsure now, I tried to convince myself that if he did anything out of line, he would be taken down by the guards. That image soothed me. I reminded myself I didn't have to be there. I *chose* to be there. I took several deep breaths to help calm myself again.

My calm was short-lived. A few more minutes went by and I started to feel anxious again. Waiting added to my discomfort. With too much time to overthink things, my mind raced. *What am I doing? Am I nuts? I am going to face my boogeyman!* I started to feel like a child again, nervously squirming in my seat as I hung onto the anticipation of each second that ticked by. *Will I recognize him? Will he still look the same?* I began to look around the large room wondering, *Which door will he come through?* I noticed two doors along the back wall. One door was labeled BATHROOM. The other door said SECURITY ONLY. DO NOT ENTER. I guessed that was where the inmates came in. My guess was right. As I glanced around the room again, the security door opened up and a man walked out. It was my father.

I recognized his profile. He wore prison garb that resembled nurse scrubs. He still had a beard, but his hair was very gray. His face was pale, and his skin looked red and blotchy. Overall, he looked disheveled as he scanned the room looking for me. When he spotted me, he began to walk over to the table. Goosebumps rose on my skin. My adrenalin was rushing, and I felt hot. He walked over to where I was sitting and began to open his arms to give me a hug. I recoiled inside and outwardly, never standing to receive it. Realizing I was not reciprocating, he paused, walked to the other end of the table, and sat down. I fought to get ahold of myself. I was trembling and didn't want to show any signs of being afraid. So while my arms lay in my lap. I began to pinch them really hard. This helped keep me alert and focused.

He initially seemed quite happy to see me. I noticed he was very excitable, talkative, and even polite. He apologized for the noise and surroundings, which I found odd. He was visibly distracted, and said he was happy when he had visits because he was able to have soda and good food.

Forget the food. I was more interested in hearing who had visited him. Finally, I uttered my first words to him. "Had visits? Oh, who visited you?"

The dialogue had begun. And my curiosity was showing.

He casually began to explain how some old friends would come to see him. He mentioned a few performers he knew from the theater. Several people he mentioned I knew, and others I did not. Before I had the chance to ask more about them, he jumped onto other topics, seemingly bored talking about people other than himself.

As the conversation continued, I found myself feeling less scared and more irritated. The minutes ticked by as we sat there, and he hadn't asked me one thing. No typical parental questions: *How had I coped with things? What was I doing with my life? How was my graduation?* Gram must have told him I was married and that he had grandchildren. But he never asked anything! Most significantly, he never said he was sorry to me for taking my mother's life, or for how he had treated me as a child. His time spent in prison hadn't inspired him to see the error of his ways and think about his choices. Instead, he was narcissistically consumed with his own selfish rhetoric. And worse, he would badmouth my mother and others when talking about the past. In his words, he was "betrayed" by my mother and wrongfully convicted.

I sat there stunned for a long time, at first too afraid and then too stunned to really comment as he lectured on. When he complained about how the courts screwed him for a crime he should have only served five years for, *I almost fell off my chair.* He went on to say how he was mentally beat down by all the trauma he had endured during the failed marriage and separation. He insisted that learning about the affair caused him great suffering and that he had a mental breakdown. That the stress of the separation, loss of his children, and Mom's involvement with Jim, drove him mad. He babbled on and on. As if he was still trying to convince a jury, he even talked about how his alcohol consumption had caused him to block out the events, and he was not aware of what he had done. As I continued to sit there dumbfounded and queasy, listening to his rambling, I wanted to break in and tell him to shut the hell up. But instead, I just sat there. I still felt uncomfortable. So I let him spit out all his bile.

It was remarkable that he seemed to forget I was old enough to remember all the things he had done, prior to the murder and after. Did he forget I was at the trial? Little did he know I had read the trial transcripts several times. I had also read a few of his appeals when given the opportunity. I already knew the details of his intoxication and supposed "diminished capacity" defense, and I had come to my own conclusion. In my eyes, the alcohol just gave him the fuel and courage to execute his plan. However, I wasn't going to tell him that.

He then told me about how he had taken two sodium pentothal tests, and proclaimed that each test proved he had no memory of particular moments from the shooting. He said it like it was a great revelation. I nodded like a bobblehead, letting him know I understood what he said, but not revealing my thoughts on the matter. In truth, I already knew from the court appeal transcripts that he had these tests done. *So what!* His efforts to exhaust all his appeals got him nowhere. He was denied a change in his sentence every time. Having selective memories of that morning doesn't change the fact he carried out the crime. I was becoming aggravated. It hadn't taken long during the visit for him to be up to his typical behavior: shedding the blame.

As he moved on to the topic of how my mother, his mother, and my grandparents provoked his actions, it took every ounce of my composure not to freak out on him right then and there. Instead, I chewed on my lip. I couldn't let him get under my skin. I was there to get him out of my head, not let him back into it.

After more than an hour of listening to my father talk nonstop, I realized I no longer felt afraid of him. Instead, I was numb emotionally and exhausted from all his ramblings. I came to the realization that, without a doubt in my mind, this man had no conscience. No remorse. That was the reason he sat in prison. The world he lived in, in his mind, was not reality. Nor would it ever be.

I interrupted him and said I needed to eat something. He agreed to pause for some food and drink. My father was required to stay in the seat at all times, so I got up to use the vending machine. I purchased soda and food for both of us. As I gathered the items for lunch, I thought about how

I would respond to some of the things he had said during our visit. I really needed to break my silence. But I didn't want him to think he was getting under my skin. I would have to be smart about it. When I reached our table with the food, I finally spoke up. Interrupting him as he was thanking me for the lunch, I let him know I wanted to say a few things. He stopped talking mid-sentence.

"Sure."

So I asked him, "Don't you want to know how my life has been? Especially after what you did? You haven't asked me about anything. Not one question." I paused and waited to hear a response. He looked at me with a blank stare.

His face looked annoyed at the questions. Then he spoke, "I didn't want to impose asking you about your life. I assumed it would be best to avoid asking." He folded his hands on the table to signal he was finished with his response.

*That's it? That's his reply to me? After eleven years of not seeing me. After all the terrible things he's done to me and my family, that's all he has to say?* I was stunned and angry at his indifference. He was so disengaged from anything that was not about himself. Knowing how his children were faring was not a priority. It wasn't even a thought in his head. My mind reeled, and all I could do was think to myself, *he has no empathy.* Why did I care what he felt or thought? Was it my own need to know? Nausea overwhelmed me yet again. *Have I not learned my lesson by now? This man is a black hole. He just sucks the life out of me, and I need to stop letting that happen.*

Recognizing he was not taking responsibility for his actions, and was not going to answer my questions, I understood it wasn't important anymore. Nothing I said was going to make him care or faze him in the slightest. I was still invisible to him. Instantaneously, I realized I had done fine without him all these years. His abuse to me as a child and his murderous act in taking my mother's life did not break me. Though deep down it had, it was vital that I didn't show him that. I was not a child anymore, and sitting across from him, I felt different. A surge of energy filled my body and I felt gigantic in front of him. I didn't cry or get angry. Instead, I shrugged off his insensitive disinterest and took a completely different approach.

In a stern but calm voice, I told him, "Despite what you took away from me and my siblings, we have carried on and have good lives. My children are happy, and I am a good mom. I thought by coming here I would get some kind of closure and possibly an apology from you. But now I realize, I really don't need one. I'm doing fine without it."

Following my short speech, he sat there in silence. He was almost stoic. He was looking at me and then looked down. He seemed to be in thought. Maybe I surprised him. Maybe he expected I would be the sniveling pea-brain child of the past. Never again. I had faced my boogeyman and he was not scary anymore.

After some silence, he spoke. "Suzie, I knew you would get through it all. You were always so strong and stubborn." He sat back in his chair, sighed, and was silent again. We sat there for a few additional awkward seconds. As usual, he managed to stump me. I had to take a second to digest what he had said. *Since when did he think I was a strong person?*

Not to be thrown off my game, I arrogantly responded with the first thing that popped into my head. "Yes, thanks to Mom's memory and my grandparents' strength through the years, I am a stronger person now."

Well, that got his attention. Immediately he seethed with anger and disgust as he blurted out, "Yes, yes, I guess you would think that! But if you knew the lies your grandparents and mother told you, you would think differently, Suzie. They are all liars!"

*There it is.*

There was that vicious nature. That ugly, nasty person I was used to. He lashed out at my comment like a reflex. He couldn't stand hearing me say anything nice about the people I loved. He couldn't even muster up a second of regret toward his wife whom he claimed to adore and then murdered.

The heat of anger welled up in me. My hands were trembling and I'm sure my face was beet red. I almost gave in to anger, so ready to scream something hateful at him. Then I thought of my mom and why I was there. A calm came over me. I need to stand strong against his lies. I spoke to my conscience, soothing myself. *Wait, wait, don't react. Do not react the way he wants. I don't need to defend Mom or my grandparents. I already know they are good people. Do not give in and play his game. Remember where you are. He is in prison, not me. I chose to come here, and this is my stand.*

All my therapy, advice from my Grandpop, and courage from my mom came flooding back to me. My father is not allowed to beat me down. He would love to know he put doubt in my mind about the people I love. But I was not there to try and find a reason why he was the way he was. His words were the affirmation I needed that he didn't care. I felt overwhelming peace knowing I could leave him at this prison. I was the one who prevailed. I was the one who was free.

I didn't know what having control was, until now.

Right then all the fear, pain, and anger I had held onto for years seemed less important. Because from where I sat, he was the loser. At that moment and on that day, I had finally taken control of me. I had pushed myself to face my demon, my father the boogeyman, in that prison. I was taking that fear back, and I wasn't going to allow him to damage my life any further. I was reborn.

It was time for me to leave. After ignoring his horrible remark, it was clear the conversation had unraveled and there was nothing more to say. I told him I had a long drive home and wanted to get on the road. He seemed surprised at my sudden request to go. I pushed my chair out from the table and prepared to stand. He quickly responded in a childlike tone, "Thank you for coming, Suzie. It was so good to see you." He continued on about how I had grown up so much and had a good head on my shoulders. He wished I would stay longer. I was too preoccupied looking for the exit to acknowledge him.

Interrupting him, I asked, "Which door is the exit?"

He reacted with a quick glance over toward a prison guard sitting at the desk near the door where I had entered earlier. It was apparent my swift departure had caught my father off guard. As I walked away from the table, he blurted out, "Good-bye, Suzie, may I write to you? May I?"

I quickly responded, "Yes, I guess so. That's fine." I really didn't have time to think about what he had asked. I was more focused on getting out of there, getting some air, and putting some distance between us. As I walked out, I glanced back and saw my father being led back to the door he had come out of earlier. Then I turned away and left the visitor room, walking the pathway of high fencing and barbed wire toward the security office. My arms felt so heavy as I pulled on the door to leave.

When I reached my car, I got in and sat there for a moment. I was physically and emotionally drained but felt calm. The visit was an eye-opening experience. Confronting him further solidified my stance on what a dangerous and deluded man my father was. I took a deep breath and began my long ride home, thinking about what my visit had accomplished. It made me realize I would never be like him. His DNA was a part of me physically, but not spiritually. I wasn't doomed to repeat his evils. Finally, I had the clarity I needed to move on with my life in a positive way. Just like my mom and my grandparents taught me.

# Chapter 29

# Guiding Light

After facing my father, I could feel a huge change. This surge of confidence after standing up to my boogeyman had changed my life for the better. I kept a steady correspondence with him. It provided a feeling of safety and command that I needed. Allowing him to write to me was informative and that was also soothing for me. I could respond back to him whenever I felt like it. I was tolerating him and doing it at my comfort level. I also felt safer knowing what he was doing and thinking. I learned quite a bit from his letters. How his health was, appeals and status, and his general state of mind. Communicating with my father kept him aware of how wonderful my life was without him. My grandparents and my sister had a difficult time understanding my mindset, and each of them requested that I refrain from discussing them in any detail with my father. They were coping with their grief in their own way, and I respected that.

For me, staying in touch with my father made me feel I had authority over my life. It was empowering to finally feel in control. Thinking about Mom's strength and what that had taught me, how I had faced my father and stood up to him, I was being strong like she was. I wanted to stay strong for my children and show my grandparents that I took my life back. I felt even more empowered to keep my mom at the forefront of everything. With every struggle I faced in my life thereafter, her inspiration filled me with strength and helped me through.

And there were struggles.

After my divorce, I remarried a few years later, and I was happy. However, my kidney disorder continued to plague my life for years. I had countless surgeries and other medical anomalies that afflicted my physical health. The unrelenting medical procedures and the stresses I endured were hard on me and my family. I often cried out to my mother for strength, and I know she was with me during those scary and debilitating times. I managed to survive through them all, and the love from her and my children kept me grounded.

*Me and my youngest son*

My youngest son was born in July 1994, premature but healthy, thank goodness. Throughout several hospitalizations, procedures, and complications during his birth, my mom spiritually was there. She was the warm blanket that comforted me when I was scared. Caring for my three amazing children, happy in my relationship, enjoying my nanny jobs, I was living a good life. I began to open up more, allowing myself to express and explore my love for music, the Gothic genre, comics, movies, and Halloween (the only holiday for me that wasn't tainted by bad memories). I may not have been performing like my mom, but my love for music and dressing up in my kind of fun way was how I expressed my love for the arts. It was different but it was me, and I know she would have been proud to see this side of me emerge.

Unfortunately, everything came crashing down around us in 1997. My marriage was shattered when I learned my husband was in another relationship, wanted to leave the marriage, and was preparing to move out. I was devastated and went to my Grandpop for guidance. My Grandpop was a deeply religious man with strong convictions that molded his seasoned personality. I trusted him and needed his advice. He told me that the good Lord will show me the way and he will pray for me. With his usual quiet candor, he said I need to do what is best for the kids. He reminded me that my Grandmom had gone through similar circumstances and knows how hard it is to manage such things based on her past experience. My grandparents were a constant source of support and strength, and I truly needed their wisdom during this difficult time.

After my husband moved out, I was leveled emotionally and physically, I began to go through a psychologically grueling separation. During this time, I lost a scary amount of weight. By spring I weighed ninety-four pounds. I had already gone back into therapy and was back on medication. I desperately struggled with which direction my life and the lives of my children should go. The stress was enormous. I was physically emaciated and emotionally depleted. Eventually, my husband and I attended counseling and tried to work things out, but we struggled to build trust in our relationship again. Before we had firmly decided whether we would move forward with the divorce or try to mend our marriage, my husband was seriously injured in a car accident while making a delivery for work. His injury was serious, and recovery was going to be a very long, life-changing event. This incident pushed us to reconsider our options. So we stopped the divorce proceedings and we tried to start over. But emotional struggles seeped in little by little as the years went by. Through the slow deterioration of my marriage, I sometimes felt so lost, but thoughts of my mom's courage and my grandparents' wisdom never left me. In the end, years later, I filed for divorce and had to move on.

In 2004, my Grandpop fell and hit his head, which changed his normally strong, independent character. After the fall, the swelling from his brain injury sadly altered his usually polite and endearing personality. The family came together to care for him, and we all held out our hand to be supportive. By this time, Grandmom was already in a nursing home at the same facility, recovering from her own medical setbacks. During the six weeks Grandpop struggled with his ailments, I would lovingly make foods he requested and bring the dishes to him when I visited. I tried to give him as much encouragement and love as possible as his conditions overcame him, just like he had done for me when I needed it.

Pop was able to come home on hospice, and he was happy knowing he would rest in his own bedroom. Grandmom was approved to come home at the same time. Together as a family we all spent as much time with Grandpop as we could. A few days later, Grandpop died, and another piece of my heart went with him. I often wonder if he knew how much I loved him. He was a hard worker and a remarkable person who left an everlasting impression on everyone who met him. He was a true gentleman with a gentle soul. He had a way of making you feel welcome and appreciated. If you ever had the pleasure of meeting him, you would not have forgotten him. He adored his family, and I will always remember how much he loved my mom. My Grandpop's wisdom and guidance kept me alive after Mom's death. He helped me realize I could use my mother's memory for support in the future. I can only hope that I honor his life, love, and wise inspirations by being the best I can be every day. I miss him terribly.

Five years later in 2009, my grandmother succumbed to her long battle with Parkinson's. She always had a profound way of saying what she thought, and that kind of honesty is hard to find. I miss her amazing flower arrangements and desserts, pound cake, and Scottish shortbread cookies. The memories of moments shared with her, I will always carry with me. My Grandmom's tenacious character also gave me strength. There were moments in my life when I had to embrace harsh things she said. Though her personality was a challenge at times, I was able to learn so much from what she taught me. She helped better my life, giving me wisdom to carry with me for years to come.

*Grandpop and Grandmom*

My grandparents' deaths left a huge void in my life. My worldly connection to my surrogate parents was gone and I missed them both very much. But to this day I am comforted when I think of all the wonderful things they did for me, and how they both instilled valuable lessons that helped me grow. Each never gave up on me and helped me through heartbreaking times while they struggled through hardships as well. I found comfort in knowing they both believed they would see Mom again. Their faith gave them that absolute assurance in their heart that they would embrace their daughter in heaven. They knew they would hear her sing once again. I remember how happy that thought made them. Knowing they felt at peace brought me peace.

Preparing my grandparents' home for sale after my second divorce was depressing. It had been in our family for more than fifty years, and it was heartbreaking to let it go—the home my mother grew up in, the home my grandparents raised me in, and the home I purchased after my Grandpop passed away. Over the years I lived there with my family, the house had become the one place that was always a staple in my life. I recalled with nostalgia taking my two eldest children's prom pictures at the house, and later graduation. It made me think of how I wished my mom could have taken pictures of me for my prom or been at my graduation. I wished she could have seen her granddaughter, and later grandsons, graduate. So many missed moments to share together. In my mother's honor, I would wrap my thoughts around making the best of everything, making sure my children knew how proud of them I was, keeping a smile on my face and not letting the pain of my own losses bring me or them down. It's what Mom would have wanted.

*My three amazing children when they were little.*

As my children grew, so did I. By their teenage years, I had learned being a parent was not all rainbows and candy. I didn't have a very strong foundation for raising children, and I desperately fought the memories of my own upbringing as I dealt with each challenge. Whenever I was feeling tested, I tried to channel my frustration and anger, and remember how my childhood *could not* be the same for my children. I wasn't perfect. Despite my best efforts I got upset and angry like all parents do. But I would recall how my father made me feel defeated by his words and actions. I kept my mother and my Grandpop in mind, using their example as a guide. The determination to honor my mom and my grandparents was always coursing through my blood. The immense love for my children, family, and friends kept me focused and strong. In difficult times, all of them were by my side channeling inspiration to me along the way. Always, the ghosts of my past, those who had helped me understand what it was to be loved, provided me support and reassurance in times of extreme distress. Subconsciously they were always there guiding me.

When I think back in my life to times I felt loved, Jim also comes to mind. The last time I saw him was shortly after I moved into my first apartment. My siblings and I met up with him and had a nice time catching up. I will never forget our happy reunion. We lost touch again after that. I always struggled with whether I should reach out, thinking I was being selfish or disrupting his life by trying to reconnect with him all the time. I knew we were a constant reminder of the tragedy for him, and I wrestled with these emotions a lot. I tried to move on and think about how he must feel every time we saw each other. It was hard to let go. Time marched on and new life events kept me busy.

One day during a very difficult and emotional time, I was feeling so much loss and needed to fill the emptiness with a connection to my past. I Googled Jim's name. The search got an immediate hit. But it was not the information I had hoped for. I began to cry uncontrollably as I saw his obituary. Jim had passed away suddenly three months earlier in July 2016. He was fifty-eight years old. My heart ached for days after this discovery. I decided to reach out to his wife. She was very receptive, and we reminisced about how loving Jim was. I shared some pictures of him with her and told her how all those years ago he brought joy to our lives. I learned he had reentered the US Navy Reserves following 9/11 and had been a police officer for more than twenty years. It was clear he was loved by many people in his lifetime. I was stunned to learn he lived one hour away from me all that time. All these years he was so close spiritually and physically. He remains always in my memories and heart.

Looking back, my life has undeniably been marked by loss. But I have also been blessed with moments of overwhelming joy. These moments have filled me up and brought me back into the light more times than I can count. Moments like seeing my eldest son graduate from Marine Corps boot camp before serving for four years. Or when my youngest son took time away from his friends or a favorite video game to spend time with me while I suffered the loneliness of his two siblings living far away. Hearing my daughter was pregnant and realizing I would be a grandma for the first time! While painful life lessons have at times stripped me down to the core causing heartaches from which I will never fully recover, I have learned to take each day one at a time. I try desperately to manage the pain that has plagued my life, whether brought on by myself or by life's general cruelty. In moments like these I remember all my inspirations. My mother, my grandparents, my beautiful children. I keep them tucked away in a safe place, using them when the light is dimming away. This is how I survive. This is how I find happiness amidst all the pain.

I wish so much that I could have helped Teddy find light in the darkness like I did. When we were growing up I knew Teddy was unhappy, but after I moved away we didn't connect as often. When I lived on my own, I would drive back to the old neighborhood to visit with him. He would tell me he was angry at so many things and struggling. It was very hard on me to hear his pain. It would bring out my own grief, and I would suffer emotional setbacks after a visit with him. It would take me days to reset and get back to feeling like myself again. Selfishly, I began to avoid visiting with him. I always kept Teddy in my thoughts, but I also needed to stay positive. When I became a mom, I started reaching out to let him and his family know I was thinking of them. In February of 1996, Teddy responded back to me and together we arranged a visit. I went to see him at his home. He still lived in Pennsylvania and I was happy to learn he had a family of his own. His wife was charming, and he had two beautiful girls. He was very open about his mental recovery and anxiety limits, but he seemed happy. He explained that he was on medication and that his horrible anxiety arose if he was put into certain situations. We were able to understand each other so well. Even with all the years we were apart, we still connected so deeply. I am so grateful to have had that visit with him. I never thought it would be the last time I ever saw him.

Three years later in 1999, I received the tragic news that Teddy had committed suicide. I was heartbroken and angry at him all at the same time, especially since he had so much to live for. But I tried to focus on the good times. I recall a song he loved: "My Life" by Billy Joel. He always turned that song up and sang it out loud. Now, every time I hear it, I always think of him. As always, I clung to my mother's spirit and imagined that if there were an afterlife, she would welcome Teddy with a big hug and together they could find a quiet place to talk.

My mother's strength and the memory of my grandparents have seen me through many a loved one's passing. It has also been what I cling to during other devastating forms of separation. When my youngest son moved to Alaska with his father after our divorce, my heart broke into a million pieces. His absence shattered my heart and even years later, my heart still aches being so far away from him. Now, as I live with the distance between us, I always keep faith and love. I choose to embrace what I have. I can talk, text, and write to him, and occasionally I can visit. I think about how proud I was to watch him walk during his graduation, and how we strolled around Ward Lake together taking in breathtaking views during a visit in 2012. The moments we spent together then or during any visit are forever etched in my memories, and they sustain me until the next time. I never give up hope that one day we will live closer to each other. I continue to look beyond the immense heartache, and value what each loss has taught me, hanging onto every moment, and having faith in tomorrow.

At forty-six years old, I took another chance at love after the pain of my past marriages. My eldest son walked me down the aisle. I had never felt so sure about things as I did that day. My husband walks the walk. He is my best friend. He showed me that you can trust again and feel loved again. I am very blessed to have such a loving, kind, and peaceful man in my life. I have never known this kind of calm. What we share is truly inspiring and I am tremendously grateful. Though they couldn't be there physically, I believe in my heart my mom and grandparents were with us on our wedding day, surrounding us with added positivity.

*Our wedding day*

I am now four times a grandma. Life has given me wonderful gifts, and despite the struggles I've experienced, I try every day to be grateful for what I have. I am so blessed to be able to experience new journeys through my grandchildren and welcome the immense happiness of having them in my life. As they grow, I often reflect how my mom would have adored them too. I share my happy memories of my mother and grandparents with them. They know how their Grandmom Bunnie was a wonderful mom, singer, and person. How she would have adored them and would have been a huge part of their lives if she were here today. Her essence and light are inspirational to me and them. I know they will carry my mother's memories into their future and pass her memories on to their children.

Life-altering changes have overwhelmed my life on a number of occasions. I've had to use every ounce of energy I had to push forward each time they happened. The courage I learned over the years is what kept me going. There were forces helping me get through each day. I just had to keep listening to them. Although my wounds have started to heal, I still have the scars from my tortured past. Those emotional scars are my reminders that life is precious. The memories of the past will never leave me but have given me added wisdom in my life. Not allowing the suffering from my past to extinguish my positive thoughts, I continue to take each day as it comes. It's what I have to do to keep my mother's beautiful life and light alive.

# Chapter 30

# **Last Words**

On January 29, 2020, my father collapsed in his cell. Age had finally caught up with him, and he was suffering from sepsis due to kidney failure. As his health-care proxy, it was in my power to consent to treatment. Although my father never gave my mother the same dignity, I didn't want his hate to ever be the focus of my actions. So I approved the dialysis. After his treatments, fate made its decision and the doctor told me his death was imminent. I decided to go see him and asked my brother, who also had prior visitation permission, to come with me for comfort and support. A small spark lingered inside that maybe, just maybe, my father may have some humanity left inside his rotten mind. Maybe with the end near, he would want to say he was sorry for what he had done to our mother and family, for shattering our lives, and for being so cruel to all of us. The need to know ran deep within me. I wanted to hear it from him.

When we arrived, we walked over to the bed and the nurse moved him a bit. His eyes opened. I said my name out loud. "Your daughter, Suzie, is here."

He recognized me right away, saying, "I know who you are." I told him his son was there too. He looked at us both and acknowledged us. I did my best to explain to him why we were there, that his condition was critical and that this was a last visit. He appeared to understand the severity of things but didn't want to accept it. I made the effort to offer him the opportunity to say any last words to us. I asked him numerous times, "Do you have anything to say to me or your son? Did you want to let us know anything?"

There were long periods of silence. Finally, he spoke, and his last words were very clear. "I missed out on so much and I know why I am incarcerated. It was because of the company I kept. It's your mother's fault that I am in this position."

After he finished speaking, heavy silence hung in the air. My brother and I locked eyes, knowing now for sure he would never apologize or accept that what he had done was wrong. Our father was going to his grave believing that what he did to our mother wasn't a crime. As for me, my heart and mind spoke out subconsciously to use every ounce of dignity for my mother and her parents and our family not to let anger guide me. He would die knowing he did not break me. My loving, beautiful mother and grandparents showed me how to forgive and live a blessed life.

I looked right at him and said, "Can you hear me?"

He nodded weakly. "Yes, I can hear you."

In a loud voice I told him, "Good, I want you to hear what I have to say. I want you to think about your opera, your classical music, and baseball. I want you to close your eyes and go to sleep. We are going to leave now . . . good-bye. Did you hear me?"

He responded, "Yes."

My conscience was clear. Trey and I turned away and walked out of the room. A peace came over me as I walked away, knowing I did not let his hate win in the end. My mom and my grandparents were walking there with me.

Forty-eight hours later on February 4, I received the call in the middle of the night that my father had died. After I hung up the phone, I stood in my kitchen waiting to feel something. When emotion came, it could be defined simply as . . . *unbelievable peace.*

A few days after my father's death, the prison superintendent called to inform me that my father had left behind many pictures and thought I may want to see them. I was making one final trip back to the prison anyway to scatter his ashes, a decision made about a year earlier when his age and health issues brought my thoughts to that subject. There was only one place his ashes belonged, in prison. That is where he was sentenced to in life, and in death that is where he should stay. Returning him to the place he belonged. It was settled. My brother accompanied me on the trip and so did our father's ashes—the product of a cremation his mother had prepaid for years earlier.

Upon arrival at the prison, I signed for my father's property, thanked the superintendent for his help, and we left.

On the drive back down the road toward the prison exit, Trey pulled over to a safe place along the road. I grabbed the bag of ashes, cut the bag open, crouched down, and poured them onto the ground. I stood up and looked at Trey. Then we simply turned away, got back in the car, and made our way out the prison exit. There were no words, no sorrow. It was a moment of conclusion. And I felt the weight falling off my shoulders with every inch of road that took us away from that place.

In the box of my father's possessions were a number of photographs of people I didn't know. One after another, I put them aside. Suddenly, among all this trash was a treasure. A white envelope with a few pictures I recognized, including one picture taken February 1981 of Mom, me, my siblings, and our dog Monique. My heart leapt. The twenty-eight years I kept in touch with my father had given me a few comforts, knowledge, control, a few family heirlooms, and this picture that captures a time with my mom and siblings when we were together, and life was beautiful.

Susan Hathaway-Saurman

Dear Mom,

I don't remember what I wrote in the letter I placed in your casket all those years ago. But today, years later, as I write my heart down on paper, I feel many emotions. Sadness, missing your physical presence in my life. Feeling the huge void of not having you here to wipe my tears or comfort me when I'm needing my mom. Missing all the opportunities we could have had, sharing my problems or hearing your advice. However, I do feel blessed to have the memories of you, and gratitude to you for spiritually giving me the strength, courage, and willpower to never give up. Although you didn't get the chance to see me grow into an adult, you were spiritually with me every day. Despite my grief, you have been my lighthouse in the storm.

You live in the hearts and minds of so many: family, friends, and all of your children. While we feel deeply the void of your physical absence, many good things have blossomed because of you. By celebrating your life, your memory, and your energy, you have given your children the strength and courage to become stronger, better people. Your love is our guide, and thanks to you, we have the strength to carry on your legacy. We carry you everywhere we go. You give us the courage to smile each day, keeping hope alive, paving the path of future days full of love. You're gone but you are so vibrantly alive in each of us. You will not be forgotten. Your memories, stories, and the pictures we hold dear will forever be a part of this world. Celebrating with my children and grandchildren the joyful recollections of how amazing you were, ensures that your memory will sustain on and on, until the end of time. We miss you, Mom. We think of you every day. We love you.

Love your daughter,
Susan

# Acknowledgements

With love and gratitude to my siblings. Through it all, we made it! I love you both. You are my forever connection to Mom, and you are invaluable to me. You each had to overcome many hardships to blossom into the amazing people you are today. I am so proud of you. Your upbringing after our mother's death was challenging and painful, and you each encountered emotional difficulties in your new surroundings. You individually had to heal and rebuild your lives. Your roads were just as difficult, and yet you have broken free and paved new paths for yourselves and your families. You too are survivors.

Immeasurable love to each of my children. You are my greatest accomplishments. I love you all unconditionally. Each of you is remarkable, independent, and wonderful in your own way. Your love changed the blueprint of violence that haunted my childhood. You provided me the unconditional love I needed in my life from the moment you arrived. Each of you are my inspirations to never give up on being positive. I vowed to never let my father's ugliness prevail, and I believe having your devotion in my life gave me the strength to always try harder. You are the one great thing I have ever done. I am so unbelievably proud of each of you. I can only hope I live long enough to see each of you reach your aspirations. Always remember how much I love you, and that my door is always open to you. My connection to you all will be with me until I die. Just like my mother's love will always be with me. Always remember Grandma Bunnie's legacy, know how much she would have adored you, and keep her spirit alive in your hearts.

To my husband, thank you for your unwavering support. I am so blessed to have you in my life. You have given me the love I longed for. My heart is whole because of you.

Enormous gratitude to my editor, Stephanie Viola. You guided me through the entire editing process with grace and professionalism. You embraced my story with immense empathy and your direction was invaluable. Your expertise shines throughout the finished product. You also became a friend, a part of my heart and family. I am so blessed to have worked with you and to have you in my life.

To Erik Hornug, thank you for your time, talent, and sincere kindness in designing the incredible book cover.

To my family and friends, I am so thankful to you all. Your endless support and encouragement in my life will always be deeply appreciated.

Thank you to the Laurel House for allowing me to promote your amazing organization. You have inspired me.

To myself. **You are a survivor.** Your childhood taught you cruelty, and for a good portion of your life you had your heart pulled from your chest. You and your siblings didn't know what it was like to have a *normal* family life. What is normal in the eyes of a child? You sure did not know growing up. Now all these years later, you truly understand that what you learned as a child does not have to define you as an adult. You learned to take control and actually change your path to become something better than what you suffered. You refused to let the hate your father brought into your life outline your existence. You fought back just like Mom did. Mom's essence lives in you. Her memory filled you with the will to never let go of life. She is the faith you follow each day. Her love and the love of your grandparents, children, and family shines inside like a bright light, giving you the courage to always press forward. Today as you face another health hurdle—kicking cancer's ass—Mom's strength burns fiercely inside you always.

*Against all odds and despite all the obstacles, I am going to make it.*
Unknown

# Need help?

## LAUREL HOUSE

### *Learn about Domestic Abuse*
### **www.laurel-house.org/learn**

Domestic abuse is an "equal opportunity offender." It can happen to anyone of any race, age, sexual orientation, religion, or gender. It affects people of all socioeconomic backgrounds and education levels. Domestic violence is a pattern of abusive and coercive behavior used by one person to gain power and control over another in an intimate relationship.

Although most closely associated with physical abuse, domestic violence can take many other forms such as psychological, emotional, verbal, financial abuse, sexual violence, and isolation. Laurel House staff members and volunteers are trained to help victims of all types of domestic violence, and to support their loved ones.

### *Does your partner:*

- Put you down, call you names, or criticize you?
- Make you feel nervous or like you are "walking on eggshells?"
- Control everything you do or constantly check up on you?
- Try to stop you from talking to or seeing friends or family?
- Take your money, make you ask for money, or refuse to give you money?
- Try to control what you do or who you see?
- Tell you that you are a bad parent, or threaten to take away or hurt your children?
- Act like the abuse is no big deal, it is your fault, or even deny doing it?
- Destroy or threaten to destroy your things (phone, clothes, car, etc.) or threaten to kill your pets?
- Intimidate you with guns, knives, or other weapons?
- Shove you, slap you, hit you, push you, choke you, or hold you down?
- Pressure you to have sex or go further than you want?

- Threaten to hurt themselves because of you?
- Threaten to kill you, your family, or friends?

If you answered "yes" to any of the above questions, you may be in an abusive relationship.

*Help, support, and information are available to you through Laurel House and other resources:*

**Laurel House: www.laurel-house.org**
*Please call the toll-free 24-hour confidential hotline:*
**1-800-642-3150**

The National Domestic Violence Hotline: www.thehotline.org
**1-800-799-SAFE (7233)**
*Experienced counselors are available to help you.*

Portions of proceeds will go to Laurel House from sales of this book.

*Please leave a review of my book, thank you.*

65339628R00149